# Successful Digital Transformation in Law Firms

## A Question of Culture

Isabel Parker

Globe Law
and Business

**Author**
Isabel Parker

**Managing director**
Sian O'Neill

*Successful Digital Transformation in Law Firms: A Question of Culture*
**is published by**

Globe Law and Business Ltd
3 Mylor Close
Horsell
Woking
Surrey GU21 4DD
United Kingdom
Tel: +44 20 3745 4770
www.globelawandbusiness.com

Printed and bound by CPI Group (UK) Ltd, Croydon CR0 4YY

*Successful Digital Transformation in Law Firms: A Question of Culture*

ISBN 9781787423824
EPUB ISBN 9781787423831
Adobe PDF ISBN 9781787423848

# Table of contents

# Dedication

*For my brilliant and beloved mother, Pat Parker (1941–2018).*

# Acknowledgements

When I agreed to write this book 18 months ago, I did not anticipate what an undertaking it would be, or that it would coincide with the most turbulent 18 months of so many people's working lives. It has been quite a journey.

I want to thank everyone who agreed to be interviewed for this book or who allowed me to bounce ideas off them. In particular: Jack Shepherd; Alex Smith; Nikki Shaver; Crispin Passmore; Wendy Butler Curtis; Noah Waisberg; Drew Winlaw; Richard West. Thank you for being so generous with your time.

Thanks to Sian O'Neill and Lauren Simpson at Globe Law and Business for commissioning this book and for bearing with me and guiding me through the process. Thanks also to Michael Faulkner for editing the manuscript.

The ability to concentrate for hours at a time and an obsessive focus on the end goal were among the many things I learned during my long tenure at Freshfields Bruckhaus Deringer. Along the way I met some incredible people who helped me on my journey. In particular, I would like to mention three people who welcomed me back after a long career break and three children, who believed in me and who supported me to be successful. Ted Burke, who gave me the opportunity to move out of fee earning and start my life as an innovator and builder of new things. Paul Lomas, a brilliant lawyer and an inspiring leader, also the most cultured of men, who helped me cut my teeth on Project TOM. Nick Bliss, who welcomed me back into Freshfields after an eight-year break and trusted me not to mess it up.

There was never a dull moment working in the global technology and innovation team at Freshfields – and I want to give a shout-out to the entire team there. The guiding star of the team is Charlotte Baldwin, Chief Digital and Technology Officer, who taught me so many things – the most important of which is that great leaders can be fully human. Much of this book is derived from what I learned under Charlotte's guidance, so many thanks to her. Thanks also to the brilliant Nick Bell, who constantly challenged me to think differently, to Graham Browning, friend and conscience, who kept me grounded through some tough times and to Olivia Balson, an inspiring leader and woman of integrity.

Life after Freshfields has been a steep but exciting learning curve. Thanks go to my friends at Panoram, Rick Seabrook and Greg Wildisen, for giving me the confidence to try a new path. To Liam Brown and John Croft at Elevate, who helped me to see the world through the customer's eyes. To Dan Reed at UnitedLex, and Bill Deckelman at DXC Technology, for confirming that my thoughts on digital transformation made sense and could be realised. To Mark A Cohen at the Digital Legal Exchange for inspiration and friendship.

Writing a book does, of course, impact those around you. Thanks to everyone I bored with my theories, rants and hypotheses. In particular, Nina and Phil Stafford for allowing me to hibernate – and then hammer out tricky issues around their kitchen island with several glasses of wine. To my three children, Livia, Hester and Leo, who put up with me disappearing into the study for many hours at a time for well over a year. A massive thank you and I love you. And I promise I won't ever make you read this book!

Finally, and most importantly, I want to thank my husband, Darren. He has always supported me, always 'leant in', and always believed in me. He is my inspiration and rock. ▮

# Foreword

**Mark A Cohen**
Executive chairman, Digital Legal Exchange

Digital transformation has fundamentally altered business and its relationship with customers and society. It is a multidimensional, enterprise-wide, integrated re-imagination of product and service delivery from the customer perspective. Digital transformation is a journey, not a moment in time. It is an ongoing change process whose North Star is customers and whose goal is elevation of their end-to-end experience.

Digital transformation predates COVID-19. It has been a top corporate priority for several years, yet most in the legal industry have scarcely taken notice. This has created a 'digital gap' separating law from business. The gap has widened during the pandemic because of the accelerated pace of digital transformation. As Microsoft CEO Satya Nadella remarked during an earnings call: "We've seen two years' worth of digital transformation in two months."

It is against this tectonic business paradigm shift that legal industry change is best, though seldom, considered. That is one of several reasons why Isabel Parker's book is a meaningful contribution. Parker demystifies digital transformation and draws a roadmap for its application to legal.

The author addresses three main issues in her book:
- the meaning of digital transformation;
- the characteristics of digitally advanced companies; and
- the development of a digital strategy and vision.

These three topics are treated separately for organisational and pedagogical reasons, but the author makes clear that they are interrelated and essential to the success of the digital journey.

Parker starts by unpacking key elements of digital transformation. Offering examples, data and crisp commentary, she thoughtfully explains why digital transformation is as much about culture, human adaptation, collaboration, teamwork, process, alignment of purpose and integration of functions as it is about technology.

Parker next delves into how and why certain companies have separated themselves from the pack. She probes into their culture and leadership, and the unwavering customer centricity that informs everything they do. She explains why no corporate function – legal included – can be exempt from the digital process and stresses that the digital journey is a team sport.

The author then focuses on large corporate law firms. Parker's professional background has produced her interesting mix of admiration and exasperation … She knows the world of the elite corporate law firm from the inside, having spent nearly a quarter-century at Freshfields. She spent the first half of her tenure as a fee-earning (practising) solicitor. The balance focused on the business of law – she was co-leader of the firm's award-winning innovation team. Parker's practice/business of law mix positioned her well for addressing her subject. Her perspective is derived from the trenches, not from afar, and this makes it all the more insightful and passionate.

Parker makes a strong case to law firms that they align with their business clients. This requires them to regard digital transformation as a strategic priority, not a tactical experiment. She is equally clear in her message that firms can learn from their clients, many of whom are well along their own digital journeys. To be successful in driving value to digital clients requires the firm itself to operate digitally.

The author stresses the importance of cultural change in the digital transformation process. She well understands the stress this places on the firm partnership model. This brings to mind Richard Susskind's quip: "It's very difficult to tell a room full of millionaires that their business model is broken."[1] But if clients say it's broken, firms had better listen.

One of the fascinating aspects of legal change is that it is not being driven or architected from within the profession. It is business – and more specifically C-suites and boards – mandating that legal align and integrate with business. Law is a passenger in its own change process. Business is the driver. This irony is consistent with legal culture that has long been reactive and risk averse, not proactive and innovative.

Parker holds out hope that firms will rise to the cultural challenge confronting them. Her personal transformation story from practitioner to legal business alignment catalyst suggests that lawyers – especially those with a passion to do better for clients and society – can adapt to new mindsets, models and metrics. Perhaps this is why Parker's message is more hopeful than ominous. ■

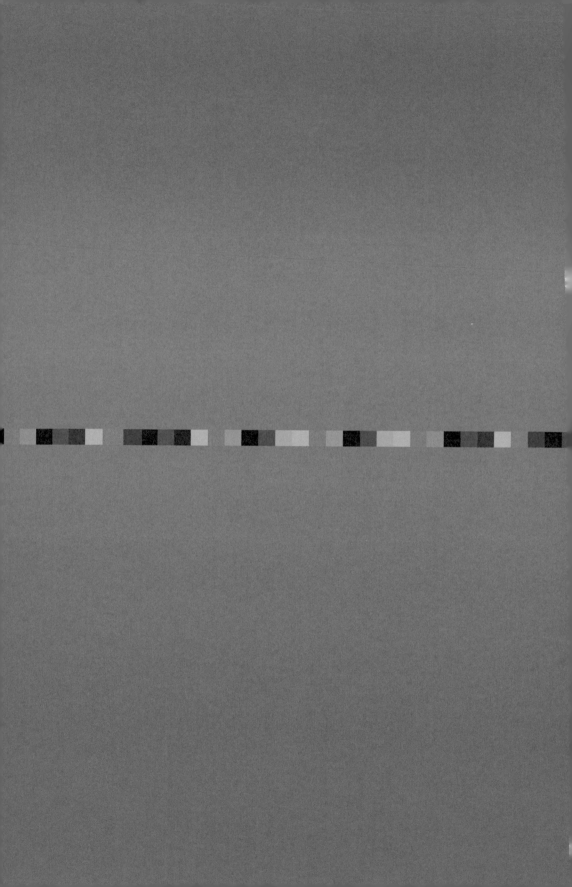

# Introduction

I was approached to write this book in February of 2020, on my last day at the law firm that had been part of my working life for 24 years and just before the coronavirus pandemic hit the United Kingdom in earnest. Writing during the long weeks of lockdown, I questioned what impact the pandemic would have on the appetite for digital transformation in law firms. Pre-COVID, the legal sector lagged far behind other industries in terms of digital maturity. Although some firms had innovation teams and others were experimenting with digital product development, investment in genuine digital transformation was rare and many law firm initiatives were tactical rather than strategic. As the pandemic hit and the lawyers went home, initial signs were encouraging. Lawyers who had resisted using digital tools could resist no more. The move to remote working was, in general, considered to be a success. As the dust settled and the lockdown dragged on, I wondered about the longer-term effects of the crisis on law firm operations. Law firms are high-fixed-cost businesses; faced with a global recession, would they look to further squeeze their cost base, retreat to a safe place, and defer the financial and cultural investment that digital transformation demands? Or would they seize the moment and take the opportunity for radical business model change?

It is too early to answer these questions with certainty. History has shown that providers of legal services to the corporate world tend to survive downturns better than other sectors of the economy. Indeed, the first publication of financial results by large UK law firms following the lockdown demonstrated that most had performed better than expected.[2] In a way, this is unsurprising; strong law practices have counter-cyclical capability (so that, for example, they can ramp up areas like restructuring as the amount of work in big ticket M&A declines). The resilience demonstrated by large law firms through the pandemic and the consequent increase in profitability is to be applauded. Law firms now have an opportunity to reinvest those profits for the longer term, to future-proof themselves for a post-pandemic world in which digital plays an ever more significant role.

The global nature of the COVID-19 crisis, the speed of its spread and the continuing nature of the threat it presents will have far-reaching effects, both on the economy and on our individual and corporate psyches. I have worked in Big Law for my entire career, starting as a trainee lawyer in 1996 and moving into a number of different roles, in strategy, transformation, innovation and knowledge. I have seen the profession change significantly over those 24 years. Even before the crisis hit, commentators who watch the legal services sector were calling out the increasing fragility of incumbent law firms. With new competition from the Big 4 and emerging law companies; new technologies and platforms coming online; the spectre of the 'Amazon of law' always lurking; and clients ever more forensic in slicing up the supply of legal work, law firms were undoubtedly under threat. And yet … most law firms, particularly the so-called Big Law firms, do not take these threats seriously. When lots of money is being made there is no compelling reason to change. Many traditional law firm partnerships, that are still highly profitable, consider themselves exempt from the pressures that have beset so many of their clients. Put simply, they do not buy the message about disruption.

Will the COVID crisis change this mindset? Possibly. It is not the first crisis to have impacted the legal sector. In the wake of the financial crisis of 2008, many global law firms changed the focus of their business to weather the storm. Brexit required firms with a significant UK and EU presence to make structural changes to their operations. The difference between these crises and the pandemic is the immediacy of the change. Law firms could plan for Brexit – but coronavirus has not afforded anyone that luxury. For perhaps the first time, law firms have been forced to pivot at speed and to work very differently.

The compulsion to work in a new way will not disappear when lawyers return to the office. It seems very likely that corporate and individual behaviours will need to change permanently as a result of the pandemic. A survey of chief executives conducted by KPMG in March 2021 showed that a quarter of respondents think the pandemic has changed their business model forever.[3] As law firms' clients change, so must law firms, and the pandemic may prove to be a genuine inflection point; it is certainly an opportunity for law firms to rethink their operating model for the next decade and beyond.

Digital transformation has a critical role to play in this new model. Now more than ever, digital transformation is not an indulgence, but a necessity. This is about much more than remote working – to evolve to a digital operation model in a volatile and unpredictable world requires a shift in culture. Law firm leaders will need to cultivate the kind of culture that innovative and transformative companies have already developed – a culture that is curious, adaptive, transparent, democratic and comfortable with change. Law firm leaders will need to ask themselves new kinds of questions. How will partners forge and nurture client relationships without jumping on a plane for a face-to-face meeting? What are the implications for the high-touch client service law firms are accustomed to deliver? How will lawyers collaborate, train juniors and build culture with reduced time in the office? Recognising that their clients' businesses will change radically, will lawyers have the confidence to show vulnerability and ask the questions required truly to understand new client needs? During a global recession, how can any law firm create a sense of purpose and mission beyond the generation of partner profits?

These are questions of good leadership as much as digital readiness. However, in times of unprecedented volatility, an analogue approach to leadership is not sufficient. Any leader looking to future-proof a law firm must learn lessons from the operating model of successful digital businesses.

There is a tendency to conflate digital transformation and technology. This book is not about 'legal tech'. I am not a technologist and those looking for a definitive guide as to which technologies to choose and how to implement them in a law firm should look elsewhere – there is no shortage of helpful material on that subject. I do touch on technology in the book, because technology is of course an intrinsic element of digitisation. However (and I don't claim to be the first person to say this) becoming a digital business is not just about technology. It is much wider than that. Digital transformation touches every element of the organisation, from governance and organisational structure right through to the mindset and diversity of employees. Put simply, capacity to change depends on culture, and culture is the biggest barrier to digital effectiveness. For this reason, the book concentrates on the cultural, organisational and strategic aspects of digital transformation in law firms, rather than on which technologies to implement.

I do not address corporate legal teams here. Of course, in-house legal functions also need to rethink their business model for a digital world, and there are some very helpful books that directly address this issue.[4] Although they share some of the same challenges as law firms, as a rule corporate legal teams are culturally better attuned to how the world is changing and how they will need to adapt. This is because they operate in organisations for which digital is already a strategic business imperative. Increasingly, they are more business-focused and less insular than law firms, and more diverse and forward thinking. In fact, much of the cultural change that is happening in law firms has been driven by the agenda of client legal teams. This is welcome; however, law firms cannot delegate to their clients the responsibility for driving change. Law firms must own their digital agenda and initiate the cultural change to support it.

This book focuses on law firms that provide services to corporate clients, not consumers. Corporate law firms tend to be larger than those that serve consumers. This is not to suggest that digital transformation is not essential to all law firms, regardless of size and client base. Nor should it suggest that it is somehow more difficult for smaller law firms to achieve digital transformation; in fact, research shows that organisations with fewer than 100 employees are 2.7 times more likely to report a successful digital transformation than are very large organisations.[5] I have focused on corporate law firms because this is the world that I know best. My hope is that smaller law firms or those with a consumer-facing practice will also find the book helpful, and that many of the learnings will apply across the board.

There are three key learnings that I hope readers will take away from this book. The first is that law firms need to approach digital transformation as a strategic exercise, not as a tactical experiment. The second is that to execute on the strategy, law firms need to look outside the legal industry and learn lessons from digitally effective organisations (many of whom will be their clients). The third is that sustained digital transformation requires cultural change, which may put strain on the traditional law firm partnership structure – but that with commitment, this cultural change can be achieved.

I have divided this book into three parts. Part I defines digital transformation and explains why it is important, gives examples of best practices adopted by successful digital companies and offers practical guidance on how to go about defining a vision and strategy. Part II addresses two important elements of digitisation, product development and technology, in more detail. And Part III focuses on culture, exploring which elements of a traditional law firm partnership might need to be reframed to enable a law firm to be successful in sustaining digital change. Recognising that law firms are all at different stages of digital maturity, and that some parts of this book will be more relevant to certain readers than others, I have attempted to make the chapters relatively self-contained so that they can be read independently. I certainly don't claim to have all the answers, or to have reflected every perspective, but I hope that this book will provide a useful starting point for law firms looking to drive and sustain meaningful digital change.

This book reflects both my respect for the traditional law firm partnership and my frustration with the model. There is so much to admire in a profession that is full of intelligent, committed and often creative people. There is also some complacency and inertia that leads to wasted opportunity. I hope and expect that large law firms will continue to thrive, but a retreat to the status quo by those same law firms would be a missed opportunity. The law firms that emerge as successful when the clouds clear will be those that have used this humanitarian and economic crisis as a time for self-examination, and made bold management decisions to reshape their businesses as a result.

At its heart, digital transformation is all about cultural change. Just as you wouldn't sow seeds without first preparing the soil, so no organisation should embark on digital transformation without first having ensured that the right cultural elements are present to create a fertile environment for change. The time is right, now more than ever, for law firms to embrace these cultural challenges with renewed energy. ■

# Part I: Why digital transformation matters – and how to get started

# Chapter 1: What is digital transformation?

*All businesses operate by some set of unstated rules and sometimes those rules change – often in very significant ways. Yet there is no flashing sign that heralds these rule changes. They creep up on you as they crept up on us, without warning.*[6]

## 1. Meaningful change or management speak?

Lawyers love words. In law firms, a high value is placed on correct and consistent use of language. It's all about precision; the quickest way to lose credibility with a group of law firm partners is to present a slide with a typo on it. Although the legal sector has its own lexicon (which is pretty much impenetrable to those outside the profession), lawyers remain deeply sceptical of vocabulary used by professionals in other industries. The language of business that is standard outside of law may simply not resonate in a law firm (or worse, may be viewed as management speak, and an instant turn-off).

For this reason, if you were to ask a typical line lawyer in a corporate law firm about the firm's digital transformation strategy, you would likely be met with a blank look. If you were to speak to a GC of a large corporation about digital transformation, however, she or he would probably understand exactly what the term means. This is because digital is integral to the strategy of most large corporations, and in many cases is driving the business strategy itself. This is not the case in most law firms, where digital transformation is still far from central to the strategy. Law firms may be familiar with the term 'digital transformation' in the context of advisory work, as most firms are advising clients on the legal and regulatory implications of their digital initiatives. Many lawyers, however, remain unaware of (and often disinterested in) the law firm's own digital transformation.

So let's start, in a lawyerly fashion, with the definitions section. What is meant by 'digital transformation', and how is it different from 'innovation'?

## 2. Innovation vs digital transformation

Corporate innovation means the creation by a business of something new (to the business, to the market or to the world) that meets three criteria:

- desirability (customers/clients want it);
- feasibility (it can feasibly be created); and
- viability (it creates value for the innovating business).[7]

At the intersection of these three elements lies successful innovation. Anything that is outside the intersection cannot be considered true innovation (it's not innovation if you invent something completely new that no one wants, for example; nor is it innovation if you have an idea for something people want and which would add value, but cannot feasibly be built). The term is often applied to the creation of new products and services. It is also, though more rarely, used in connection with the creation of entirely new business models.

In the law firm context, innovation is widely used to describe initiatives to modernise existing legal service offerings to clients. For this reason, innovation has become associated with the adoption of legal technology. The association rather devalues the term's currency. Innovation in law firms did not start when 'legal tech' came onto the radar in 2012. Its roots are in the more prosaic world of process efficiency and the offshoring/nearshoring of commodity legal services. Although it may seem very old school now, the move by a number of large law firms to establish captive centres[8] to deliver more process-oriented legal work was the first (and perhaps the only) truly radical and lasting change to the traditional law firm operating model. It was also a genuine exercise in responding to customer needs.

For the purpose of high-level definitions, we can think of innovation as new ways to deliver legal services, using process, people and technology, usually to drive greater efficiencies, increased profitability and lower risk.

'Digital transformation' goes further than innovation, encompassing wholesale operating model change to future-proof a business. Its objectives are new revenue generation as much as cost reduction and efficiency gains. Digital transformation is expansive. It touches the entire operating model of an organisation: client-facing delivery and product development; data management and exploitation; the client experience; tooling and software; cloud strategy, data centre strategy; and the other fundamentals of IT infrastructure. It also touches delivery of the new operating model, including the capabilities to implement the model and the cultural change to sustain it. There are many ways to define digital transformation, but I like this definition, from Salesforce:

> *Digital transformation is the process of using digital technologies to create new – or modify existing – business processes, culture, and customer experiences to meet changing business and market requirements. This reimagining of business in the digital age is digital transformation.*[9]

This definition hits the essentials. It is sufficiently broad, reflecting the fact that digital transformation requires attention to technology, process, culture and the customer experience. It also contextualises the reason why digital transformation is so urgently needed – because in every industry sector, the market, the economy and the competition are changing so rapidly.

## 3. Why should law firms change?

The World Economic Forum (WEF) white paper on digitisation of professional services, produced in collaboration with Accenture as part of the WEF's digital transformation initiative, contains some interesting analysis of the impact of digital transformation on professional services.[10] Their research shows that of all professional services categories, Big Law is the laggard in terms of digital disruption.

The white paper was published in 2017 (a long time ago in the digital world) but the results still resonate. Why is it that law firms have not yet experienced the kind of disruption that has impacted other industries – and other professional services providers? Why is it so difficult to find examples of successful radical change?

Sceptics in law firms commonly give three answers to this question. The first relates to revenue. Law firms are making a lot of money, which suggests that the model works. Why try to fix something that is not broken? The second relates to expertise. Legal expertise, the argument runs, cannot be commoditised, and consequently law firms are not vulnerable to disruption in the same way as other businesses. The third relates to brand. The established brand and deep client interactions that many law firms enjoy create a relationship of trust that cannot easily be copied or eroded.

These important challenges need to be met head on.

### 3.1 Money, money, money

It is true that many law firms, particularly those at the top end of the market, continue to be very profitable. Partners in these firms will tell you their business model is working just fine, and that there is simply no need for change. In some cases, they will be right. If I were to walk into the boardroom of Kirkland & Ellis and tell them that they urgently need to become more digitally effective, I would certainly be laughed out of the room. 2020 was kind to Kirkland:

> *Insiders at the Chicago-based firm said that its turnover was approaching $5 billion for the twelve months to the end of January [2021], up from $4.45 billion in the previous year. One partner described the firm's performance as "eye-watering".*[11]

The issue here, though, is one of conscious strategic choice. The law firms that stand to gain the most from digitisation (and that have the most to fear from disruption) are not the Wachtells or the Kirklands – these firms have made a clear strategic choice to focus all their energies on a particular market segment and to do this very well. The firms that need to think seriously about digitisation are those that have not yet made a conscious strategic choice about where to play in the market, have not recognised the immediacy of the threat to their traditional business model and are at risk of sleepwalking into a strategic vacuum. Loitering in a no-man's-land between bespoke, high-touch legal advisory and being a 'full service' law firm is a dangerous place to be without a winning strategy.

### 3.2 Law firm expertise

It is certainly true that some elements of legal services, particularly corporate legal services, can be highly complex and unique. There is also some logic to the argument that the bespoke nature of high-end legal work makes wholesale disruption, through a challenger provider or platform, harder to achieve. Certainly, law firms are not accustomed to thinking of their services as 'products' as would be the case in the B2C sector. The concept, common to a product world, of developing and packaging up 'reusable components' – that is, common elements or approaches that can be applied to different clients with similar issues – is a much less familiar concept in a law firm setting.[12]

However, even in a global elite law firm, not everything that the lawyers do is complex and unique. A relatively large proportion of legal work (and often the elements that are the most profitable) can be

*Lawyers are justifiably proud of their professional expertise, and it can be uncomfortable for them to admit that a significant portion of their work is not really all that special.*

standardised to some degree. Lawyers are justifiably proud of their professional expertise, and it can be uncomfortable for them to admit that a significant portion of their work is not really all that special. There is also an element of professional arrogance at play here, which suggests that elite law firms are exempt from disruption because of the exceptionally high quality of their people and the bespoke nature of their work. In the digital world, however, complacency is a warning sign. McKinsey (ironically, perhaps, given their own global elite status and reputation) puts it like this:

> In our experience, arrogance and an unwillingness to listen to others is an early indicator of a company ready to head off the rails.[13]

Regardless of whether law firms choose to recognise it, the world around them is changing very rapidly. Law firms cannot continue to deliver in the same old way, insisting that their expertise is too special to be touched by technology, or their relationships too deep to be threatened by a competitor. Law firms will have seen from their own clients, who are themselves subject to disruption (think of financial services and challenger banks) the potentially disastrous results of this kind of complacency. Although the legal services sector has not yet seen the emergence of one 'Amazon of law', change is manifesting itself, gradually and inexorably, in different ways. Clients are pushing harder for better value and are increasingly looking to find that value from providers who are not traditional law firm partnerships. Process engineering approaches are being more frequently used (and are used as standard by law companies and other emerging competitors) to identify those elements in legal matters, including bespoke or complex matters, that can be commoditised – or even productised. Technology is being deployed to drive efficiencies in delivery, with a fierce battle to develop the industry-defining legal services platform (see Chapter 4).

Take the familiar example of due diligence, a contract review process undertaken as part of a corporate merger or acquisition. Due diligence was historically a time-intensive service, provided entirely by a law firm using a tiered resourcing model. I well remember my early days as a trainee, before the arrival of digital data rooms, being locked in cavernous cellars reading hard copy documents for ten hours a day. Due diligence may be only one small piece of a complex M&A matter but, as with document review in litigation, it is the area where law firms have traditionally made their biggest profit.

Today, a combination of machine learning-enabled extraction technology and alternative (lower-cost) resourcing, supported by defined processes, is the standard approach to M&A due diligence work. Expensive law firms have been put under pressure to deliver this service much more cost effectively than was historically the case, and this has opened the field to other, non-law-firm, providers. By using technology (often proprietary technology) at scale to deliver this kind of work, and leveraging cost-effective resources, these 'alternative' providers can capture the commoditised end of the market by driving significant cost efficiencies. Law firms that are seeking to be full service need to be alert to this threat. If alternative providers have access to sufficiently skilled people, and can establish a sufficiently strong relationship with the client, they can then move up the value chain, capturing client work higher up the scale. The capability to do this will only increase over time as regulation relaxes and technology improves, allowing alternative providers to take on a much broader cross-section of legal work. In fact, Noah Waisberg, CEO of Kira Technologies (one of the pioneers of machine learning-enabled software as a service model in the field of due diligence) has seen M&A due diligence data volumes increase significantly over time:

> From 2017 to 2020, the average number of documents in a cloud project inside Kira has doubled. Though there are a few reasons this might be so, we think the most likely explanation is that people are doing bigger projects now because AI technology allows them to.[14]

The larger law firms have recognised this and mirrored the model; the use of contract review technology as part of the due diligence process is now considered a hygiene factor for Big Law, as is the establishment of a captive centre with lower cost resource. The reality for small or mid-sized corporate law firms, however, is very different, as these firms may not have the capacity to make the investment required to compete.

Of course, the Big 4 legal teams and new law companies are highly alert to these opportunities. With Deloitte and EY rapidly scaling up their legal managed services arms, and KPMG and PwC already having sizeable legal divisions, competition from the Big 4 is becoming increasingly fierce. Not to be outdone, law companies such as UnitedLex, Elevate Legal Services and Factor are developing proprietary technologies and nurturing the digital capabilities required to support corporate legal functions in driving their digital transformations. Add to this the fact that corporate legal teams are sending less work to external counsel. They are doing more of their work themselves, using flexible resourcing to scale when they need to. Some are automating workflows and knowledge, and making their own investments in technology solutions, either sourced themselves or purchased as a service from third-party providers (some corporate legal teams are even starting to develop and sell their proprietary technology solutions to their corporate peers). For law firms there is less high-end, cerebral work to go around. The argument that high-end legal expertise is inviolable no longer holds water.

### 3.3 The mythology around law firm brand

The third justification for maintaining the law firm status quo is the protective moat of the law firm 'brand'. Could the fact that we still have not seen significant shifts in market share from incumbent law firms to challenger providers be explained by the unique relationship of trust between a client and an established law firm brand? Certainly, in times of crisis (a large regulatory investigation or an insolvency, for example) or significant risk (a hostile takeover), clients seek the stamp of approval that a trusted brand will deliver, even if it comes at a much higher price. Law firms, of course, seize this opportunity to make sure they remain, as a partner at one global law firm was heard to say, "reassuringly expensive".

Many large law firms have built up trusted client relationships over hundreds of years – and these are not easily dislodged. However, as Mark A Cohen, a respected and thoughtful critic of the traditional law firm partnership model, points out, client views are also changing. As in-house legal teams come under pressure from their own C-suite to "function at the speed of the business", longstanding loyalty to external counsel can quickly be eroded:

> *Data is replacing conjecture; customer satisfaction is paramount; and in-house teams are increasingly provider-agnostic provided that the source delivers expertly, efficiently, measurably, consistently, collaboratively, and cost-effectively.*[15]

I believe this, and many of my peers and other commentators believe it; but the message that the world is changing is not loud enough to penetrate the walls of the traditional law firm partnership. In fact, law firms have two distinct vulnerabilities when it comes to digital transformation. Not only do they need to consider the way in which their own business and sector might be disrupted, but they also must be aware of how their clients' businesses in multiple sectors are being disrupted, so that they can respond ahead of the competition to those changing demands. According to the WEF paper:

> *Digitalization is ... affecting the Professional Services industry both internally and externally. How digital disrupts other industries will impact the clients of Professional Services firms, who, in turn, will have to adapt their offerings accordingly. Transforming business models to better meet client expectations, pre-empting disruptive competition, and creating the right ecosystem of partners will become a source of competitive advantage.*[16]

We might layer on top of all this the impact that the coronavirus pandemic is likely to have on client loyalty to an established brand. As noted above, law firms are high-touch businesses, with personal relationships at the core of their proposition. If global business is likely to be subject to social distancing rules for extended periods, will remote working start to dilute the power of the individual law firm brand? If the client can't see the smartly suited grey-haired lawyer, can't visit the marble-clad central London office or join the annual golf tournament, will that client make their choice of lawyer on a more democratic basis, placing more importance on price point, fixed fee certainty and the right level of skill (not paying for a Rolls Royce when you only need a Mini)?

*Digital trends indicate that technology is slowly levelling the playing field: automation is lowering the cost to serve, global collaboration tools are allowing freelancers to work from anywhere, and platforms are bringing clients closer to freelancers. These developments, coupled with data ubiquity, are empowering the client, marking a shift in the way expertise will be procured and shared in the future.*[17]

Expertise and brand, then, may not be enough to carry law firms through turbulent macro-economic times. Certainly law firms should not be complacent about increased competition, or underestimate the readiness of clients, themselves under pressure from their own business, to look beyond traditional law firms for value. But do law firms really believe it?

## 4. "Only the paranoid survive"

Not all law firms are entirely blind to how the world is changing. Some get it, and are committing to digital change and embracing a radical rethink of their business model. But these firms are in the minority. Many other firms are adopting a wait and see approach, or innovating at the edges without investing, financially or culturally, in genuine change. However, as is evidenced by the experience of businesses (and, ironically, law firm clients) in other sectors, this is a dangerous approach. If firms wait for hard evidence of disruption in the legal industry before taking action, it is likely to be too late:

*The need to see the big picture and take bold actions flows from an uncomfortable reality: in the technology age, disruption is just over the horizon ... or even closer. It's notoriously difficult for companies with a long history of success to see catastrophe looming. Often they have been lulled into a belief that the protective moat around their business is a lot wider and deeper than it actually is.*[18]

It would appear that law firms, many of whom continue to be extremely successful and profitable, are lacking in one of the qualities that defines sustainable success in the digital world: paranoia. The former CEO of Intel, Andy Grove, wrote a book in 1988 called *Only the Paranoid*

*Survive,* in which he talks about the importance of keeping an eye on potential threats and adapting to them quickly.[19] Responding to what Grove calls 'strategic inflection points' has never been so important, and the book resonates powerfully in today's climate. Law firms, particularly those at the Big Law end of the scale, are of course deeply wary of their immediate and obvious competitors, but not terribly worried about disruptive competitive threats.

## 5. The disruption test

The law firm that considers itself immune from disruption should apply the test below to challenge the established view.

Consider the following list.[20] If the answer to *any one* of the following questions is yes, this may indicate that your law firm is open to disruption:

- *Are your customers subject to intermediaries and their associated fees?*
- *Do your customers face long lead times to complete transactions or to receive products?*
- *Are your margins higher than in other industries?*
- *Is there an opportunity to unbundle products and services?*
- *Is the user experience you provide below the level of the best global practices?*
- *Is supplier information less than fully transparent to customers?*

Most law firms would have to answer yes to at least four of those questions. So why aren't they more paranoid about disruption?

In fact, law firms *are* paranoid – but the paranoia is focused elsewhere. Law firms are exceptionally paranoid about their partners – about keeping their star performers happy and not losing them to established competitors. It is easy to see why that might be. The competition for the best legal talent is very hot indeed. Take the UK market. *The Lawyer's* most recent report on the top 50 US law firms in London, published in June 2020, shows that revenues generated by the 50 largest US law firms in the UK rose by 6.1% in 2019, while the partner headcount increased by only 1.7%.[21] This translates to only one thing – even more money for partners at US firms in London. US firms can (and do) pay extraordinary amounts to poach lateral partners from UK Magic Circle firms. And those firms put extraordinary amounts of energy and management time into trying to prevent this happening.

Law firms need to redirect their paranoia. I would argue that they have taken their eye off the ball and are paying insufficient attention to more pressing competitive threats: from their own clients, who are beginning to leverage technology and alternative resourcing to do more of their legal work themselves; from law companies and the Big 4, who are scaling quickly and with purpose; and from technologies and platforms that might further disaggregate the highly profitable churn work that supports a large proportion of law firm revenues. A relentless focus on the best legal talent will of course continue to be a crucial success factor, but firms should give equal attention to hiring the best digital talent and to the long-term digital strategy they will put in place to counter the competition.

## 6. The art of persuasion

As highlighted above, there is work to be done to convert law firm sceptics to the need to commit to digital transformation. People who work in law firms can perhaps be divided into two camps: those who operate in the innovation/transformation space and those who 'do law'. The decision makers (in a law firm partnership, the partners) are usually in the second camp, for a host of complex reasons that I explore in more detail later in this book. For those operating in the law firm innovation world, it is easy to forget that the lawyers in the firm probably know nothing about the firm's digital transformation, and are too busy to invest time in learning about it.

Education is a significant part of the remit of the team leading digital change. That team will need to convince a partnership of highly intelligent, sceptical individuals to invest in entirely new ways of working – potentially to change their entire business structure – and to sacrifice drawings into the bargain. It won't be enough simply to tell partners that competitors are making investments in digital. Partners will need proof that digital transformation is crucial to the continued success of the firm. In short, they will need to see a persuasive case for change.

The rest of Part I of this book addresses how that case for change can best be made: that is, by learning from successful digital organisations and applying these learnings to the development of a digital strategy that aligns with the firm's broader strategy.

In the next chapter, we focus on examples of digital best practices, and how they might be applied in a law firm context. ▪

# Chapter 2: Five defining elements of successful digital companies

## 1. Framing the challenge

The unpalatable truth about digital transformation is that it is difficult to achieve – 70% of transformations are not successful. Transforming into a successful digital business is a huge commitment:

> *[T]he painful reality is that most transformations fail. Research shows that 70 percent of complex, large-scale change programs don't reach their stated goals. Common pitfalls include a lack of employee engagement, inadequate management support, poor or nonexistent cross-functional collaboration, and a lack of accountability. Furthermore, sustaining a transformation's impact typically requires a major reset in mind-sets and behaviors – something that few leaders know how to achieve.*[22]

This may not sound very encouraging, but it is important to be realistic about the level of commitment required to effect meaningful change. Add to this the fact that there is no rule book that you can follow to guarantee digital success – each organisation will need to tailor its transformation to its own ambitions and align it to its core business strategy.

The good news is that many organisations have made significant progress with their digital initiatives and there is plenty of valuable insight into how this can be achieved. There are numerous examples of practices and approaches that work (some from the legal sector, some from other more digitally mature industries) that can be applied to the law firm environment. These examples are not just drawn from digital natives and start-ups. There are also powerful examples of more traditional, incumbent organisations that have changed their culture and the way they operate to become more digitally effective.

Examples from incumbent organisations are particularly helpful for law firms considering the investment in digital transformation. Digital natives may be more agile, but there are advantages to being part of the old guard. Long-established and highly profitable, incumbent law firms enjoy strengths and advantages that law companies, the Big 4 or new law firm entrants do not, including hard-won brand loyalty and trust (I discuss this in more detail in the context of the partnership model in Chapter 6). This translates to real opportunity. For the law firms that genuinely commit to digital transformation, the rewards could be very significant. However, these advantages will not last forever and are rapidly being eroded, as competitors move faster, invest more and commit more seriously to digital change. Law firms should recognise that there is an imperative to act and that a wait and see approach carries risk.

## 2. Adapting best practice to the law firm environment

My approach to finding examples of digital best practice was twofold. First, I looked outside the legal industry (essential given the relative digital immaturity of the legal services market). Second, I looked for examples that could actually be applied in a law firm environment. It isn't difficult to identify examples of successful digital practices, but some of these approaches would simply never work in a traditional law firm partnership environment. Many successful digital companies, particularly digital natives, are digital by design. They don't have legacy systems. They create their culture from scratch, and have always been agile in the way they work. They don't have to contend with the challenge of enterprise-wide mindset change. Traditional law firm partnerships are not built that way, and have a distinct culture that has developed over many years. So although it may be the case that a digitally native organisation might spend up to 40% of revenue on R&D, it would be unusual (and probably ill-advised) for a law firm to do the same. To be helpful to a law firm embarking on transformation, examples of digital practice need to be adapted to the reality of the law firm environment. This is not to suggest that law firms can't be ambitious and create meaningful change at scale; but it pays to be mindful of the challenges that are unique to the law firm partnership model (which are explored in detail in Chapter 7).

### 3. Beware of innovation theatre

I have done a fair amount of horizon scanning, of the legal sector and beyond, to find examples of digital effectiveness that will be helpful in a law firm context. Such scanning, indeed, is a critical success factor for innovation. Sometimes, however, the horizon can be a bit fuzzy. Having spent many years at a Magic Circle law firm obsessing about what competitors were doing, and a very concentrated eighteen months of research while writing this book, I have found that immersing yourself in the literature around law firm innovation can be more exhausting than illuminating. As David Rowan, the founding editor of *Wired UK*, puts it in his book, *Non-Bullshit Innovation*:

> *Too often what is celebrated as innovation inside ... large organizations is in fact 'innovation theatre' – a box-ticking, public-relations-led, self-reassuring alternative to radical changes in mindset and culture.*[23]

We must accept that there is a marketing value to innovation. However, too much hype is simply unhelpful. It breeds scepticism and resistance amongst the people that really need to change – the lawyers. Lawyers are trained to be precise and critical, and are deeply sceptical about exaggeration and puffery. Too much hype, and the lawyers will simply disengage, and 'innovation' will be reduced to an echo chamber for those tasked with driving change within law firms.

In an attempt to cut through all of this, when researching this book I spoke to a number of key people involved in digital transformation in the legal services sector, whom I knew to be the real deal. I am very grateful to those interviewees, all of whom were incredibly open and honest about the challenges they had encountered during their organisation's digital journey. Some of them appear in this book as case studies, and others wished to remain anonymous. The legal profession can be sceptical about collaboration (not least because of the obligation to avoid crossing the line into potentially anti-competitive behaviour). However, sharing insights and war stories with others in an honest way will help law firms move beyond 'innovation theatre' to genuine digital effectiveness, and for that reason I am very grateful to everyone who agreed to be interviewed for this book.

## 4. What does 'good' look like?

I mentioned above David Rowan's book, *Non-Bullshit Innovation*. It is an insightful, engaging read in which the author, frustrated with innovation theatre, travels around the world in search of examples of genuine corporate innovation in different industries and jurisdictions. What is striking is that although the examples of corporate innovation are drawn from radically different industries, all the organisations that are featured share certain characteristics. It is never a good idea to generalise, and reducing digital transformation to a formula is lazy and should be resisted. However, the learning on the subject of innovation and digital transformation, ranging from scholarly articles, to thought leadership, to conversations with those on the ground, right through to one-liners on Twitter, demonstrates a surprisingly broad consensus about what constitutes best practice for digital change.

## 5. The five elements of successful digital transformation

What is it that unites successful digital companies, either those who are digital natives or incumbents who have undergone a successful transformation? There are, of course, multiple factors. For the purposes of this book, though, they can be distilled down to the following five elements. Successful digital companies:

- focus on *customer/client* needs and the customer experience above all else;
- take a *strategic* approach to digital transformation;
- *commit* to seeing the transformation through;
- hire the *best people* to make the change happen; and
- create a *culture* in which transformation can continue to flourish.

The diagram on the next page shows these five elements. Below each of the five are high-level practices or approaches that need to be put in place in order for transformation to take root and flourish. Underpinning all of this are incentives and organisational structures, which must be aligned to the strategy, and communications and change management – the foundations of successful change in any organisation.

Certain of these elements are so important (and in some cases, conceptual) that they need to be unpacked in more detail. They are explored more thoughtfully later in this book (Chapter 3 discusses strategy, and Part III of this book focuses entirely on culture). This chapter looks at each of the elements at a high level, bringing them to life through a case study and analysing how law firms might be able to apply them in practice to their own transformations.

### 5.1 Element 1: digital companies are customer-centric

*(a) Start with the customer*
Although it is always tempting to jump to technology as the solution for digital transformation, we all know that technology should not be the starting point. Successful digital companies start with the customer,

**Figure 1. Digital success factors**

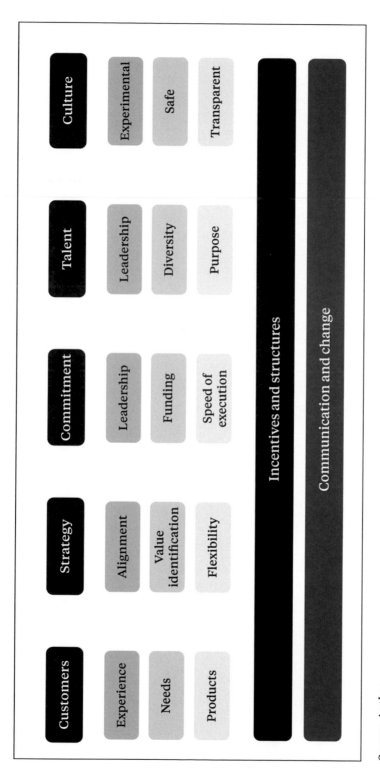

*Source: Author.*

focusing on customer needs before everything else. Some even anticipate what customers will need in the future: by understanding what customers value, they can identify unmet needs and move proactively to satisfy them (Tesla is an excellent example of this principle in action).

Any law firm thinking seriously about its first steps in digital transformation will be faced with strong and divergent views about priorities. Some will advocate creating data lakes, others will suggest that the firm copy its competitors; some will argue for accelerating AI adoption, others for hiring a chief transformation officer. These may all be excellent suggestions, to be implemented along the journey, but they are definitely not the starting point, and can act as a distraction from the foundational issues. The highest priority and the starting point must be the law firm's clients:

> *Frustrated executives wonder, "To transform my business through digital, how do I get started, and how do I orchestrate the digital transformation?" Responding to the loudest voices within the organization is not the way. Instead, established companies that are reaping the greatest benefits from digital begin with the customer – his or her needs, priorities, points of pain and points of delight. Customers may not always know they want an innovation (few customers were clamoring for the first cars or computers), but they do know what they value.*[24]

There are law firms who have plunged into 'innovation' without having asked a single client how (or whether) this would deliver value to them. This mistake can easily be avoided. Law firms should not rely on anecdotal evidence – an increase in questions about law firm technology use in RFPs, for example, or press releases about how other firms are innovating – to inform their strategy. Law firms must speak to their clients, openly and regularly, and understand their pressure points and needs, so that the strategy can be designed around what every other industry refers to as 'the customer'.

Digitally effective businesses practise empathy – speaking frequently to customers, testing new approaches with them, learning from their responses, eliciting feedback on performance and working to understand (and design for) the client experience. This human-centred design thinking methodology, first made famous by the global design company IDEO,[25] has been established as an essential part of the digital toolkit.

*(b) The power of human-centred design*
Human-centred design, which focuses on customer experience (or CX), may sound a bit Silicon Valley for a law firm. In addition, it may not be immediately clear what is new about CX, and what it has to do with digital transformation. Isn't customer experience just about talking to your clients, which is what law firms do all the time? Not quite. When done well, human-centred design involves much more than a typical law firm post-transaction review. It is a structured approach to understanding customer needs and designing services and products to respond to them, and is an important building block for becoming more digitally effective. Organisations that specialise in advising on digital transformation advocate adopting CX at scale, through establishing CX 'factories' to really shift the digital dial. But CX is an intensely human experience, and is equally effective when implemented at a small scale. Even in a CX factory, human effort must precede technology adoption:

> *Digital technologies can help make customer episodes scalable and low-cost, but digital is not sufficient by itself. Human judgment and communication still matter for many high-stakes moments. And behind the digital veneer, factory teams will have to redesign the supporting processes and policies in order to simplify customers' lives and keep them returning for more – all while improving the company's economics.*[26]

What makes CX design so appealing is its focus on the human element of an organisation's interactions with its customers. Although IDEO, the originator of human-centred design, started out as a physical product design company (famously designing the first computer mouse for Apple), it is best known as a company that solves problems by observing the customer and putting them at the centre of the solution. This is a deceptively simple approach, that starts with listening to what your customer has to say.

As IDEO's founder, David Kelley, said in interview in 2013, "[T]he thing is to really build empathy – try to understand people through observing them."[27]

*(c) Designing a legal service*

It is relatively easy to think about design in the context of a product, but perhaps less obvious to see how one might 'design' a professional service. Yet product thinking can be used to design services as well as tangible products. Service design links together human, digital and physical (spatial) interactions to create a differentiated client experience. To bring to life how human-centred design can inject humanity into a bureaucratic and complex environment, and completely redesign a service, consider the case study below. The case study explains how, way back in 2011, IDEO helped a public sector behemoth (the Singapore government) evolve its work visa process to put customers at the centre of the design.

**Case study: IDEO and human-centred government**[28]

In 2008, IDEO was approached by the government of Singapore to work with a number of government agencies. The brief was a redesign of policies and practices to put the needs of the government's customers – the public – first.

Singapore has a high number of foreign workers, and the process for issuing work visas needed a radical overhaul. Although highly efficient (the fastest in the world), users reported that the process was anonymous and cold – not the atmospherics a country would want when welcoming its future workforce. IDEO worked with the Singapore government's Ministry of Manpower to humanise the process, using its human-centred design approach.

IDEO focused on both the end-to-end visa process and the physical space in which visas were issued. Part of IDEO's approach is to map the journey of the customer, in this case from first entry into the ministry buildings to finally receiving the piece of paper that allows the application to work in Singapore. Starting with the physical building, IDEO worked with ministry staff and customers to transform the space, from a cold bureaucratic office with plastic chairs and authoritarian signs to a welcoming space with a doughnut-shaped 'enrolment bar' (in place of a sterile desk), and comfortable 'cabanas' for family appointments. No detail in the process was overlooked; instead of being called by number, the new process had customers called by name, further personalising the experience.

The process of issuing visas was also given a makeover by IDEO, with a focus on simplification at every stage. This included redesigning the appeals process to make it less cumbersome, streamlining the back-end system, reducing the number of different types of passes and making it easier to register for and collect a work pass. The tone of communications became warmer, clearer and less 'legal': the letter the worker received when the visa was issued was changed from a long missive peppered with legalese simply to read, "You can come to Singapore."

The principles that IDEO applied to humanising this process were simple:
- Start with citizens (understand their needs and aspirations).
- Map the journey (understand each step in the customer journey, including what happens before and after the interactions with the ministry).
- Forget the 'average' (there is no average customer – design must be inclusive).
- Visualise change (prototype and visualise rather than use long documents to describe the change).
- Simplify in the face of complexity (look for the root of the issue, even where the system is complex).

*(d) Human-centred design in a law firm environment*
It may sound far-fetched and removed from the reality of legal practice,

but human-centred service design is morphing into legal service design and rapidly gaining currency. LegalGeek, the organiser of the biggest and most influential lawtech start-up conference in the world, hosted a sub-conference entirely dedicated to legal design in both 2018 and 2019. Stanford Law School has a lab dedicated to legal design. Legal design has even made its way onto the curricula of law schools in the United Kingdom.

Despite the growing profile of legal service design in academic circles, and despite the column inches that are increasingly devoted it, legal service design is not routinely put into practice in law firms. (Some are experimenting. In 2020 Linklaters launched a legal design competition that resulted in 45 ideas being submitted from across the firm's global network. The winning idea, which was developed by lawyers in collaboration with clients, was a simplified pre-closing memorandum – a guide for client teams on their legal obligations after an acquisition has been agreed but has not yet closed.)

Experimentation aside, it is my experience that most law firms do not take a structured, human-centred approach to solving their clients' problems. This is because the design approach requires a level of openness with clients that does not come naturally, and for which lawyers are currently not trained. There are three common barriers to adopting human-centred design in law firms:
- Lawyers assume that clients expect a 'Rolls Royce' approach to delivery.
- Lawyers are reluctant to show vulnerability.
- Lawyers are generally transactional thinkers – they are not curious about the end-to-end client experience.

**The Rolls Royce approach:** It is not that law firms don't care about their clients. They do care, and deeply. Lawyers will work exceptionally hard, over extended periods of time, to deliver the best results. Clients will often get Rolls Royce service from their counsel whether or not they need it or ask for it. The tendency is to throw everything the firm has at delivery of a mandate, and to deliver perfection, regardless of the financial or human cost. The problem is that clients often don't want a

Rolls Royce, and would be perfectly happy with a Mini. At the risk of straining the metaphor, clients certainly don't want to pay for delivery of a car they didn't order. The just-work-harder-to-deliver-faster school of client care is not sustainable at a number of levels. It is expensive for the law firm's clients. It has a negative impact on the law firm's people. And it is often not what the client really wants or needs.

As the long hours and culture of presenteeism continue to take their toll on those who work in traditional law firm partnerships, with mental health becoming a real issue in the profession, some clients are actively campaigning against the Rolls Royce culture. In October 2018 Barclays introduced its Mindful Business Charter. The Charter set out guidelines for a new way of working (originally for Barclays and their external counsel), with the aim of removing the 'always on' culture and unnecessary stress prevalent in the legal community. The Charter covers openness and respect, smart meetings and emails, respecting rest periods and mindful delegation, outlining best practice for each area. This is an extract:

> *The intention of the Mindful Business Charter is to remove unnecessary sources of stress and promote better mental health and wellbeing in the workplace. We recognise that there will be times and transactions when long-hours and stress cannot be avoided, but this isn't always the case, and we want it to become the exception rather than the rule.*[29]

What is telling is that the push to manage work more effectively and efficiently (which is at the core of the Charter) comes not from the law firm, but from the client. One has to question whether, left to their own devices, law firms would ever have developed a document of this kind – or if they would ever have suspected that such a document might be welcome. If they had been listening to their clients and asking them the right questions, putting humans at the centre of design, law firms could have led the way, rather than being pulled along.

**Showing vulnerability:** Another reason why law firms are reluctant to practice human-centred design is that, in general, lawyers do not like to show vulnerability. Lawyers are used to advising, to having all the answers, and have an unshakeable belief in the inviolability of their expertise. A human-centred design session will require them to leave that expertise at the door, and to come to clients with questions rather than with answers. This is a really hard sell in a law firm.

This is not an issue for lawyers alone – it could be considered a characteristic of professionals working in regulated industries. IDEO has done a lot of work in the healthcare sector, and has this to say:

*In healthcare, as in many tightly regulated industries, expertise is held sacred, which means nobody wants to feel like – or appear as if – they don't know how to arrive at a solution. But the purpose of using design to solve problems is to allow uncertainty and open questions to drive new thinking. The point is to explore possibilities through prototyping and learning.*[30]

The closest law firms get to a service design conversation is likely to be a post-transaction review, or a questionnaire sent to clients to elicit feedback on a particular area or – my absolute favourite cop-out – conversations with 'safe' clients who are alumni of the firm. Taking feedback in this way about very specific individual client touchpoints is not sufficient to get an overview of the end-to-end client experience.

**Mapping the end-to-end client experience:** Law firms can undoubtedly form very close bonds with their clients, particularly if they have worked side by side with them through moments of crisis (a restructuring) or moments of triumph (a landmark acquisition). Lawyers are likely to have a very deep understanding of the pain points and client expectations associated with those particular transactions. What they generally do not have is a good enough view of the day-to-day operations, the business as usual, the politics and challenges of the client's organisation. This level of insight is critical to human-centred design.

Consider this example, from a pay TV provider who was looking to manage churn, new competitive pressures and escalating costs. The

*This is the key – not just taking feedback from a client on the transaction you have just closed, which will probably result in positive reflections on the performance and hard work of individual lawyers – but looking at the whole experience, from the client's perspective.*

provider had a deep understanding of discrete issues relating to particular touchpoints with clients, but was still not managing to keep its customers. The provider's leadership team decided to look at the end-to-end customer experience, rather than focusing on individual known problems:

*As they dug in, they discovered that the firm's emphasis on perfecting touchpoints wasn't enough. The company had long been disciplined about measuring customers' satisfaction with each transaction involving the call centers, field services, and the website, and scores were consistently high. But focus groups revealed that many customers were unhappy with their overall interaction. Looking solely at individual transactions made it hard for the firm to identify where to direct improvement efforts, and the high levels of satisfaction on specific metrics made it hard to motivate employees to change.*

*As company leaders dug further, they uncovered the root of the problem. Most customers weren't fed up with any one phone call, field visit, or other interaction – in fact, they didn't much care about those singular touchpoints. What reduced satisfaction was something few companies manage – cumulative experiences across multiple touchpoints and in multiple channels over time.*[31]

This is the key – not just taking feedback from a client on the transaction you have just closed, which will probably result in positive reflections on the performance and hard work of individual lawyers – but looking at the whole experience, from the client's perspective. Some of the most important moments from a client's perspective might precede or follow the transaction itself – indeed, the billing processes is a known pain point for most law firm clients. Many lawyers are simply not curious about what happens before and after their involvement with the client. They do not like to participate in open sessions in which clients explore in detail the strengths and weaknesses of the client experience, because it feels uncomfortable. But to really understand your customer, you have to embrace discomfort:

*No matter the industry, it can be highly uncomfortable to do things differently, even when everyone is aligned on the ultimate goal of innovating and creating change. So much of healthcare is about following protocol. Billing. Process improvement. Hierarchy in healthcare adds to that discomfort. Often, there are big divides between roles and status, and people are more often judged on their mistakes, rather than their successes. Can department chiefs and front desk receptionists work as peers on a team? Can we prototype a new service experience with real patients going in for surgery? Leaders who want to effect change need to explicitly acknowledge and address that discomfort.*[32]

This is a description of the healthcare industry – but it is eerily close to the situation in law firms.

*(e) Getting started with customer-centred design*

In summary, although all law firms will tell you that they are client-focused, and will believe themselves to be so, in reality there is a lot of work to be done really to understand their clients' needs, current and future, and to deliver a seamless client experience. So, what can law firms do to address this, and to build their digital muscles in the area of client experience?

A practical way to introduce human-centred design into a law firm is to invest time in mapping the client experience. This involves convening a group of willing participants, including clients with whom you have a good relationship (or, even better, a client with whom you are forging a new relationship) to map out the full end-to-end journey in relation to a particular area or aspect of an interface with a client. The ultimate aim should be to map the entire law firm client experience from beginning to end; however, this is a significant undertaking. It would need to cover each part of client-facing and professional support in the firm, across a number of different areas:

- horizon scanning for new client opportunities;
- new relationship building and marketing;
- pitching;
- client and matter opening;

- matter delivery;
- matter closing;
- billing and recovery; and
- document management.

Every element, that is, of what a law firm does that touches the client.

Bain & Company tell us that "trying to tackle the entire customer experience at once, to infuse digital elements throughout, is an overly broad and complex goal",[33] and recommend the approach of looking at customer 'episodes', which can be a series of interactions which make up a particular service or experience.

As this is not necessarily a comfortable exercise, it helps to have a third party facilitate, not least to bring some challenge into the room. It is also very important to make sure the mapping is led by a multidisciplinary and diverse team from the law firm, representing all areas of client delivery (not just the lawyers). Ideally there should be some diversity on the client side too – the experience of general counsel is not going to be the same as that of the line lawyer, the legal operations professional or the procurement team.

Customer experience exercises are not in themselves hard to do – but they do require a commitment of time and energy. Anyone who has worked in a law firm will recognise that carving out substantial amounts of time from busy lawyers' schedules is a perennial challenge. If help is needed to persuade partners to commit to a customer experience initiative, then the economic argument may be useful – the rewards of institutionalising a focus on the client justify the effort:

*While the effect of [customer experience] design has been hard to measure, suggestive links between design and business performance do exist. The Design Management Institute found that design-led, publicly traded companies outperformed the S&P 500 by 211% over the 10 years ending in 2015.*[34]

**Case study: Alex Smith**[35]

**From service design to systems design – the untapped power of the product mindset**

Alex Smith knows a thing or two about listening to customers. Previously innovation manager at Reed Smith, and before that senior product lead at LexisNexis, Smith is now global AI product lead at iManage (which supplies a large number of law firms with their document management services). Smith is unashamedly passionate about service design. He is an expert on knowledge, data and search – and is also a vocal critic of the 'innovation theatre' that prevails in some parts of the legal sector. Smith has also spent a significant amount of time thinking about how law firms can achieve better client proximity by identifying the real problems that need to be solved – and designing a solution that delivers a superior client experience.

**Identifying the real problem:** Smith emphasises how crucial it is to understand and contextualise the real problem that needs to be solved. The lawyer or client may think they know what the problem is, but the key is to challenge those assumptions and look for the genuine root of the issue. Building a product or a solution for only part of the process without context will not deliver the right result.

**'Jobs to be done':** There are number of descriptors for this approach: service design, user journey mapping or, the most recent coinage, 'jobs to be done'. Whatever you call it, the approach is pretty much the same. Smith describes the method used by Riverview Law, an early play alternative legal services provider (ALSP), UK-based, now acquired by a Big 4 consultancy. Called 'moments of truth', the approach involved mapping out the end-to-end process for delivery (of alternative legal services, in this case) and giving everyone three stickers. The participants were told that they had only three moments on the map that they could influence or change, and to place their stickers on those three moments. This approach is an effective way to focus the mind on what really matters.

Smith emphasises the importance of getting to the root of the client problem, not its manifestation:

*You need to get to a realisation of where the real problem moment is. When a client is distressed and turns to a law firm for help, that moment of engagement is not where the problem lies. The problem came before, as did the opportunity to solve it.*

Smith gives the example of working with a client whose legal team was having issues with managing the negotiation of contract terms with third parties. The client thought they had identified both the problem (the form of the contract was difficult to navigate), and the answer (automation according to a playbook). When the process was mapped out, end-to-end, and the team identified the 'moment of truth', the real problem emerged: the sales team was agreeing to terms with third parties without consulting the legal team. The answer, it turned out, was not complex contract automation, but a simple checklist, provided to the sales team by the legal team, setting out five points to bear in mind before agreeing contract terms.

**Another kind of listening:** Reflecting on his time at Reed Smith and on the work he has done subsequently with law firms, Smith is of the view that law firms "leave a lot at the door" without ever realising it. He suggests there are many simple and inexpensive ways to gain insights into a client's business. He gives the example of a large client in the financial services sector with a labyrinthine internal structure and a reputation for being demanding of its panel firms. As with all demanding clients, they asked for a lot of secondee support. Smith's solution was simple: programmatically to interview all present and past Reed Smith secondees to the client, in the process extracting valuable insights about the client's structure and tacit power base. This sounds obvious, but is not something law firms always do. In Smith's words, it is "another kind of client listening".

*(f) Lessons for law firms*
Coming to clients with questions rather than answers can be an uncomfortable experience for lawyers. However, the rewards of

focusing on the client experience can be significant. By thoughtfully adopting the principles of legal service design, law firms can get closer to their clients, deepen relationships and derive new insights. Adopting an entirely new approach to interacting with clients is ambitious – start small, with trusted clients, and prove value. Below are three lessons from our case studies.

**Define the service you are focusing on and only design the details that matter:** For example, if you are designing the closing mechanics of a large transaction, you might focus more on practicalities, such as digital signatures through mobile devices, transparency around progress to completing the signing process, and creating a sense of order and control to put your client's mind at ease. If you are designing for taking a witness interview, you might concentrate more on the human and emotional elements, the physical space and the atmospherics.

**Map the client journey for the service, factoring in the before and after:** Truly to empathise with the client and to put yourself in their shoes, you need to think not just about the 'service moment' but also about what precedes it for your client and what comes afterwards. For example, if you are presenting the client with the results of a due diligence review, think about the context of the review. What outcome is the client's business trying to achieve, and what will the client do with your report once they have received it? Present it to the board? Stick it in a desk draw? Use it to create a risk matrix? Understanding the context in which you are delivering the service informs the best way to deliver it for your client.

**Involve your clients and your people at different levels:** Effective design of services must be done collaboratively, and without making assumptions about the client's needs. Taking the views of a number of different people who are involved in delivering and receiving the service will help to build a more accurate picture. This means thinking not just about the GC as your client, but bringing in the GC's business colleagues and external end clients too. On the law firm side, it means designing not just with partners, but with lawyers at all levels, other business professionals and any third parties (such as relationship firms) who might be involved in the process.

*5.2 Element 2: Successful digital companies have a digital strategy (aligned to business strategy)*

*(a) The importance of strategy*
The development of a strategy for continuous digital transformation, aligned to the firm's core business strategy, is absolutely critical to success. The next chapter of this book explores in detail the practical steps that law firms should take to develop, support and communicate a vision and strategy. Here, I outline the basic building blocks that need to be considered, and share a case study of a bold and customer-focused approach that has proved highly successful.

*(b) Serendipity vs strategy*
Digitally effective companies are strategic in their approach to digital transformation. By this I mean that they make investments in technology, digital talent and cultural change to support the organisation's overarching business and growth plans, rather than making those investments tactically or speculatively. Innovation (which is an important element of any digital strategy but is not the strategy itself) is often more undirected, involving placing bets on speculative technologies, investing in R&D, and experimenting with entirely new and transformative business lines. This is the former head of innovation at Autodesk, a company that makes software for designers of products as varied as smartphones and supercars, describing how his innovation team operates:

> *[T]he group is entirely undirected, no one tells us what to do. From time to time, I'll tell the leadership, "Here's what we're working on and why." There's a lot of trust, little oversight, zero direction. Which is important if you're trying to break out. Creating a strategy will by definition fail.*[36]

A similar story from Spotify co-founder, Daniel Ek:

> *So many companies talk about innovation, and they try to put processes in place … I don't think that works. I don't think any innovation happens at a desk – by someone structuring a creative brainstorm. Innovation is serendipity. It happens when people get totally new influences or ideas that come totally from the sidelines.*[37]

There is a place for experimentation in an overarching strategy, certainly. But serendipity cannot drive an entire digital initiative. Digital transformation differs from innovation in that it cannot be separate from the business and must be aligned to a broader business strategy. This is not to suggest that strategy should be static and monolithic; it is important for it to evolve, allowing an organisation to pivot in response to unforeseen events. An overarching plan, however, is essential. Like a complex jigsaw with many pieces, it is easier and quicker to complete if you plan how to put the pieces together (start with the corners, build the edges) rather than picking up random pieces and discarding them if they don't fit. A deliberate strategy is essential, not least because speed and the ability to execute are such important differentiators in the digital age.

### (c) The first steps towards developing the strategy

A digital strategy is not a back-of-the-envelope exercise. It takes time and careful planning. However, pressure to move quickly can be the issue that prevents law firms from approaching this exercise in a considered and thoughtful way. It is essential to invest the time to get it right.

> *Crafting a deliberate strategy that unlocks real value may take a bit longer at the outset, but can massively accelerate your transformation down the road.*[38]

Taking the first steps to developing a digital strategy can feel overwhelming. There are many conflicting views on the 'right' way to approach it. My own research into best practice followed by successful digital companies, and my experience as part of the team developing Freshfields Bruckhaus Deringer's award-winning digital transformation strategy, suggests the following eight practical steps to strategy development (which are not necessarily interdependent or sequential):

- Understand your law firm's business strategy.
- Undertake a diagnostic of your current strengths and weaknesses and identify opportunities to create digital value.
- Undertake a comprehensive review of the competitor landscape.
- Talk to clients.
- Create a business case for funding.
- Create a roadmap for delivery.
- Create your vision and strategy document and communications plan.
- Communicate widely.

Chapter 3 goes into some detail around the practical actions that need to be taken to accomplish each of these steps.

### (d) Strategy must be inclusive

To ensure good governance and cohesion, the strategy needs to be owned by the team leading digital transformation, but must not be developed in a vacuum. To drive business value, the strategy needs to be very close to the business itself, developed in consultation with the lawyers on the front line who generate revenue. To be actionable, the strategy also needs input from different operational parts of the firm. One practical way to achieve this is for the C-suite member leading the transformation[39] to establish an extended leadership team structure that includes senior representation from the other key business functions: marketing, finance, pricing, operations and HR. This multi-functional approach is relatively unusual in law firms, as business functions can be very siloed. However, provided the other business function heads are supportive of their people joining the extended leadership team, it can be an effective way of ensuring that the strategy has buy-in from all the business leaders before communicating out to the partners. The extended leadership team should not be established simply to navigate law firm politics; digital transformation is most definitely a team sport and touches every part of the firm. Every function needs to be part of the change (and benefit from the upside).

*(e) Digital strategy must be aligned with firmwide strategy*

Digital delivery is not a technology or 'IT' exercise; it should be an intrinsic part of how the law firm's core services are delivered to clients. For this reason, digital strategy must align with and reflect (and over time, even drive) the firmwide strategy. As law firms reflect on how their business and delivery models will need to change in response to a shifting market, and work to respond to their clients' changing needs, the digital strategy will evolve to support the model. The case study below illustrates how this can work in practice.

---

**Case study: Ping An**[40]

Ping An Insurance (Group) Company of China, Ltd started out as an insurance company in Shenzhen in 1988. Since then, it has grown into a digital powerhouse. In 2020, Ping An was ranked seventh in the *Forbes* Global 2000 list and 21st on the *Fortune* Global 500 list, reporting revenues of $155 billion, assets of $1.2 trillion and profits of $18.8 billion.

The driver for Ping An's success is its bold digital strategy. Ping An is widely lauded for having developed and executed one of the most successful digital transformations in the financial services sector, the company's digital strategy being held up as a model of best practice.

The strategy is multi-layered, and the company is constantly evolving. Over the years, by executing on a deliberate strategy, Ping An has shifted from being an insurance company to a technology-led company:

- Ping An's roots are as a traditional insurance company (the first in China, established in 1988).
- The company moved into financial services, establishing a traditional banking and asset management business line in 2003.
- Ping An then diversified into fintech and healthtech.
- In recent years, the company has invested heavily in technology to create a 'technology ecosystem' that encompasses a number of successful new businesses, including:

---

- Lufax, the world's largest digital wealth management platform;
- Ping An Financial Cloud, a third-party cloud environment providing cloud-based services to financial institutions operating in China;
- Ping An Good Doctor, listed on the Hong Kong Stock Exchange, the world's largest telemedicine platform;
- Ping An OneConnect, an open platform that provides business technology services developed internally at Ping An to other financial service stakeholders, in China and internationally; and
- Ping An's smart city ecosystem, which promotes sustainable city development with self-developed AI, blockchain, cloud computing and other leading technologies.

What is most compelling about Ping An's strategy is that it has been shaped, as Jonathan Larsen, the company's chief innovation officer puts it, "from the outside in":

*It's one thing to be a major and an innovative financial institution today. But I think we have to recognise a lot of innovation is being driven from outside of the financial industry. 30 years ago, most innovations were initiated by the industry, by a small number of large players, and also by a small number of technology vendors. That has completely changed. Today most innovation is coming really from the outside-in.*[41]

By looking outside the industry and learning from companies such as Tencent and Alibaba, who were driving a new digital economy in China during the financial crisis of 2007/8, Ping An changed its strategy, pivoting to become a technology-led company and committing to the investment needed to achieve this:

*It is important to grasp how Peter [Ma, founder and Chairman and CEO of Ping An] and the company look at the future. On one hand, he believes the advent of digital economy is rendering the capabilities that have made us successful in the past, 1.4 million insurance*

> *agents, a great brand, a lot of capital, less and less relevant –*
> *although these are, of course, critical to our business in the near*
> *term. On the other, our ability to access data, to be able to make*
> *great value out of data to serve client needs is going to become more*
> *relevant. That insight is powering all of our strategies going*
> *forward.*[42]

### (f) Lessons for law firms

This example may feel very far removed from the reality for most law firm partnerships, who are not ready to transform into technology-led businesses any time soon. Rather than being overwhelmed by the success stories, law firms should follow the lead of companies like Ping An, learn lessons from outside legal and scale them to apply to their own digital journeys. Below are three lessons to start with.

**Be bold:** An incremental approach to digital change, with no strategy supporting it and no vision of the desired end state, is unlikely to deliver real business value.

**Look 'outside-in':** When developing a strategy for digital change, radical answers are unlikely to come from other law firms, or other legal services providers. Corporate law firms have privileged access to some of the most innovative companies in the world. Ask to speak to clients about their digital strategies – learn from them.

**Align digital strategy to firm strategy:** For Ping An, business strategy and digital strategy are one and the same. This is very unlikely to be the case for law firms. When developing a digital strategy, start with the firm strategy and align the digital strategy to support it.

### 5.3 Element 3: Successful digital companies commit to digital change

### (a) Positioning the investment

Even when the firm has a clearly defined digital strategy that has been approved and adopted, digital transformation is a long, hard road. As noted above, 70% of digital transformations fail. Transformation can be costly, and take a long time. Those that succeed commit to the change, see it as a permanent part of the firm's strategy, and sustain momentum through good times and bad.

This would be challenging for any organisation, and is particularly so for law firms, who have a relatively short-term approach to investment (see Chapter 5). Most law firms will have seen their fair share of 'IT projects'; many will have gone through an upgrade of their practice management system or finance systems. These programmes can be horrifically complex, slow and painful, not to mention expensive. Many will have been delivered using a waterfall methodology, which essentially involves gathering customer requirements up front, then designing the solution before testing and rolling out to customers.[43] Although this approach has its merits in certain situations, it is generally considered to be outmoded, slow, expensive and insufficiently customer-focused. Many law firms will have been burnt by the experience of this kind of programme and will recoil at the thought of a multi-year digital transformation programme that depends heavily on the firm's technology teams.

Given this context, when the team leading transformation is communicating its digital transformation strategy, the first questions to which partners will want answers are likely to be:
- How much will the transformation cost?
- How long will it take?

The answer to both, frustratingly, is "It depends". Firms with a lot of legacy IT will need to modernise as a priority, and this can take a long time to achieve.[44]

*Business leaders consistently underestimate the timeline, which can lead to nervousness after about 12 to 18 months and pressure to pull the plug on the transformation or massively scale back. In a global survey, 87% of senior executives said they felt under pressure to demonstrate financial results within two years. We know of a number of cases where transformation budgets were cut by as much as 50 percent within the first year of the program.[45]*

Transformation teams will need to manage expectations very tightly and to be realistic about the level of commitment that is involved. They will need to work closely with their communications teams to make sure that a realistic message lands in the firm – without making the digital transformation sound unachievable, and without squeezing all the excitement out of it.

*(b) The importance of a robust business case and committed leadership*
Commitment means both financial commitment and commitment of leadership time. In terms of financial commitment, it is important to secure budget for the transformation and to protect it as far as is possible, to avoid the budget-slashing exercise referred to above. The transformation must be positioned as a multi-year investment. Part of this comes down to preparing a really robust and convincing business case for digital transformation, which is realistic about costs but also sets out the anticipated benefits (business case development is discussed in detail in Chapter 3).

Of course, when times are hard, it is likely that budget will come under threat. This is where the firm's commitment will really be tested, and the digital team will need to go into battle. Digital leaders should be prepared to challenge other capital initiatives (new premium office space could be a contender, given the anticipated seismic change to the way law firms are now working) to make sure that sufficient funds and leadership attention are committed to the transformation. Other investments (for example, the costs of hiring a lateral team) will be harder to challenge, which makes the benefits case for the digital change even more essential and underscores the importance of very strong and experienced leadership that can clearly articulate the urgency for the change.

Commitment of leadership time is just as important as funding, and perhaps even more difficult to achieve. Digital is a hot topic, and firm leaders like to talk about it, not least because it is high on law firm clients' agendas. Launching new digital solutions and winning awards makes everyone feel good. But commitment and interest need to be sustained over a long period, which can be difficult, particularly when (as is inevitable) the transformation isn't going to plan.

*(c) Establishing governance*

The right governance can be very helpful in sustaining leadership interest. To avoid an upwards reporting trap, with digital initiatives relegated to the last agenda item at firm board meetings, law firms might consider establishing an advisory board that is dedicated to digital change. The primary aim of the board should be to act as supportive digital advocates, working with the CTO to advise on firm strategy, to make recommendations to management about significant digital investments and to make sure the client voice is central to the decision making.

The composition of such a board is very important to get right. It should not be too large, or it becomes unwieldy and slow. It should not be self-selecting, or you will end up with only partners who are interested in technology, which can be dangerous. In fact, it is useful to have some partners who are sceptical about digital change (provided they are open-minded) as they are likely to be more representative of the partnership as a whole. The board should not make technology decisions (that is the preserve of the CTO); it should ensure that technology decisions are being made in a way that aligns to client and business strategy. Finally, the board members ideally need to be as diverse as possible (tricky in a traditional law firm partnership), covering different practice areas and, in an international firm, regions.

It is worth investing time in putting a digital advisory board together with the right partner composition. Do not underestimate the challenge. Partners in law firms are incredibly smart, very powerful, and often opinionated. Some working in the law firm innovation space advocate limiting the involvement of partners, and investing more deliberately in talent from outside the legal sector. One innovation team member at a global law firm has this to say:

> *There is a danger at any law firm that partners can have a significant say over matters, yet they are not equipped with the skills to make informed decisions. This is perhaps why point solutions, rather than strategic solutions, emerge so commonly. A partner is brought up to respond to client demands, no matter what. Usually, they are not*

*required to think any more strategically than that. But when venturing into product development, it is essential to be strategic. You cannot approach these problems like you would a legal matter.*

*I believe law firms must look to other industries, rather than partners. Bringing in a person with experience in product development would not only ensure the right decisions are made, but would serve to up-skill others.*

The optimal composition of the digital board will depend on the culture of the individual firm and its partners. My own view is that, wherever possible, partners should be involved in digital initiatives at the strategic level, with clear terms of reference around the expectations and limits of their role. When the governance is right, an effective digital advisory board can help to speed up funding decisions so that momentum for digital change is maintained. The board can also be a valuable channel for communications about the progress of the digital initiative (see Chapter 3).

*(d) 'Killing the puppies'*

With apologies for the slightly distasteful heading, commitment does not end with securing multi-year investment for the digital transformation initiative. True commitment requires not only staying power and leadership to push delivery through numerous challenges, but also requires leaders to kill off digital activities that are not delivering value. This can be difficult, particularly if those initiatives have been announced to the firm and the public with great fanfare.

**Case study: Walmart**

Walmart is a great example of digital commitment in action. The US retailer is, at the time of writing, the largest in the world, with 11,400 stores globally. The road to success has not been easy. Walmart, in common with much of the retail sector, faces fierce competition from Amazon, which continues to dominate the US online retail market. There have been times over the last five years when Walmart's prospects have looked dim. In 2020, however, Walmart revenues were up at $524 billion, with its e-commerce business,

Walmart.com, growing rapidly. This is the result of a tenacious commitment to digital transformation – and some good timing.

Walmart has displayed the right kind of paranoia, refusing to rest on its laurels as the successful incumbent of US retail. The retailer has made a number of investments in the digital space, some of them speculative and risky, and persevered in the face of significant challenges. The strategy is multi-layered and required significant investment, running into the billions of dollars. It included acquisitions of digital natives in the e-commerce space (acquiring Jet.com in 2016 and a 77% stake in Flipkart, an India-based web marketplace operator in 2018) and a technology investment of $5 billion year on year since 2014. It also involved some experimentation in new ways of delivering the best customer experience. In 2019, Walmart launched its 'Intelligent Retail Lab', a showcase store in Levittown, New York which, according to the Walmart website, offers a "unique real-world shopping environment designed to explore the possibilities artificial intelligence can contribute to the store experience".[46] Sensors, cameras and processors are used in the space to give real-time information on stock inventory and availability, including the freshness of the produce on offer.

This is all exciting stuff, but it could be argued that any big corporation with dollars to spend can easily throw money at a problem and come out on top. Yet Walmart's commitment is not demonstrated solely by the money it has invested. The corporation has also shown its tenacity by backing its strategy in the face of criticism, and persevering until the time is right to switch gears in order to sustain success. The story of Walmart and Jet.com is a great example of this.

In 2016, with Amazon rapidly gaining traction, Walmart acquired a relatively small e-commerce start-up, Jet.com, as part of the strategy to expand its portfolio of e-commerce sites. Walmart paid a whopping $3.3 billion for Jet.com, a new digital native without significant traction in the market. Jet.com's primary innovation was a real-time pricing algorithm that displayed to customers the price of goods on the basis of the goods' location (if the customer purchased multiple goods from the same distribution centre, the price would reduce in real time). Its other innovation was a laser focus on customer satisfaction. What Jet.com really offered, however, was insight into the future of e-commerce and a new way of thinking that could re-enliven the oil tanker mentality of the incumbent Walmart. Jet.com's employees were transferred over to Walmart, and Jet.com's founder, Marc Lore, was appointed head of Walmart's e-commerce business in the United States.

The market reception for the acquisition was mixed; some called it a frolic and many market commentators considered Jet.com to be massively overpriced. In 2018, Walmart reported drastic slowdown in its online growth, prompting market speculation that it was faltering in the war against Amazon and that Walmart's online business was unlikely ever to catch up. Walmart continued to commit to the investment, however, and in 2019 Walmart's online sales shot up by 40%, accounting for approximately half of its US growth.

The acquisition was a gamble that paid off, kickstarting a serious focus on e-commerce and importing the energy and customer focus of a start-up into an established brand. In the three full fiscal years since the acquisition, Walmart's e-commerce sales have increased by 176%. Grocery in particular has been a stellar success story. Walmart now has approximately 3,300 stores offering grocery pickup and more than 1,850 offering grocery delivery – an investment that was both strategic and serendipitous, given the limitations on traditional grocery shopping resulting from the coronavirus pandemic.

In the spring of 2020, Walmart announced that Jet.com was being wound down and the brand phased out. When he announced that this particular puppy was to be terminated, the CEO of Walmart, Doug McMillon, paid tribute to the contribution Jet.com had made to Walmart, crediting it with jump-starting the progress Walmart had made over the last few years:

*[I]f you look at the trajectory of our business, it changed when we made that acquisition.*[47]

In acquiring Jet.com, Walmart had spotted an opportunity to accelerate change within the company. But Walmart also showed commitment by refusing to abandon its established business model simply to become another Amazon. Walmart retained its physical presence by keeping its stores, which turned out to be a masterstroke.

Walmart has put its stores to very good use. Not content with simply reaping the rewards from increased online sales during the pandemic, Walmart pivoted to delivering coronavirus vaccinations in-store.[48] In January 2021, Walmart announced that it expected to be able to deliver 10 to 13 million doses per month of the vaccine when at full capacity, using its network of more than 5,000 pharmacies in the United States and Puerto Rico. Its unique network meant that Walmart could deliver the vaccine to the places that needed it most, the 'health case deserts' (mostly rural locations where there are few options for customers to access health care, designated by the US government as 'medically underserved areas'). Amazon could not compete with this. Quite apart from the greater good to which Walmart was contributing by delivering this service, think of the customer experience opportunity. One can only speculate as to the level of customer loyalty engendered by being the brand that delivered a lifesaving vaccine. You can't put a price on that.

### (e) Lessons for law firms

Walmart was an incumbent, with all the legacy that comes with it. The leadership took some calculated risks and committed to them, which paid off handsomely. Walmart pivoted to a new business model while retaining the strength of the brand. Below are three lessons to take from their journey.

**Commit to the strategy even when times are hard:** If you have invested time (and money) in developing and implementing a strategy, commit to that strategy and see it through even when returns are not immediate. Do not scale back at the first hurdle. If Walmart had listened to market criticism and given up in 2018, they would not have reaped the rewards of their sizeable investment.

**Know when to stop:** Commitment also means showing leadership in knowing when to stop. When part of the strategy is clearly not working (and subject to the lesson above), kill it, even if this means going back on a public announcement.

**Don't destroy what you have built:** In committing to a digital strategy, do not lose sight of your traditional strengths. Incumbents have strengths that digital disruptors do not – brand and relationships amongst them. Walmart did not acquire Jet.com and then move entirely into e-commerce – they kept their stores, which has been a masterstroke for engendering customer loyalty.

*5.4 Element 4: For successful digital transformation, you need the best (digital) people*

*(a) The challenge of Generation Z[49]*
Historically, law firms, particularly corporate law firms, could take their pick of the best graduates. Law firms pay well, the benefits are good, the work is interesting and the brand is great to have on the CV. Who would not want to work at an Allen & Overy, or a Kirkland & Ellis?

It would be overstating the point to suggest that talented graduates are no longer attracted to working in law firms. Having been part of the graduate interview team at a Magic Circle firm, I know from experience that both the number of applications and the standard of candidates remains extremely high. However, the competition to recruit and retain the very best candidates is fierce.

As Gen Z come into the workplace, they are likely to be highly attuned to issues of culture and diversity, as well as looking for a sense of purpose in the work that they do.[50] They will certainly expect to join a digitally effective, forward-looking organisation, and might legitimately expect a more flexible approach to office working than was standard in the pre-pandemic world. These factors will be significant when the very best candidates are making a decision about where they want to work (see Chapter 6 for more on this). On issues of diversity and inclusion, as on culture, the corporate law firm gloss is somewhat tarnished. Firms are going to have to continue to work hard over the next few years to address the organisational and cultural biases that have emerged with such clarity in recent years. The same is true of law firms' digital effectiveness.

### (b) The battle for digital talent

Leaving Gen Z and the future workplace aside for a moment, it is already the case that the market for digital talent is quite different from that for legal talent, and requires a correspondingly different approach. The brightest and the best digital graduates (not to mention the digital 'stars' at the senior level) will not automatically be attracted to professional services, and are even less likely to be attracted to a traditional law firm partnership. Law firms need to work hard on their employment proposition for digital talent.[51]

### (c) Hiring for new skills

In practical terms, to have any chance in the battle for digital talent, the law firm talent team itself will need to develop (or hire) new skills and capabilities (I discuss the role of the HR and talent function in more detail in Chapter 8). Systems and processes will need to change too. Finding the best people means challenging established processes and precedent (including around remuneration and incentives). Law firms will need to be prepared to move quickly and with purpose when they have found the right candidate.

The profile and number of new hires will of course depend on the firm's digital strategy. If new product development is a priority, then product management capability will be essential. If the firm has a lot of legacy systems to retire or migrate, then IT systems transformation, cloud skills and programme management experience will be needed. The key to success is to find a stellar digital leader (who does not need to have experience in legal) and empower her or him to build the strategy and the team to deliver it.

## (d) Reskilling your workforce

Having the best digital people is not just about spending money on new hires. Effecting the cultural change that is needed for digital transformation to be a success requires law firms to invest in reskilling their existing people, including their lawyers, to create a more digitally literate workforce. This is not an easy task for a law firm. Building digital skills is a challenge faced by all companies, regardless of sector. However, some industry sectors, such as technology, media and telecom (TMT), are of course significantly more likely to attract people who are interested in technology and who will be open to experimentation and new learnings in the digital space. Lawyers are (traditionally) not of this mindset.

Lawyers are, however, good learners. And it is possible, with deliberate effort, to create an environment in which people can acquire new skills and be incentivised to do so as part of their career progression, as the next case study demonstrates.

**Case study: Procter & Gamble**

Procter & Gamble is a company with its roots in manufacturing, a household name that we associate with consumer products and big brand names like Gillette and Pampers. P&G is not a brand you would immediately think of as being a digital leader. However, as with the Walmart example above, over the past five years P&G has been consciously and successfully changing its business model, with e-commerce sales increasing year on year, up by 40% in the fiscal year 2020 (unsurprisingly, given the impact of coronavirus) and accounting for over 10% of total company sales.[52]

A significant part of this successful business model pivot can be attributed to the culture of learning that P&G has consciously fostered throughout the company. At a time when e-commerce was only 2% of the business, and the threat from digital sales was becoming ever more real, FD Wilder (now retired but formerly senior vice-president of global go-to-market strategy and innovation at P&G) was tasked with leading an e-business growth strategy, which involved increasing the digital IQ of the company. Wilder recognised that successful digitisation requires a mindset change, diffused across the entire company. In Wilder's own words, "If digital expertise is concentrated in too few people, that's a risk for the enterprise."[53]

The key driver for this change was a learning environment to which all employees would have access, delivered in a snackable format that was less of a drag on employee time. The first step taken by P&G was to create a thought leadership platform called Fastest Learner Wins. The name of the platform is unfortunate (it makes learning sound like a competition rather than a benefit) but the thinking behind it is sound: to get every employee at P&G learning and developing so that the company could secure competitive advantage. For P&G, corporate learning is not an esoteric exercise but an investment from which the company expects a return. As Ann Schulte, chief learning officer, says:

> At P&G, we believe that the 'fastest learner wins' because we see in uncertain and changing markets that experimentation, rapid-cycle feedback, and the ability to adapt are competitive imperatives – and all require learning. To help our people learn faster, we are disrupting how we manage learning and development to focus more on the immediate business context and personalized needs by providing easy access to information, performance support aids, and carefully curated training that is relevant and can be directly applied to work.[54]

Faster Learner Wins was an initiative directed at changing the culture of P&G from 'knowing it all' to 'learning it all'. The platform offers a series of videos lasting no longer than five minutes. Interestingly (and echoing Ping An's 'outside-in' strategy), 80% of the modules feature interviews with people outside the industry. This recognition, that the company does not know everything and needs to learn from others, is very important for changing the established culture (a consistent theme running through this book is frustration that law firms are too busy 'advising', and miss the opportunity to learn from their clients).

Developing a healthy learning culture is one part of the P&G strategy. The other part is to develop targeted and specific digital skills that will support the company's e-commerce drive. P&G rolled out a Digital Genius Academy across the enterprise, which aggregated the very best bits of digital training that various business units had already created, then honed that training to focus on the specific areas that are most important to P&G's online customers (search, website navigation, online content).

The third element to the training is intensely practical – a programme called Eyes on Consumer, Hands on Keyboard. Kirti Singh, the chief analytics and insights officer at P&G, explains the thinking behind the initiative:

> Technology is omnipresent, so teams must now have the competencies to win in both the old and the new worlds. During the last four to five years, we have worked on transforming skills and competencies in the world of data and technology to ensure the organization is relevant for the future.[55]

The emphasis of the initiative is on learning by doing, empowering each employee by giving them the technology tools, support and coaching they need to take practical steps to understand and respond to customer needs. Employees can learn how to design their own direct-to-customer website, for example, or how to use analytics to optimise their sales performance, using P&G's data management platform. Learning by doing is a highly effective approach. Remember how quickly digital learning was accelerated by lawyers being forced to use digital tools while working from home during the COVID-19 lockdowns?

The final piece of the learning strategy at P&G was the introduction of an accelerated learning programme (ALP) targeted at high-potential managers. The ALP is a kind of mini-executive MBA, focused on the particular skills P&G wants its best people to acquire. Twice a year, high performers are taken to P&G's largest e-commerce market, China, to learn more about 'new retail' (that is, the digital integration of offline and online commerce). Future leaders are effectively immersed in the technologies and approaches shaping the future of P&G's business.

*(e) Lessons for law firms*

As discussed in detail in Chapter 8, the battle for the best talent is a fierce one. Recruiting the best is important, but is not sufficient to create sustained cultural change. An important part of the strategy should be to create a growth mindset across the organisation. The good news is that lawyers and business professionals in law firms are generally smart people and effective learners, and will respond to a well-designed learning programme that integrates into the flow of their work. P&G had a multi-layered learning and reskilling strategy. Below are four lessons law firms could learn from P&G's approach.

**Create a firmwide digital learning culture:** Break the mindset of lawyers knowing it all. Don't shirk from telling lawyers they need to acquire new skills to be relevant to their clients in a digital world and to be successful in the firm. Incentivise the whole firm to learn new digital skills and create a hunger for ongoing learning.

**Make it snappy:** Lawyers don't like spending time away from billable work, so adopt the P&G approach of bite-sized learning that is baked into lawyers' workflow and reaches them at critical points in their career (for example, just before making partner, or at the point of qualification/becoming a senior associate).

**Look 'outside-in':** Use your clients to inspire all employees with examples of their own digital journeys. Law firms have access to world-class companies – there is simply no excuse for not learning from your clients.

**Get hands-on:** Create opportunities for lawyers, partners and business services professionals to play with technology and experiment with analytics. Give them access to tools to create simple applications and dashboards (any firm that has introduced Microsoft Office 365 will already have access to enterprise tools). Let employees do this in their own time, but incentivise and reward participation.

## 5.5 Element 5: Create a culture in which transformation can continue to flourish

We have heard it said many times. Digitisation requires a new way of working; for organisations to work differently they must change; change can only be successful if it is adopted; adoption depends on mindset; and mindset is inextricably linked to culture. It is not a new insight to observe that digital transformation is not just about technology, but about a change in mindset.

It may be trite, but it is true. As Part III of this book explores in detail, there can be no successful or sustained digital transformation without the right culture to support it.

But what is meant by organisational culture, and how can it be measured or assessed? Culture has been described as being how people act when no one is looking. It shows itself in how people in an organisation behave towards one another, particularly in a hierarchical structure. Corporate culture informs how employees think, and influences both their formal and informal interactions.

In the case of a traditional law firm partnership, where culture is the product of norms and behaviours established over many years, it is tempting to throw our hands up in despair and claim that culture is immutable. It is not; culture is dynamic, and like anything else in an organisation, it can be managed and influenced.

> *You shape the culture of your firm by the decisions you make or facilitate, which then affect behaviour, which subsequently becomes part of 'how things are done here'.*[56]

Not only *can* culture be managed – it *must* be managed. It is important to be deliberate about culture, not only because this is the right thing to do, but also because organisational culture is under close scrutiny. Recent events, in particular the Black Lives Matter and #MeToo movements, have taught us that a positive and inclusive culture is something we have an obligation to work at and strive for. Organisations that do not pay attention to their culture will be held to account, and this has reputational – and ultimately economic – consequences.

Culture change can be brought about by necessity, through the impact of external forces. The coronavirus pandemic is one such force (Satya Nadella, CEO of Microsoft, famously said in April 2020 that Microsoft had seen two years' worth of digital transformation in two months).[57] It is still too early to be sure how law firm culture, with its focus on presenteeism and face time, has been impacted by the pandemic. There is some evidence of a positive effect:

> [M]any firms have found that the pandemic has served as a needed reminder of the importance of creating and maintaining a strong firm culture through renewed emphasis on the firm as an intentional and supportive community for its lawyers and staff. Indeed, leaders of a number of firms have commented on how the shared experience of the pandemic has actually strengthened their firm cultures.[58]

It remains to be seen whether this observation holds true as law firms return to the office and revert to the status quo. Although using a crisis as a catalyst is one way to drive cultural change, it is no substitute for sustained effort in managing culture as part of business as usual. The fact that we recognise that culture can and should be managed does not make it an easy task; cultural change is particularly difficult in law firms, for reasons I discuss in detail in Part III of this book. Before we get to the challenges, however, I want to try to identify the cultural attributes of a digitally effective organisation, and to explore what defines a culture in which digital change can continue to flourish.

Many of the cultural attributes required to be a digitally effective organisation are those we might associate with a 'good' or healthy corporate culture: attributes like organisational diversity (which fuels innovative thinking); transparency (which unites teams around a shared vision); and agility (which allows organisations to be responsive to change and serve customers better). Of course, this does not mean that all digitally effective companies are intrinsically 'good' companies. Facebook's reputation is far from golden, beset with accusations of tax evasion and failure to protect data privacy, not to mention an advertising boycott led by the advocacy group Stop Hate for Profit.[59] But it must be the case that establishing culture at a new, digitally native company is a different (I would argue, a lesser) challenge than changing the culture of an incumbent. A start-up's culture will be influenced by its founders and funders (generally a pretty small group), and can be moulded for the digital age. The culture of an incumbent organisation, such as a large traditional law firm partnership, is influenced by 400+ owners, and will have been shaped over many years, without the injection of much new thinking. Long service and a commitment to the established culture is prized at law firms. When I was at Freshfields, people used to compare particularly loyal partners of long standing to a stick of rock – "Cut him in half and he will have the word 'Freshfields' running through him" (this was intended as a compliment, of course). Other long-established law firms have similar stories.[60] Although long tenure has its advantages, it is unlikely to deliver cultural dynamism.

For this reason, although there are many inspiring examples of digital natives designing their organisations deliberately to create a positive working culture, those examples feel too far away from the law firm reality, and therefore are unlikely to resonate. More relevant are examples of incumbents who have successfully turned around the cultural 'oil tanker' – as is the case with Autodesk, profiled in the case study below.

**Case study: Autodesk**[61]
Autodesk is a world leader in designing software for computer-aided design and 3D visual effects. The company was founded in 1982, just as the technology world was changing, with the advent of the desktop PC disrupting the sale of mainframe computers. From its roots as a small software company selling discs in boxes, Autodesk has grown into a successful digital company with a market capitalisation of around $62 billion. To get to this point has not been easy; Autodesk has had to constantly reinvent itself to secure its place in a world where cloud services and AI have rapidly replaced traditional software services. The company's organisational culture has had to change, too, to keep pace with this reinvention.

Managing culture is not necessarily a touch-feely exercise. To turn a legacy organisation into a successful digital contender takes cultural agility, which means embracing change as a constant. To make this happen, the leadership of Autodesk had to confront some difficult truths and deliver some hard messages over the years.

The first of those messages was in 1983, after Autodesk had successfully launched AutoCAD, a new product designed to be used on an IBM personal computer. The company experienced very rapid growth, such that it simply could not meet demand for the product. John Walker, then CEO, wrote to shareholders warning them that the company could collapse in the next 60 days:

> *Our company is in very deep crisis. Each single segment of the company is overloaded to the point of collapse. We cannot return all the calls from people who want to do business with us, not less plan a coherent advertising campaign ... We have no business plan, even an informal one ... This is a prescription for disaster.*[62]

Walker did more than just complain about the problem – he issued a call to arms, asking the shareholders to contribute whatever skills they had to help Autodesk professionalise quickly. This paid off, and the business grew rapidly, from a valuation of about $200,000 when Walker's letter was written to $500 million four years later. Walker had recognised that a start-up culture was not going to enable Autodesk to scale – it had to become more disciplined and professional as an organisation. Recognising this fact, and uniting the company around the organisational change required to fix it, could only be achieved through a culture of self-awareness, pragmatism and collaboration.

In 1991, when the company had grown to a value of $1.4 billion, Walker wrote another letter, this time to senior management. The problem that Autodesk was facing was quite the opposite of the problem it had faced eight years before. Now professionalised and successful, Walker perceived Autodesk as resting on its laurels. His memo to senior leadership issued a stark warning against complacency and the dangers of failing to prepare for the future. The memo was explosive, and widely leaked. Here is an extract:

> *I am writing to you because I am deeply concerned for the future of our company ... Autodesk possesses all the prerequisites to lead the next generation of the PC industry, yet it seems to have become stuck in the past, mired in bureaucracy, paralysed by unwanted caution, and to have lost the edge ... on which the success of AutoCAD was founded.*[63]

Autodesk had moved rapidly from start-up to scale-up to 'fat and happy' incumbent. Walker's memo sparked another cultural shift, an enterprise-wide commitment to being alert to and protecting against disruption from competitors. The company, under the direction of its leadership, switched its focus to identifying its blind spots and shoring up against them.

The Autodesk of today has regained the edge that characterised its origins. The leadership has cultivated a culture of experimentation, while at the same time respecting and protecting Autodesk's core business and nurturing its emerging businesses. Andrew Anagnost, the current CEO, explains:

> *Our key advantage is running multiple experiments, and having a mechanism for mainstreaming some of those experiments.*[64]

Much of Autodesk's focus is on the future of software and technology and the company's place in that future. Autodesk has established a number of research labs and workshops (the lab in San Francisco, for example, is experimenting with the future of robotics); it has also made a sizeable financial commitment to research and development, ring-fencing investment of more than one third of total annual revenues every year. As software moves entirely online and customers consume services on a subscription model, Autodesk has morphed into a cloud-centric subscription company, placing bets in emerging technologies such as AI, self-programming robots and virtual reality design.

It's not just technology that is shaping the culture. People is another area of focus: Autodesk has consciously recruited diverse talent. The teams in the lab, for example, are 50% female and the team is deliberately cognitively diverse. As Maurice Conti, the former director of strategic innovation says: "Diversity on the team is absolutely critical ... even their hobbies are diverse. No person on the team is a one-trick pony."[65] And there is an enterprise-wide push to become more customer-centric, to shift from shipping known products to a more human-centred approach. As Anagnost puts it: "We don't sell software now. We sell outcomes."[66]

### (a) Lessons for law firms

The Autodesk story shows that it is possible for successful incumbents to change their culture provided they have the foresight and self-awareness not to rest on their laurels. Large law firms in general have been performing well through the coronavirus crisis; in order to sustain that success they must plan for the future. Most law firms do not have the funds (or the appetite) to make big bets on technology in the same way Autodesk has. However, all law firms can invest time in identifying their blind spots and in thinking how to protect against them. To become more forward-looking, traditional law firm partnerships need to inject dynamism into their culture. If Autodesk had stayed 'fat and happy' following sustained growth in 1991, and had continued to be "stuck in the past, mired in bureaucracy, paralysed by unwanted caution" it would not have gone on to achieve the success it did – indeed, it could have become entirely obsolete. Below are three lessons law firms could learn from Autodesk's tenacious commitment to cultural change.

**Culture is defined by leadership:** If the leadership is not open to change, the rest of the organisation cannot follow. Law firms must lead from the front, with confidence. Senior management and partners must model the cultural characteristics they want to cultivate at the firm, inject new thinking (from outside the legal sector) and celebrate and reward diversity of thought. Managing culture requires more than an annual firmwide culture and values programme, or a glancing reference in the senior partner's address. The Autodesk example shows the criticality of sustained leadership and active messaging in shaping a dynamic culture.

**Cultural change is not a 'soft' objective:** Cultural change is a business imperative; a law firm's culture is as important to the bottom line as revenue targets, and should be afforded equal weight. Changing culture is not a touchy-feely exercise to be delegated to the HR professionals. Facing up to shortcomings in firm culture may involve facing some hard truths, for leaders in particular. Honesty and self-awareness are of paramount importance.

**Cultivate a culture of experimentation and focus on the future:** Autodesk made a significant commitment to experimentation, but not at the expense of the company's core business. Law firms should cultivate a culture where experimentation can happen, safely, and celebrate and reward it, so that new thinking can start to influence legacy attitudes and approaches. ■

# Chapter 3: Developing the vision and strategy

## 1. Introduction

Chapter 2 looked at the five key elements that define successful digital companies, and explored how to take them from esoteric concepts to practical actions that can be shaped and scaled for the law firm environment. Client centricity is (rightly) first on that list; the second of those elements is strategy. Successful digital companies take a strategic approach to digital transformation, and align the digital strategy to the organisation's enterprise strategy. For companies that have fully embraced digital, such as Ping An,[67] there is no distinction between digital strategy and business strategy – the two are one and the same. Law firms may get to this place over time, but most are not there yet. Digital is still a footnote to law firm strategy – the more forward-thinking firms may see digital as a strategic priority, but there are very few that see it as leading the strategy.

For law firm leaders who have recognised the digital imperative and who are keen to get started, developing a digital vision and strategy may feel like an indulgence, the kind of exercise a consultancy might convince you to do at great expense. Why waste valuable time? Why not just get on with it? There are four primary reasons why the effort is worth it:

- Digital change is multi-faceted, touching many different elements of the firm (technology, people, governance, process, to name a few). Launching into digital initiatives without taking the time to think about each of these touchpoints means that the firm will not get value from its investment.
- Investment, of time and money, is part of the journey. Tactical or hasty investments that have not been thought through can be very expensive to remediate.
- Articulating a vision and strategy allows the firm to set goals to be achieved and metrics to measure success, which in turn allows for course correction if value is not being delivered.
- Ultimately, digital transformation requires a change in culture and mindset. To achieve this requires a vision around which the firm can unite. Developing a coherent strategy is part of the change effort, and will help the firm understand what it is aiming for.

In summary, taking the time up front to develop a strategy will save time and cost further down the line – and help prevent expensive mistakes.

This chapter outlines the steps a law firm might take to develop a strategy for digital transformation. One caveat: just as listing the ingredients won't tell you how to make a cake, so there is no one formula for strategy development that will work for all firms. A carefully considered digital strategy will be proprietary to each individual law firm. The aim of this chapter is to frame digital transformation as a strategic exercise and, hopefully, to ensure that nothing gets missed or overlooked when undertaking that exercise.

## 2. Eight steps to digital transformation

There are eight steps to developing the kind of digital transformation vision and strategy outlined in Chapter 2:

**Step 1:** Understand your law firm's business strategy.
**Step 2:** Undertake a diagnostic of current strengths and weaknesses and identify opportunities to create digital value.
**Step 3:** Undertake a comprehensive review of the competitor landscape.
**Step 4:** Talk to clients.
**Step 5:** Create a business case for funding.
**Step 6:** Create a plan for execution and assemble the right team.
**Step 7:** Create your vision and strategy document and communications plan.
**Step 8:** Communicate widely.

### 2.1 Step 1: Understand your firm's business strategy

One of the most difficult challenges for the team that is accountable for developing digital strategy is one that ought to be the easiest – understanding the law firm's overarching business strategy. Outside the legal bubble, most corporations will have a clearly articulated strategy for the business, which (certainly in more progressive companies) will be widely communicated to all employees and shareholders. This is not an assumption that can be made about law firms. Although there may be a shared sense of where the firm is headed and the clients, sectors and geographies that are important to growth, this cannot always be found in a written strategy document. If there is such a document, it is not often accessible to all employees. For those leading digital change in a law firm, the hardest task might be trying to intuit what the firm is actually trying to achieve.

This is one of the unique characteristics of a partnership. The consensus-driven nature of the partnership structure, in which all partners are equal owners of the business with (at least in theory) an equal say, makes development of an overarching strategy difficult. Partners may consider themselves to be autonomous agents with the freedom to develop their own practice as they see fit. In large firms, with a number of global offices and practice groups, individual partners or regions will often have their own views about the work they should do and the clients they should pursue. Sometimes this will accord with the wider firm direction, but not always – there is a lot of potential for conflict.

Then there is the question of who is responsible for developing the strategy. Most law firms have a management team (a senior partner and a managing partner) and governance boards that will be notionally responsible for developing and signing off on firm strategy. This paper structure does not give the full picture. There is an informal power base in law firms, which wields a great deal of influence over decisions impacting the direction of the firm. These informal influencers are often the most profitable partners (the so-called 'rainmakers') who are bringing in a lot of revenue. Alternatively, they might be office managing partners of a particularly large office or high-performing region. There are also culture-carrying partners, who may not be the most profitable but who have been at the firm for a long time, are well liked and respected, and represent the spirit of the partnership. A colleague in a large global law firm shared with me that she was once present at a meeting in which partners were discussing a potential HR consultation process that would impact people in a 'support' function. One of the (male) partners turned to the only female partner in the room – a well-respected 'culture carrier' leading a small practice group – and said, "You represent the heart of the firm – what do you think?" This is revealing on so many levels, but it gives an indication of the different kinds of power that can influence firm strategy in a partnership. There is very little command and control.

Historically, in good times, law firms have not had to put too much thought into strategy; it has been enough simply to keep on delivering excellent quality for the best clients, while keeping an eye on what the competition is doing. An article from Harvard Law School's *The Practice* expresses the historic problem neatly:

> *Strategy as an explicit concept and worthwhile consideration is rather new to law firms. "For a long time, law firms didn't need to have a strategy. Or to be very fair, the implicit strategy was: do excellent work," says David B. Wilkins, a professor of law at Harvard Law School and the faculty director of the school's Center on the Legal Profession. He continues, "The thinking was that if you do excellent work for your existing clients, not only will those clients continue to come to you, but you'll get new clients, and if you have enough clients,*

*good lawyers will want to come and join you." This implicit strategy of doing good work was considered more or less enough to ensure overall firm health, prestige, and profitability.*[68]

Nothing sharpens the appetite for strategy development better than hard economic times, however, and when the credit crunch of 2008/9 hit law firms, many were forced to rethink, and to make tough decisions about what work they should do (and stop doing). A number of law firms responded with aggressive partner performance management and culling of practice areas.

However, those who have worked in law firms for many years will recognise with a degree of weariness the cyclical nature of these events. Once the crisis has abated, firms very quickly revert to the status quo of allowing partners to do their own thing without adhering to a defined strategy. When strategy is invoked, it tends to focus on two areas: partner expertise at one end and cost control at the other. I discussed in Chapter 1 the (arguably disproportionate) focus on partner expertise, and the paranoia around losing rainmakers in an overheated lateral market. Lateral hiring is of course essential to growth; absent a merger, it would be impossible to expand into a new market or practice area without it. Similarly, retaining your best legal talent has to be high on management's agenda. But, as clients focus more on delivery and value, legal expertise is only part of the picture. Unless the firm's strategy is purely to do high-end work at high-end prices, Wachtell-style, firms cannot afford to focus on finding and remunerating legal expertise at the expense of factoring in other competitive threats to the business (of which digital disruption is arguably the most pressing).

**Key points**

Law firms are not always disciplined about defining and executing their strategy, particularly when times are good. But, one way or another, the team leading digital change will need to piece that strategy together. The best way to do this is to talk to as many people as you can: the line lawyers, the rainmakers (if you can get hold of them!), the heads of function, the COOs. Look at the firm's financials to understand which practice areas and regions are growing. Collate all the written documentation you can find from each region about different areas of focus for the firm: target clients and sectors, for example. Do not overlook the documentation about the firm's stated values and mission – this will also be important for shaping strategy. Find out who the culture carriers are in the firm, and spend time with them. Your digital strategy will need to appeal to and build on the positive elements of the firm's culture if it is to be adopted and executed.

## 2.2 Step 2: Undertake a firm diagnostic and identify digital opportunity

*The starting point for any change is self-knowledge. You need to understand your current strengths and weaknesses before you can figure out what you need to do to improve. Running a diagnostic or self-assessment is the natural answer, but the truth is, getting a good picture of a company's current performance is surprisingly difficult for most businesses.*[69]

Having understood firm strategy (where the firm is headed) the next step is to get a picture of where the firm is now and what new opportunities or value digital can create or support. This is the hard yards of strategy development. It involves reviewing how the firm is operating at every level, and looking for opportunities to improve using digital solutions and new ways of working, to help the firm deliver faster and more efficiently. It also involves creativity – to envision how the digital strategy can support any firm strategic plans to open up new lines of business or develop products to generate new sources of revenue. This is an area where the team leading digital transformation may need help, and where investing in consultancy support could be an option, for firms that can afford it. Many consultancies offer digital diagnostic support. This can be through traditional consultancy (putting resources on the ground in the firm to gather data)[70] or through giving access to a digital diagnostic tool, which will ask a series of questions, the answers helping to build up a picture of the firm's digital maturity and areas of opportunity.[71]

The aim of the diagnostic is to identify both revenue-generating opportunities and opportunities to work more efficiently and to lower costs. Opportunities will of course depend on the firm's strategy and how far it has progressed already in terms of digital change. When undertaking this exercise, law firms should look at both their internal processes and their client service proposition, to try to capture as much potential value as possible.

### (a) Cost efficiency and cost control

Digital tools can be used to streamline a firm's operations (lowering its cost base), and to meet client demand for more efficient delivery (keeping the firm competitive, enabling it to retain existing clients and acquire new ones). Most large corporate law firms will already have looked at both these areas: efficiency because it is high on clients' agendas, and internal cost control because this is the most effective way for law firms to increase their profitability. Many large law firms have established lower cost captive delivery centres, or have offshored or outsourced back-office business or legal processes. Others have partnered with other organisations to provide a more cost-effective delivery option. As part of that exercise, firms should have looked in detail at efficiency opportunities, and analysed the target operational profitability that these efficiencies will drive for the firm. Alternative resourcing, either through establishing a captive centre or through third-party partnering, is an established model (Orrick set up their centre in 2002, for example, and Clifford Chance in 2007). The economics at the time are likely to have been focused on process efficiency and labour arbitrage, rather than on digital solutions, which have proliferated over the last five years. Opportunities for cost efficiency should now be reviewed afresh through a digital lens. Below are some examples of low-hanging fruit that will likely be common to most law firms. The good news is that there are tried and tested digital solutions to help to deliver efficiencies for most of these areas:

- intelligent automation of certain legal processes, for example:
  - development of automated workflow processes for collaboration between teams and offices (particularly relevant if the firm has a captive centre for process-oriented legal work);
  - the due diligence process (reviewing documents to identify risks and confirm value prior to a merger or acquisition); and

- the verification process (checking documents produced in connection with a share issue to make sure that the contents are accurate);
- the document review process in the context of an investigation or litigation;
- creation or adoption of a platform for matter management, either for internal purposes only or for collaboration with clients and other delivery partners (for example, local counsel in jurisdictions where the law firm does not have an office);
- automated generation of first draft documentation and basic negotiation to support transactions;
- automated drafting of chronologies and timelines for contentious matters;
- electronic document or trial bundling;
- automated market scanning, collation, updating and reporting of data relating to changes in law or regulation affecting particular sectors, clients or products (for example, rules affecting cross-border marketing of financial products);
- automating certain corporate housekeeping services for clients, such as keeping statutory books and records, maintaining a history of the company's structure, or monitoring contractual risk; and
- collation, retrieval and sharing of legal knowledge.

It is an encouraging list – but the object of the exercise is not to look for a point 'legal tech' solution for each of these areas. Two considerations should be front of mind. First, technology is not a strategy – for a technology solution to deliver value it will need to be supported by the right data flows, processes, governance and change management. Secondly, simplification is key. Simplification is an important principle when creating a digital transformation strategy, and it is crucial to work with the technology teams to make sure that applications are streamlined and integrated and that digital transformation plans do not add unnecessary complexity to the technology environment (more of this in Chapter 5). Some investment in new tools will be inevitable; however, it is likely that increases in efficiency and some automation can be achieved using the tools and technology the firm already has.

For example, the Microsoft Office 365 suite, used in many law firms, has functionality that is often not fully utilised, and is improving all the time.

The diagnostic exercise is about more than simply identifying technology solutions. It must be supported by an assessment of the value that digital solutions can bring to each area of law firm activity. This will depend on how often the firm undertakes the activity and how profitable that activity is for the firm. For example, it may be easy to identify a digital platform that can streamline the generation and negotiation of prospectuses, but if the firm's securities practice is tiny, the investment may not be worth the return (unless the firm's strategy is aggressive expansion of that practice). The diagnostic must factor in the current and projected volume and regularity of identified activities.

*(b) Revenue generation opportunities*

More challenging to identify than efficiency gains, but equally important, are opportunities for new revenue generation. These opportunities must again be tied into the firm's strategy. There is little point building product development capability if you can only identify one client for whom this is a priority (unless it is a really significant client for the firm). Even if the firm's paper strategy is to move into new service lines, new products or other new adjacencies, before building a digital strategy around this, the team leading digital transformation should verify that there is indeed client demand for these services. Has anyone actually asked clients whether these new services would deliver value to them? It may sound obvious, but there are many examples of strategy built on assumptions rather than on data – often clients are simply not consulted.

I discuss client-facing products in more detail in Chapter 4, and developing a business case for digital transformation later in this chapter. For the purposes of this overview, it is enough to note that the team developing the digital strategy should look to identify a wide range of client-facing digital opportunities:
- those that drive higher efficiency, better quality and lower risk;
- those that generate new revenues; and

*Although it may be tempting to leap straight to highly disruptive, cutting-edge technologies, and not to direct investment to support standard services and processes, this is inadvisable. Digitising the core should take priority.*

- those that have the potential to be transformative or disruptive in the future.

Although it may be tempting to leap straight to highly disruptive, cutting-edge technologies, and not to direct investment to support standard services and processes, this is inadvisable. Digitising the core should take priority:

> *Digital reinvention only works if companies master the right digital technology architecture ... we found that digital reinventors ensure that they have adopted the full range of digital technologies, and diffused them across their organization to support mission critical applications and processes. Further, they are already investigating emerging artificial intelligence technologies, such as upgrading machine learning algorithms to deep learning ones, or investing in new generation of smart robotics, as a way to have an edge. Surprisingly, we see no evidence of leapfrogging in our data: companies that kickstart AI without mastering the first wave of digital technologies, such as social media or mobile, are not only rare but also do not get full return on their investments. Companies must master each generation of technology, and fast, in order to become digital reinventors and obtain good returns on their technology investments.*[72]

The key is to aim for a balanced portfolio that reflects the firm's strategy and its risk and investment appetite, but which also does not rule out experimentation with technologies at the more transformative end of the spectrum. There are a number of ways to experiment without hiring in an army of £2,000/day data scientists or building your own blockchain. A number of start-ups and academic institutions are very keen to collaborate with law firms on research projects or partnerships that require only the contribution of legal expertise. Collaborations of this kind are a cost-effective way to build digital knowledge and confidence. Think of the example of Autodesk in Chapter 2 – the company made a significant commitment to experimentation, but not at the expense of its core business.

*(c) Digital opportunities within business functions*

In addition to client-facing opportunities and efficiencies in the delivery of front-line legal work, the team leading the transformation should look at digitising processes that support client work. The hope is that the shift to remote working forced by the coronavirus pandemic will have significantly accelerated digital in this area. Opportunities can range from the foundational (building resilience into the environment by improving security and reviewing the data centre strategy, for example) to a focus on modernising the user experience for all law firm employees (better collaboration tools, easier remote working, upgraded software and tooling), through to creating the foundations for a cost-effective and secure cloud-first approach. This part of the diagnostic should be carried out in close collaboration with the leaders of the core business functions within the firm (HR, marketing and business development, finance, legal and risk). Opportunities might include:

- robotic process automation (RPA) of repetitive business processes (for example, payroll processes or elements of the billing process);
- automating and streamlining elements of the anti-money laundering and know-your-customer (KYC) process (both for the law firm's own compliance and potentially for clients – for example, automating the KYC process for investors, potential acquisitions and portfolio companies for private equity clients);
- specific opportunities related to individual functions ('martech' (marketing technology), for example, is a growing area of interest for law firm business development departments);
- better data integration across all business functions as part of a holistic data strategy;
- data centre and cloud strategy; and
- modernisation of workplace tools and technologies to allow better collaboration (particularly when working remotely).

The importance of creating one holistic strategy that brings together all elements of digital transformation cannot be overstated. In many law firms, including some with established and sizeable innovation teams, foundational or user experience transformation is treated as being completely separate from transformation of the client experience or legal services delivery. Often, foundational/modernising work is regarded as the preserve of the CIO and the 'IT crowd', with the sexy client-facing work left to a separate team. I have experience of working with both models, and can confirm that one strategy, under experienced leadership, is much more likely to deliver a successful outcome. Of course, the leadership will need to be supported by a team with insight into legal workflows, experience of client challenges and an understanding of the work lawyers actually do and the ways in which they deliver it.

### (d) A balanced portfolio

It is essential to get the balance of the transformation portfolio right. Some elements will be non-negotiable – so-called 'hygiene factors' that have to be done as a priority. Anything relating to security of data falls within this category, for example, as does the upgrade of systems and software that have come to the end of their life and are out of support.

For other digital initiatives, which require a priority call, it can be useful to visualise the potential products or programmes to make sure you are achieving the right balance for the firm's risk appetite and strategy.

There are plenty of ways to map products and programmes, but sometimes simple is best. One approach, originated by *Harvard Business Review*, is to segment the portfolio into three sections: 'core', 'adjacent' or 'transformational'.

Initiatives in the 'core' will be those that are essential for the firm's current business to continue. These are the 'no regrets' changes – anything relating to security, cloud strategy, and the core systems that support the firm would sit here.

Also in the core area would be those technologies that automate or improve existing processes that are delivered to existing clients. An example would be contract review using machine-learning-assisted extraction technology for due diligence purposes, or automation of standard form contracts. Here, you are applying known technology solutions to improve processes that are core to the business.

The core section is most likely to contain all those initiatives that deliver better efficiencies to the client. Pricing will be key to making these initiatives viable; this is where fixed pricing comes into its own.

In the 'adjacent' section sit products and services that the firm might create to serve clients (existing or new) in new ways, for example:

- **Expanding the nature of the professional services that the firm provides.** One example might be moving from pure legal advisory work to providing business consultancy in areas in which the firm has expertise – for example, post-merger integration.
- **Serving clients in a new way.** This might include automating elements of legal advice using expert logic tools and providing the advice to clients on a self-serve basis, under a subscription model.
- **Developing entirely new products to meet changing client needs.** Examples will depend on the client and the sector, but could include using legal expertise from previous global investigations to develop a forward-looking compliance tool for a particular client or client sector (client-facing products are discussed in detail in Chapter 4).

The expectation is that products or services in the adjacent segment contribute to the revenues of the firm, rather than simply offering greater efficiency.

The 'transformational' segment is where firms should place their big bets. In this segment will sit research and development into new technologies that are not yet routinely deployed in the legal sector but which are likely to impact in the future – for example, blockchain and distributed ledger technologies.

Also in this transformational space will sit initiatives that relate to fundamental business model change. This is the space for truly radical thinking about size and shape of the firm and the future of the services it will deliver. For example, law firms might think about:

- selling their captive centres to a third party and consuming all 'business support' as a service;
- drastically reducing legal expertise to only the true 'stars' in the most profitable practice areas and sourcing any legal expertise beyond this on a crowdsourced basis; and
- acquiring or merging with a business wholly outside legal services.

Clearly, very few law firms will be comfortable with investing disproportionately in this transformational category; however, investing nothing at all in more radical thinking is short sighted. Plotting digital transformation initiatives on a matrix is a good starting point and a springboard for discussion with the firm's management. Although there is no right answer, given that each firm's strategy, ambition and level of digital maturity will be different, it is likely that most of the investment will be in the core segment, with some serious contenders in the adjacent category and relatively few in the transformational.

Regardless of where you start, the balance on this matrix should shift over time, as more of the core becomes digitised. Revisiting the spread of initiatives regularly will help the team leading digital transformation ensure a healthy balance for the firm.

**Key points**

Understanding where your firm is now in its digital maturity, and identifying opportunities for digital change at every level of the firm's operations, is a significant task – but one that needs to be done thoroughly if the firm is to unlock the potential of digital transformation. Firms may not need to start from scratch; some of the work may already have been done.

Look for the outputs of earlier process improvement initiatives or for analysis undertaken as part of cost-cutting or consultation exercises. To identify ways in which digital can add value, talk to your clients about the challenges they face in their own delivery and think about how you might solve them together. Aim for a balanced portfolio; the team leading the transformation will need to explore and map out all the opportunities, large and small, in current operations. The team should also look for cost-effective ways to explore more transformational technologies and digital investments.

It is important that all digital transformation efforts be part of one holistic strategy, under one leadership. Artificial distinctions between work touching lawyers and clients and work that is regarded as the IT 'plumbing' are entirely unhelpful. If the technology leadership is not considered close enough to the lawyers to transform client-facing work, then it could be time for the firm to look for new leadership.

### 2.3 Step 3: Review the competitor landscape

As discussed in Chapter 1 and as illustrated by the case studies of Walmart and Autodesk in Chapter 2, successful digital businesses have a healthy dose of paranoia, and are constantly looking at what the competition is doing (not only new and potentially disruptive entrants to the market, but also traditional competitors who are in the process of reinventing themselves). Competitors are everywhere:

> *Companies typically face a mix of traditional competitors, new entrants within their industry, and entrants from adjacent fields. However, we also found that, on average, three of these traditional rivals are likely to have already chosen to forcefully engage in digitization, and one of them is probably already morphing into a digital reinventor.*[73]

Sound terrifying? It is important to stay attuned to your competitors, but there is definitely a risk to shaping a digital strategy on the basis of FOMO (fear of missing out). It is easy to be misled by assumptions about what other law firms are doing. As already observed, there is a lot of innovation theatre out there, and if one were to dent the veneer of even the most innovative law firms the reality would be different from the gloss. When shaping a digital transformation strategy, law firms should focus less on competitors' public relations activity and more on their organisational strategy and the extent to which they are investing in digital capabilities. For each potential competitor (law firm, law company, alternative legal service provider or Big 4 legal team – or, increasingly, corporate legal team) the law firm should try to answer the following questions:

- Who are they hiring and from where?
- What digital capabilities are they developing?
- Who are their clients?
- With whom are they collaborating or partnering?
- What digital solutions are they developing, using or acquiring?

This information will help the law firm define its points of differentiation as it develops its own digital strategy. To be clear: law firms need a deep understanding of what the competition is doing, not in order to copy, but to get ahead. 'Fast following' won't be enough to allow a firm to differentiate:

> *First movers win. That's the hard reality of the digital age. Our research is clear on this point ... Time and again we see companies that have taken a fast-follower strategy not be able to move fast enough.*[74]

Having a good grasp of what the competition is doing can also be helpful in selling the firm's own strategy to management and law firm partners. Appealing to lawyers' sense of competition by calling out competitors' successes is one of the useful tools in the law firm change management armoury.

The team leading digital transformation will need to be disciplined in keeping an eye on what the competition is doing; strategy may need to be adjusted or revisited to take account of new information. The landscape is very fast moving, and someone in the team should be accountable for keeping competitor intelligence current and useful. Bear in mind that competitors should be broadly defined to include more than just the usual suspects (law firms of similar size and capability). There are also potential competitors outside the legal industry. Existing enterprise technology platform providers (Microsoft,

Salesforce, Servicenow, for example) have the funds and the skills to build the definitive legal services platform, acquire legal delivery expertise, and corner a significant segment of the market. Perhaps the only reason that they have not done this, to date, is that the legal services market is not large enough to merit the investment. Law firm partners will have seen from their own clients that industry disruption does not always come from the obvious places. Looking outside the legal industry is also an effective way to get a better understanding of digital best practice and new ways of working:

> *While companies understand they need to 'get better' or 'become more digital' it is often hard to know what that means in practice. Many business leaders simply don't know what they don't know. In this vacuum, leaders will tend to set their aspirations too low or focus on the wrong elements of a transformation. Understanding what the best companies are doing, and how they're doing it, can dramatically shift what leaders think is possible.*[75]

When Freshfields was establishing its global legal services centre in Manchester, the team spent a lot of time visiting shared service centres that supported a wide range of industries, from financial services to the public sector. These visits were incredibly useful, giving us insight into how successful global shared services organise themselves to drive a culture of innovation and efficiency. Similarly, when setting up the Freshfields Lab in Berlin,[76] the team visited customer experience labs established by McKinsey and Deloitte, as well as spending time in the Berlin lab's ultimate home, The Factory, an innovation ecosystem and co-working space in Berlin's Görlitzer Park. This was time well spent. There is really no substitute to walking the floors and seeing different ways of working in action. Getting to grips with the physical layout and understanding the motivation of the people who work in a different environment is worth a hundred textbooks.

Many law firm clients already have digital labs, or innovation centres. Ask if you can visit. Those that work in a digital environment are usually passionate about their space and their ways of working and happy to share insights.

Taking partners to visit new spaces and witness new ways of working can also be an effective way of managing change within the partnership. Some partners in traditional law firm partnerships will have worked in one office for their entire career – they will need help to envision a different way of working.

> **Key points**
> When developing a law firm digital transformation strategy, stay alert to what the competition is doing, but make sure you are focusing on the right kind of intelligence. Do not rely on law firm press releases and allow your team to be distracted, for example, by anecdotal evidence of technology investments – remember, technology is not a strategy. Look out for more strategic moves – for example, one of your competitors making a new hire in the digital space, particularly if that person comes from outside the legal sector. Hiring a digital 'star' is an indication that a law firm is serious about digital change. Keep on top of the competitor landscape and be sure to look outside the legal industry, both for inspiration and for potential new competitors from unexpected places. Stay paranoid.

### 2.4 Step 4: Talk to clients

In Chapter 2, we explored how successful digital companies share a laser focus on the customer. Talking to clients is essential to shaping a digital transformation strategy for two reasons. First, the client voice is very powerful when it comes to change management. Secondly, if the strategy does not resonate with clients, there is no point in implementing it.

### (a) Change management and the client voice

Not everyone in the partnership will buy into the financial commitment and cultural change required for the firm to become digitally effective, and the strategy will need to include a compelling case for change. A generic strategy will be much less impactful than one that is grounded in the lived experience of a particular firm. In my experience, bringing in the client voice is the single most effective way to influence partner behaviour.

## (b) *Creating client value*

As discussed earlier in this chapter, before launching into a multi-year investment case, it is important to test the digital strategy with clients. There is little point in creating something that customers do not want to buy. Be tenacious in probing elements of the strategy with clients. Are they interested in the firm providing services via a subscription model? Are they confident in the firm's product development capabilities? Do they see a law firm as the best source of legal operations consultancy? What is it about your law firm that clients really value and how can you use digital solutions to deliver more of it?

Choose a range of clients that are important to the firm for different reasons: a long-standing and loyal client; a newly acquired client; one in a growth sector; one that is undergoing or has undergone its own digital transformation; if possible, one in the TMT sector with a high level of digital literacy. The range is important. You may be surprised by how many partners will try to exempt themselves from engaging with a digital initiative on the grounds that digital has no relevance to their practice or their clients. For the same reasons, if the firm has an international presence, make sure to involve clients from the largest or most profitable regions – or the regions the firm is looking to grow.

The team leading digital transformation may not have ready access to clients, and this can be a problem. Partners can be protective about their relationships and some may be unwilling to introduce an untested individual to their client. This is perhaps understandable, as an open conversation over which the partner has no control can feel uncomfortable. Senior sponsorship is helpful in these situations; a respected senior partner ought to be able to persuade others to trust the team that is leading the change. Challenge whether the partner who manages the client relationship should join the session. The conversation needs to be as open and honest as possible (see the discussion of human-centred design in Chapter 2) and a relationship partner may, understandably, be defensive, which can be counterproductive.

If access to clients proves difficult, ask the marketing team for the results of past client feedback exercises. Although static feedback has limited use (it is only a point-in-time snapshot) it is a good starting point, and certainly better than nothing.

I have spoken to many corporate legal teams in different sectors about digital transformation over the years, while in private practice and while leading the Digital Legal Exchange. I have yet to meet a client who didn't welcome the conversation. That said, to extract real value the conversation will need to be tightly structured to ensure the best possible use of the client's time, and to make sure the interviewer can extract the insights that she or he needs. Set the scene by explaining what the firm is trying to achieve, and how crucial the client's contribution will be to helping achieve it. It may sound obvious, but be careful not to position the digital team as the sole change agent in a firm of dinosaurs. This is about the firm's success, not the team's own mission.

Keep the conversation as open as possible. Going back to the human-centred design approach discussed in Chapter 2, try to use the time to envision the experience that would truly 'delight' the client. Using video to record the session can be very powerful, particularly at the advocacy stage, as it brings the client voice into the centre of the room.

**Key points**

The customer voice must be the foundation of a digital strategy. Before getting too far down the line towards implementation, be bold and tenacious in testing the digital strategy with clients. Be sure that you understand what problems your clients are looking to solve. Share your developing strategy with them and ask them if they see value in what the firm is trying to achieve. If part of the strategy is improving efficiency, test whether the proposed solutions will meet your clients' expectations (corporate legal teams are likely to have their own efficiency or spend targets) and whether the proposed solutions will deliver the experience that clients associate with the firm – or, even better, an improved client experience. If the strategy involves new products or services, test whether clients are interested in buying these from you, and whether they have confidence in the firm's ability to deliver. Better still, ask your clients to be part of the design process as you prototype and test. There is no downside to making clients an integral part of strategy development – it can only be relationship-enhancing.

## 2.5 Step 5: Create the business case for funding

A strategy only has value if it can be implemented, and it can only be implemented if the delivery teams have the funds, the resources and the capabilities to execute. Before moving to delivery, it is important to understand the costs associated with implementing the strategy, and to be realistic about the target benefits. A business case is essential, because without the right level of funding, the strategy cannot succeed:

> *Having bold aspirations matters, but only when also matched by corresponding commitment. Without allocating funds and resources at sufficient scale over enough time, the value of digital will remain a mirage – promising but forever out of reach.*[77]

Most digital transformations are likely to involve a multi-year commitment. Law firms may or may not require a formal business case in support (this will depend on the governance process for each individual law firm). Regardless of firm requirements, it is good practice to prepare a business case. It is a helpful discipline, as it gives a clear view of the commitment required by the firm, and is the first test of whether the investment actually makes sense.

Law firms with little experience of what digital transformation involves might justifiably ask for benchmarks for both costs and benefits, so that the leadership can check the numbers before making a commitment. What benefits can a 'transformed' law firm be expected to enjoy, and over what period might those benefits be realised? What are the likely costs associated with an investment in digital change?

There is plenty of generic information available on this subject, but very little that is specific to professional services. This means that most available benchmarks are unhelpful. On the cost side, we are bombarded with information about the eye-watering levels of investment that many corporations are making into digital. On the benefits side, the mystique that surrounds digital companies and the dominance of the highly successful few can give the impression that if you get digital right, you will unlock the profitability of an Amazon or an Alibaba.

Of course, this is not the reality. Plenty of digital natives, who don't have the burden of legacy systems and the challenge of cultural change, have yet to make a profit. Equally, plenty of incumbent organisations in sectors outside legal that have embarked on digital transformation have yet to see a return on the investment. Digital transformation is hard work, and the benefits will in all likelihood not be realised in the short term. Recent research suggests that although digitisation has the potential greatly to increase productivity, benefits will only appear "once companies absorb digital technologies in business workflow practices".[78] This takes time.

For law firms, and indeed for corporate legal teams, there is limited data available on the hard benefits of digital transformation. This is unsurprising, given that so few firms have made the commitment to digital change. It is a real challenge to find examples of traditional law firm partnerships that have undergone a firmwide strategic digital transformation that has resulted in a measurable competitive advantage. Law firms are slow to move, because they cannot see a burning platform (by which I mean hard evidence of challenger organisations disrupting the law firm model in a way that threatens the most profitable law firms). All firms will of course have war stories about losing pitches to more innovative legal service providers on price, diversity or technology. However, anecdotal evidence is not sufficient to shift a fixed mindset.

This challenge is not insurmountable, however. When confronted with examples of multimillion-dollar digital investments, bear in mind that a law firm digital transformation can be sized to a level of investment that is feasible. There are many ways to become more digitally effective that do not involve buying expensive new technologies. Changing ways of working, being more disciplined around data, understanding clients better, partnering with others to augment digital capabilities, and making better use of the technology the firm already has are all cost-effective ways to effect change.

As an example, rather than law firms investing in building proprietary technology products, or in developing entirely new delivery solutions, they could instead partner with a third party (a technology provider or alternative legal services provider, for example) to deliver a digital solution to clients. If the law firm is concerned about potential brand devaluation associated with this partnership, they could simply 'white label' the solution and deliver it under the law firm's own banner:

> *Modern day white labeling in the context of legal services can be seen as compiling or assembling the most optimal way to solve a client's problems. There is great value in assembling the best solution for a client and firms can gain a premium and competitive advantage through that assembly and the positioning of the assembled solution under a single banner – with a single accountable partner. Law firms have, for years, bundled into their litigation practices e-discovery and ... document review providers to complement their expert advisory services. While this isn't traditional white labeling, in that the client is directly procuring, or interacting with these outside parties, the foundational drivers are consistent in that ... services within the firm and for all practical purposes an anonymous third-party solution [are] bundled together under your firm's banner to create an optimal client solution.*[79]

Variations on the partnering approach, giving firms access to technology and resourcing solutions without incurring the risk and expense of building or scaling their own capabilities, are being adopted by a number of large law firms. A good example is the partnership between the law firm Paul Hastings and the technology and legal services company UnitedLex. In 2020, UnitedLex acquired Paul Hastings' data science, analysis, and investigations (DSAI) team. The DSAI team is now part of UnitedLex, who are investing in the team and augmenting solutions with UnitedLex's own technology, enabling the DSAI team to scale. Paul Hastings benefits as the team continues to provide services to Paul Hastings' clients. This is a pragmatic solution for situations where law firms want to take a digital product or service offering to the next level, but do not have the appetite for further investment.

Sometimes, however, investment in technology is unavoidable. Firms with a high level of technical debt (legacy, outdated systems) will need to increase technology spend – it is just not possible to kick the can down the road indefinitely:

> *Our experience suggests that in IT alone, companies with outdated systems might need to double their current spending over a five-year period. That investment is likely to result in lower profits for a while – but without it there is a serious risk to profits in the longer term.*[80]

Chapter 5 discusses the challenges of legacy technology in more detail.

When searching for benchmarks for the costs and benefits of digital transformation, it is easier to find examples of downside risk than upside benefit. There is evidence that organisations that do not invest in digital grow at a slower rate than those that are more digitally advanced (see s 2.5 (j), "Risk of inactivity", below). McKinsey research into the benefits of digitisation shows, for example, that companies that fail to invest in digital will on average see a decline in revenue of 12%. Those that "lead from the front with a disruptive strategy (and at least decent execution)" will see gains of 16% above that depressed level.[81]

Quantifying risk of inactivity alone will not make a business case. Given the likely level of investment (both financial and in terms of management energy) that digitisation demands, it is important to quantify the costs and benefits.

*(a) Quantifying costs*
When building a picture of the cost of a digital transformation, the team leading the digital change will need to work in collaboration with other business functions, particularly the CFO and (if the digital strategy is not being led by the technology leadership) the CTO or CIO.

HR and marketing leadership will also need to be closely involved, as the transformation may have significant people implications (around hiring, reskilling and training, incentivisation and organisational design) and marketing/business development implications (around brand, commercialisation of products and services, and customer experience).

The costs to be included in a business case for digital transformation will of course depend on the individual firm – its size, global reach, level of digital maturity, level of technical debt, digital capabilities of its leadership – and the scope and ambition of its strategy. Two areas that are often underestimated when putting together a business case are the total cost of ownership of technology investments and the people costs of resourcing to drive and sustain digital change. (If you are a law firm COO or business functional leader experienced in developing a business case, you will know all this already. The red flags below are for those in a law firm who have not worked closely with transformation teams and who are less familiar with the hidden costs (for example, law firms in which partners are leading the digital transformation).)

**Technology costs and the total cost of ownership:** Most digital transformations will involve investment in technology. For a lay person, calculating the true cost of technology investment is more complex than it might first appear. Rather than focusing simply on the cost of the kit (in the case of hardware), or a licence or service contract (in the case of software), the business case must reflect the total cost of ownership of the investment. This means understanding the true cost of the service, including staff, maintenance and support, and the share of infrastructure used by the service (eg, processing, storage and networks). One frustrated CIO describes the consequences of failing to do so:

> *This often leads to over-inflated expectations of benefits, with savings and programmes of work that are underspecified and misunderstood. With the worst-case scenario of frustrated business users and a CFO or finance director throwing their arms up in disbelief as IT costs continue to rise even after improvement projects have completed. The*

*promised wonderful savings and benefits not delivered and a phase 2
needed. Why is this? One answer is that we find that the evidence used
to create the business case was flawed and not accurate for the basis of
defining service improvement. TCO [total cost of ownership] was not
understood.*[82]

Other technology costs that will need to be included and that can get
overlooked include the cost of remediation of legacy systems
(discussed in Chapter 5) and the change management costs associated
with encouraging lawyers to adopt new technologies or ways of working
(discussed below).

**People costs:** The people costs of a traditional transformation would
usually be divided into two buckets. The first would be the cost of
experienced leadership to direct the transformation and the resources
required to do the hard lifting to get the programme of work underway.
The second, smaller bucket would contain the ongoing costs associated
with sustaining the transformation to make it successful.

Under the old model, the first bucket would quickly be full to the brim,
with resources pouring in during programme delivery and then
draining away. Often, there would be very little in the second bucket
(because, too often, insufficient thought and energy were given to
sustaining change after the project team had moved on). A digital
transformation is different. It is not a 'project' or a 'programme', but an
ongoing and integral part of firm strategy and operations, requiring a
corresponding investment in resources. Investment in people to
sustain the change is as important as investment in people to take the
practical steps to get it off the ground. In business case terms, resource
costs for successful digital transformation must be treated, not as one-
off project costs, but as a long-term investment for the firm. Digital
transformation is now a constant. The strategy will need to be reviewed
and refreshed as market and competitive pressures change over time.
Law firms will need to invest in digital talent for the future.

Individuals with the requisite skills to develop a strategy and lead
digital transformation are hard to come by and justifiably expensive.

Just like lawyer rainmakers making a lateral move, digital leaders will often come with a team that they have worked with before and that they trust to get the job done. This will also come at a cost. Chapter 8 discusses in more detail what these digital stars look like and how crucial they are to success. For the purposes of the business case, be sure not to underestimate the people costs. Experienced leaders and other resources with specialist skills (developers, cloud architects, data scientists) are likely to be more expensive than traditional IT role profiles.

Becoming more digitally effective will inevitably involve changes to established ways of working. For those law firms with an ambitious strategy, this could extend to entirely new ways of delivering (working in multidisciplinary teams, for example, or experimenting with new ways of interacting with clients). The reality for most firms, though, is that change will bite when it hits the desktop. Lawyers are busy people, and are easily frustrated by being asked to give up time to undertake training, or to master a new system. The teams in law firm IT departments bear the brunt of this, as lawyers routinely cancel scheduled training sessions or refuse to commit time to become familiar with a new interface (then take out their frustrations on the IT helpdesk when they can't find a document). It is of course possible that coronavirus, the bluntest of change management instruments, has altered this mindset. Being forced into remote working during lockdown will certainly have exposed the most recalcitrant partners to collaboration technologies. Sadly, though, using Teams does not equate to firmwide digital literacy.

It is important to invest in change management to support the digital strategy and make it successful. The business case should make provision for permanent, professional change management capability and for dedicated communications support. This will be essential to sustaining momentum for the journey. Effective communication is discussed in more detail later in this chapter.

### (b) Quantifying benefits
As noted above, there are few industry benchmarks in legal services to

help law firms (or corporate legal teams) assess the potential benefits of digital transformation. Often, the leadership has a gut sense that becoming more digitally effective is something the firm needs to do, but has no scientific way of quantifying the benefits. This could, of course, apply to a number of law firm initiatives (sustainability, diversity, corporate social responsibility, behaviour and values) which are important for reputational reasons (and are objectively the right thing to do) but which do not immediately impact the bottom line.

Digital transformation is different. If the firm has a clear strategy for change, it is possible to form a view of the potential benefits. Depending on the strategy, benefits might include:

- cost reduction;
- increased efficiency;
- risk reduction;
- improved client experience;
- reduced client attrition;
- greater market share;
- increased revenues; and
- improved employment proposition.

The business case should aim to set measurable targets for each of these benefits.

Again, without benchmarks, setting targets is not easy. One way of addressing this is to model a best, median and worst case for benefits realisation, with the targets calibrated accordingly. Ultimately, common sense will prevail; if a median case shows a revenue increase from new product development that feels indefensible, it is probably time to revisit the assumptions.

**Cost reduction benefits:** The bottom-line benefits of digital transformation are easier to quantify (and therefore more easy to sell) than the top-line benefits. Law firms are high-fixed-cost businesses and are constantly looking to squeeze their cost base in order to achieve better profitability. With competition increasing for the best partners, who are commanding ever higher remuneration, law firm management

*Digitisation is not just about cost reduction. It has the potential to stimulate growth and open up new revenue opportunities.*

is likely to be receptive to opportunities to lower costs, particularly in the non-revenue-generating part of the business (it is this very pressure on cost that led to a number of UK and US law firms offshoring or nearshoring business services and legal services during the early 2000s).

In times of recession, law firms are likely to be even more sensitive about cost, and will tend to focus on bottom-line savings and to be sceptical about top-line growth.

Digitisation, even if only at a level to support incremental innovation rather than to drive transformative change, presents plenty of opportunity for reducing the cost to deliver. Automation will often be one of the first areas of focus for the business case. The use of RPA to automate business processes has been shown to deliver significant efficiencies in the shared services world.[83] RPA essentially involves automating rules-based processes using software that sits on top of established systems (such as a practice management system). RPA can be used for repetitive data-entry tasks (copying and pasting data, filling in forms, moving files and folders, for example). The potential benefits are significant. However, most law firms don't have the operational scale to justify the investment. Automation doesn't have to be at a huge scale to deliver benefits, however, nor does it have to be limited to back-office processes. A number of law firms have successfully automated the M&A due diligence process. Other legal processes that lend themselves to automation include document review and repapering (to take account of regulatory change, for example the IBOR transition) and document automation/generation (including basic negotiation). As corporate data volumes continue to increase in transactions such as M&A, automation (with or without the overlay of machine learning/AI) will become an even more essential part of the law firm toolkit.

**Efficiency benefits:** Making a legal process more efficient will inevitably have an impact on revenue. This has long been an issue for law firms, with some partners continuing to argue that increasing efficiency does not make economic sense for the firm – it is simply cannibalising the firm's own revenues. This is not an argument that will fly with clients, who now regard use of technology to increase efficiency as a hygiene factor. However, a business case based on increased efficiency will need to show that any revenue loss is compensated for by a corresponding reduction in headcount or by reselling lawyer time freed up by automation.[84] Another approach is to move to pricing on a fixed basis (something that clients actively want law firms to do) for legal services made more efficient by automation. This creates an incentive for the firm to increase its efficiency, as this will in turn increase operating profit.

Providing better tooling to lawyers, both software and hardware, can also have efficiency benefits. Being able to collaborate as global teams, virtually and seamlessly; being able to access key applications on mobile devices; not wasting time with latency or slow legacy systems – all of this adds up to more efficient and effective working, with the time saved resold and converted to additional revenue (or enabling everyone to go home an hour earlier).

### (c) Risk reduction and reduction in write-offs

Becoming more digitally effective can also improve profitability through reducing write-offs (the reduction in the amount of time billed at the end of the matter because of (actual or perceived) inefficiency, waste or duplication). Write-offs can add up to a significant amount annually; however, it can often be tricky to quantify the percentage of the write-off that is attributable to inefficiency.

Digitisation will also reduce risk. Streamlining and automating a process, under the right governance, should reduce the risk of error in delivery. Investment in core systems to make them more secure will shore up the firm against costly cyberattacks and breaches of security rules by employees. This should result in reduced liability insurance and fewer instances of costly litigation, both of which should be factored into a business case. The benefits to the firm of protecting its reputation (a cyber attack could be catastrophic for market reputation) cannot be underestimated.

*(d) Digital resilience*

COVID-19 has shown just how essential it is for all organisations to be digitally resilient and able to move to a remote working model without disruption. Some law firms only just made it when lockdown hit, having upgraded systems, security and hardware just in time. Others, particularly smaller law firms without the means to make these investments, are still analogue businesses and have been hit hard by the crisis. For any firm wishing to embark on or accelerate a digital transformation, resilience and disaster recovery should form a key part of the business case.

*(e) Revenue benefits*

Digitisation is not just about cost reduction, however. It has the potential to stimulate growth and open up new revenue opportunities. The degree to which a business case will lead with growth benefits rather than cost benefits will depend on the firm's strategy, its current and projected performance and its pipeline.

Revenue increase might come from any of the following sources:
- building and commercialising client-facing digital products;
- moving into new service lines or adjacencies;
- winning new clients or retaining existing clients through improving the client experience; and/or
- exploitation and commercialisation of firm data.

*(f) Digital products and new service lines*

Law firm profitability has held up very well during the coronavirus crisis. Even so, as we head into a global recession, law firms will be thinking hard about their growth strategies. If established areas of work dry up, law firms will be faced with a choice – to reduce their size and shape and concentrate on key practice areas and traditional services, or to identify new avenues for revenue generation. Digitisation opens up opportunities for growth. One option might be to build (or partner to build) digital products that could be commercialised and sold to clients or to the wider legal market. Using this approach, a law firm can leverage its technical legal expertise and scale certain of its legal services without having to invest in more lawyers.

Growth can also be achieved by moving into new service lines and adjacencies (consultancy is a good example). A number of large corporate firms have already taken this step, including Dentons (a risk advisory consulting unit), Norton Rose Fulbright (a legal operations consulting arm and a technology consulting practice), and Allen & Overy (regulatory consulting).

Law firms that make a strategic decision to develop client-facing digital products or to move into new adjacencies should consider the costs and benefits carefully. The development and commercialisation of digital products is challenging for most law firms and requires strong governance and a radical change to ways of working (I discuss products and commercialisation in detail in Chapter 4). Similarly, launching a consultancy is not just an extension of lawyering; it requires new skills that will need to be acquired or developed.

### (g) The client experience

Another benefit to consider is the client stickiness that will result from delivering an improved digital customer experience. This is not all about technology – client experience extends to every interaction with clients, from physical meetings to the visual impact of the documentation the firm produces. One legacy of the pandemic, however, is that more of our professional interactions will remain virtual. For example, the likelihood of returning to paper signings, when we have electronic signatures, is low. Digital has become an integral part of professional delivery, and global elite law firms will be expected to provide a digital experience to clients that is consistent with the firm's brand and fees. An improved client experience should be the focus of any digital strategy and, in terms of benefits, can deliver a closer and more personalised relationship and a higher likelihood of retaining existing clients (and winning new ones).

### (h) Exploitation of data

Data, which lies dormant and untouched in most law firms, has real value (I discuss data in more detail in Chapter 5). There are many ways to be creative in monetising data. Data can be aggregated from different systems and analysed to derive new insights about how matters are run, and to challenge assumptions about optimal resourcing and leverage. These insights can be used to increase operational profitability (for example, by enabling partners to price mandates on a fixed-price basis with confidence and accuracy, while maintaining a healthy margin). Data can also provide client insights. These insights could be provided for free, to enrich the client relationship (for example, giving the client a view of its negotiating position across historic transactions). Alternatively, data providing insights about particular markets, sectors or risks could be packaged up into a product and sold to clients on a subscription basis as an additional revenue generator.

### (i) 'Soft' benefits

The business case for digital transformation should not ignore the 'soft' benefits that digital ways of working can deliver. Although these are not easily quantifiable, they are still very important. Many of these benefits relate to talent and people management. I discuss talent in detail in Chapter 8; it is enough to mention here that the brightest and the best graduates will want to work in an organisation that is forward-looking and digitally effective. Generation Z's expectations of the working environment will be high; it is very unlikely that the best talent will be attracted to a firm where the user experience is far behind the experience they have at home or at university, regardless of how good the brand might be. Providing a modern digital workplace will create an environment that attracts the best people and future-proofs and modernises the law firm brand.

Another intangible or soft benefit relates to the credibility and authenticity of the law firm with its clients. In order to advise fast-growing digital businesses, law firms need to demonstrate that they both understand and relate to the way those businesses operate and the values that underpin them. This involves more than simply taking off your tie before the pitch meeting. The outward representation of the law firm brand used to be the corporate office; prime real estate in a central location, with expensive art on the walls and Michelin-starred catering. I suspect those days are gone. As we enter a new world of virtual interaction, the digital capabilities of the law firm will start to speak for its professionalism and brand far more than the corporate office **will**. Just as clients now demand evidence of a law firm's diversity statistics and sustainability agenda, they will also ask for evidence of the firm's commitment to digitisation. This cannot simply be evidenced by lawyers having the most modern kit or buying in legal tech; law firms will need to demonstrate how they have changed their ways of working, their culture and values to foster the right environment for digital effectiveness.

Perhaps the most compelling soft benefit that will result from successful digital transformation is positive cultural change. I noted above that many of the cultural attributes required to be a digitally effective organisation are the same as those we associate with a 'good' or healthy corporate culture. Consequently, for law firms committed to digital transformation, one unintended positive consequence will be that digitisation reinforces the wider cultural change that law firms are looking to drive. I explore the importance of culture in sustaining change in detail in Part III of this book. Of course, as with other soft benefits, the value of culture is difficult to measure. The Financial Conduct Authority, in its discussion paper "Transforming Culture in Financial Services", puts it like this:

> [C]hanging culture can be hard. Some still see changing culture as a 'soft' discipline; and clarifying how to define, measure, and manage it in practical terms is difficult. Its intangible nature has left business leaders pondering how to influence and transform culture.[85]

The value of cultural change is very difficult to quantify in business case terms, but should nevertheless be referenced as a positive outcome of digital investment.

### (j) Risk of inactivity

An alternative approach to making the case for change, which is helpful when challenged to find sufficient 'hard' benefits, is to model the risk of simply doing nothing. If a firm fails to invest in digital, and just continues to plough the same furrow, what will be the result? If its competitors digitise and grow market share while the firm stays static, what will be the effect on that firm's business? Law firms should use scenario planning, as part of the business planning process, to stress test this question. The risk to a law firm of simply putting its head in the sand or deferring the investment for another year could be significant:

*Choosing not to invest and use AI is already proving to put major pressure on firms' financial performance. In professional services and retail, companies that do not deploy AI are reporting digital cash flows that are 15 to 20 percent lower than their AI-embracing peers. In financial services, the gap is 30 percent, and in high-tech, a very substantial 80 percent. These figures demonstrate not only that the gap between the performance of nonadopters and adopters is large, but it is even more substantial in sectors that are more digitized and globalized, and require a higher share of cognitive skills – high tech being an example.*[86]

**Key points**

The legal services industry suffers from a lack of benchmarks to help law firms (and corporate legal teams) understand and sense check the costs and benefits of investing in digital transformation. Nevertheless, putting together a business case in support of the strategy is an important discipline and will help to test the firm's ambition and investment appetite. The business case is not the preserve of the team leading the transformation; it must be developed in collaboration with the business functional leaders and with lawyers across practice groups and regions. When quantifying costs, be sure to assess the total cost of ownership (TCO) of technology investment, and not to underestimate the people costs associated with sustaining change. Be creative in quantifying benefits, including both hard and soft benefits. Bear in mind that digital transformation is not just about efficiency and cost reduction. The real value lies in the opportunity to generate revenue from entirely new sources, and in improving the experience for your clients.

*2.6 Step 6: Create a plan for execution and assemble the right team*

*(a) "Execution is everything"*[87]

A digital vision and strategy is no use unless it can be executed. This is easier said than done; translating aspiration and ambition into action can be daunting. It may sound old school, but creating a roadmap for delivery will help to make the strategy concrete. It is also an essential planning tool; if your firm has a lot of legacy IT that needs to be upgraded or replaced, a roadmap is crucial for highlighting dependencies and making sure the teams get the sequencing right.

The roadmap should not be rigid and static, however. In line with agile principles, it should be flexible enough to allow for revisions of the strategy in response to changing markets, new competitor moves, or (once a theoretical threat, now very real) unforeseen events with global impact. The team delivering transformation should revisit the roadmap regularly.

To avoid the rabbit-in-the-headlights issue that can occur when converting strategy to action, use the balanced portfolio approach to inform the roadmap.[88] Those core workstreams that are essential to the stability of the firm's operations must take precedence. However, this does not mean that other, more ambitious elements should be postponed or delayed indefinitely – the world is changing too quickly to allow for a linear approach. Counterintuitively, you can't wait until all the foundations are built and secured before you start to consider more transformational initiatives. There needs to be delivery at every level of the strategy.

*(b) Delivery teams and ways of working*
The size and composition of the delivery teams will depend on the workstreams themselves. The team leading the digital transformation will need to take time to think about how best to resource workstreams for success, while keeping an overview of the transformation as a whole. At Freshfields, our teams were aligned to different strata of the strategy (for more on what this strategy looked like, see Step 7 below). Teams in the stabilise layer had extensive technical and architectural knowledge and experience. Those leading the modernise layer were transformation professionals with experience of running large-scale IT change programmes. The transform layer was led by teams with deep legal domain knowledge (many were former lawyers), working with

technology professionals who had delivered transformation in other regulated industries.

It makes sense to look at the firm's existing talent pool first. The likelihood is that there will be individuals already in the firm who have the necessary skills; identifying them ought to be relatively easy and should be done as quickly as possible to allow the teams to get moving. It is equally likely, however, that there will be capability gaps. There are a number of ways to plug these gaps:

- relying on traditional consultancy;
- partnering with a long-term delivery partner;
- reskilling existing staff; and, of course
- hiring new talent.

The best approach may be a mix of all of these.

Bear in mind, though, that digital transformation is not just another IT programme at which you can throw money and consultants in an effort to push it through. It must be part of the long-term strategy of the firm. Consequently, the firm needs to build permanent internal delivery and change capability that is fit for the task. Engaging the firm's HR team in undertaking comprehensive workforce planning is crucial, and should be on the digital team's change agenda – but it can take a long time to complete. Investing in training and development to help existing teams develop new digital skills or hone existing skills is also very important. Engaging the HR team early is key. I look more closely at digital talent and the importance of HR as a business partner in Chapter 8. Also essential to successful delivery is change management and communications capability, preferably dedicated to the digital transformation. Depending on the size of the investment in the digital transformation, and the complexity of the business case, it may also be advisable to have a finance business partner closely aligned to the digital leadership team.

Upskilling employees is as much about new ways of working as it is about new technology. In order to execute effectively, teams need to work together differently. However, many law firms, even those that

*When law firms professed themselves open to agile working in the pre-pandemic world, they often meant begrudgingly allowing lawyers to work from home for one day a week.*

have made significant investments in technology, are resistant to changing the way that they work – or have simply never considered it.

Digitally effective organisations work in an agile way. This concept is still largely alien to the practice of law. With a few notable exceptions, if agile is recognised at all in a law firm, it is usually misunderstood, or associated solely with the delivery of IT projects. Yet there is a business imperative to agile. Working in an agile way can have a positive impact on the bottom line. Research has shown that agile teams are 50% more likely to outperform other business teams financially.[89]

*(c) Remote working and Agile are not the same*
Law firm management have been known to use the term 'agile' quite a lot – but not in a context any software developer would recognise. When law firms professed themselves open to agile working in the pre-pandemic world, they often meant begrudgingly allowing lawyers to work from home for one day a week. Before the lockdown, law firm offices were definitely not set up for agile with a capital 'A', with its emphasis on small, co-located teams, collaboration, transparency and continuous delivery. Pre-COVID, cellular offices (for the lawyers, at least) were the norm in many large firms and lawyers were expected to work physically in their office at least four days a week. Then came the pandemic; lockdown forced remote working, and proved that law firms could still do business, in the short term at least, without everyone being physically present in the office.

A small minority of law firms have announced that they will not return to the office at all. The majority have stated that they will be open to their people working remotely, but that they want to move to a more hybrid model with some office face time still viewed as essential. Most law firms will go back; but, in the short to medium term, the office environment will look very different and not particularly progressive. Where some law firms might have been considering hot-desking or a more open-plan configuration pre-COVID, this is unlikely to be possible in the current climate. We may even see further retrenchment, a movement away from co-location of diverse teams towards more physical protectionism. Physical separation and rotation of teams may be a long-term necessity, for safety reasons; and this becomes an easy justification for the single person partner office. This is unfortunate, as practice groups in law firms often work in siloes; lawyers and 'non-lawyers' are kept physically separate, which does not encourage collaboration.[90] This approach can filter through to the business teams too, which is particularly dangerous as core support functions really do need to work together to deliver to the business. As the case study below from Paul Hastings demonstrates, working in an agile way can help teams to execute more effectively; this is essential for successful digital transformation.

*(d) What is 'Agile'?*

Agile with a capital A is a cornerstone of successful digital transformation. It is easy to mischaracterise agile as an abstruse methodology, with a kind of mythical status and its own language, making it feel foreign and inaccessible to lawyers. Lawyers are used to a linear process for delivery, and believe that anything can be accomplished if you work long enough and hard enough and have sufficient resources. For delivery of legal work, this may be true (although one has to question the quality of the output of even the most elite legal team after a couple of all-nighters). It does not hold true for agile development of digital products, however, which are increasingly becoming part of the law firm portfolio (see Chapter 4 for a discussion of the rise of productisation in the legal services sector). An example of the difference: a colleague in a law firm that was building a client-facing product watched a partner asking the product team when the product would be finished. He was told that the team "did not yet have a sense of its aggregate velocity".[91] This was not what the partner wanted to hear – he wanted a date so that he had a 'throat to choke' if things began to slip.[92] This demonstrates well the yawning gulf between the way lawyers and product teams deliver.

If you step back a little, however, the two are not so far apart. At its core, agile comes back to something that should be close to the lawyer's heart, because one of the core five elements of successful digital transformation is customer centricity:

*Agile is often thought of as a process when it's really a mind-set (supported by processes, of course). Yes, it's about testing and learning, and new ways of working, but at the heart of agile is the determination to provide the customer with something she or he wants or needs ...*[93]

There are many excellent books devoted to agile and the organisational changes that need to be made to adopt agile working practices at scale. There are agile coaches who train teams with the new skills they need to work differently. Most law firms simply won't have reached the level of digital maturity that justifies an intervention of that kind. However, the development of a culture of multidisciplinary working and shared accountability is essential if the firm is to deliver digitally enabled business outcomes.

It is worth spending a bit of time on what agile is really about, at its heart. Back in 2001, a group of developers got together to discuss the future of software development and address their frustrations over the status quo, which prioritised planning and documentation of development at the expense of the most important consideration – pleasing the customer. They developed an Agile Manifesto with four values[94] and 12 Principles. Here are the Principles:[95]

1. *Our highest priority is to satisfy the customer through early and continuous delivery of valuable software.*
2. *Welcome changing requirements, even late in development. Agile processes harness change for the customer's competitive advantage.*
3. *Deliver working software frequently, from a couple of weeks to a couple of months, with a preference to the shorter timescale.*
4. *Business people and developers must work together daily throughout the project.*
5. *Build projects around motivated individuals. Give them the environment and support they need, and trust them to get the job done.*
6. *The most efficient and effective method of conveying information to and within a development team is face-to-face conversation.*
7. *Working software is the primary measure of progress.*
8. *Agile processes promote sustainable development. The sponsors,*

*developers, and users should be able to maintain a constant pace indefinitely.*

9. *Continuous attention to technical excellence and good design enhances agility.*

10. *Simplicity – the art of maximising the amount of work not done – is essential.*

11. *The best architectures, requirements, and designs emerge from self-organising teams.*

12. *At regular intervals, the team reflects on how to become more effective, then tunes and adjusts its behaviour accordingly.*

What can we take from the Principles that might resonate in a law firm setting, and help with delivery of digital change? If I had to reduce them down to four, I would extract these learnings:

- The customer/client is the highest priority.
- Lawyers and the digital transformation teams should work collaboratively.
- Regular communication across teams will speed up pace of delivery.
- Treat people with respect and trust their professional opinion.

These are sound principles that don't sound too alien, nor do they seem unachievable. However, they are not routinely enacted in a law firm setting, where lawyers are just too busy to invest time in changing the status quo. There are organisational structures that can help to address this; in Chapter 4 I look at the development of products in law firms, and discuss the importance of the role of the lawyer/product owner, which is one approach to getting lawyers invested in the delivery of digital change. Other organisations have approached this in different ways – some going all out to adopt agile at scale, others adopting elements that work for their business.

Lawyers who are sceptical about agile, thinking it a buzzword or a concept that could never be applied to legal work, should speak to their clients. An increasing number of corporate legal functions, notably in the telecommunications, financial services and technology sectors, are moving to agile ways of working for the legal team. These corporate legal functions are supporting businesses that are themselves working in an agile way, and have made the shift in order to remain effective business partners. The mindset change and new way of working that agile requires has not always been an easy shift for these corporate legal functions, and has required investment and training. However, the benefits are justifying the effort; by breaking down siloes and working more collaboratively as part of multidisciplinary teams, lawyers are being brought into business conversations at the right time, and are able to influence the development of products or provision of services earlier in the process, leading to fewer legal issues along the way. If significant law firm clients are committing to an agile way of working, law firms must, at the very least, educate themselves on what this means for their clients and think through the implications for the law firm's own client service delivery.

I have yet to find an example of a law firm partnership that has successfully applied agile ways of working to the delivery of legal advisory work. However, some law firms have experimented with agile, typically within innovation or legal project management teams. The case study below from Paul Hastings in a good example of adopting those parts of agile that make sense for your own organisation and adapting them to improve execution and delivery of a change agenda.

**Case study: Paul Hastings**[96]

**Adopting aspects of agile**

Paul Hastings LLP is an international law firm with a presence in Asia, Europe, Latin America and the United States. Named 2020's Innovator of the Year by the International Legal Technology Association (ILTA), the firm has a strong reputation for innovation in both its technical legal advisory work and its client service delivery. The firm's managing director of innovation and knowledge, Nicola Shaver, was also recognised at the 2020 ILTA awards as Innovative Leader of the Year (marking outstanding achievement by an individual in maximising the value of innovative technology in support of legal professionals).

Shaver is one of the leaders of Paul Hastings' practice innovation department. One of the largest of the law firm innovation teams, the department is made up of 50 colleagues, including attorneys, developers, knowledge professionals and legal project managers. This diversity is reflected in the team's remit, which is wide ranging, covering knowledge, legal project management, alternative staffing, legal research and legal technology.

Like many innovators in law firm partnerships, Shaver is a lawyer by training. She worked for a number of years in private practice and in-house, before making the move to legal innovation.

Shaver is no starry-eyed futurist, nor is she a fan of innovation theatre. She is a pragmatist who is committed to delivering real change. Shaver's view is that effective change can't be achieved by looking inwards. She believes in the value of importing ideas and methodologies from more digitally mature industries into legal services, to help improve the way lawyers deliver to clients.

Shaver has been experimenting with introducing aspects of agile into the firm, starting with her own team. Her objective was clear: to shift the mindset of the team towards greater collaboration and client centricity. She recognised that certain technologies and tools would be too alien or difficult to adopt, so opted for simplicity. To encourage greater communication and transparency in the team, she introduced the use of Kanban boards. Kanban is a framework used in agile software development, involving real-time communication of what team members are working on, with full transparency around capacity and progress – allowing a team to maximise efficiency (or 'flow'). Work is represented visually on a Kanban board – either an old-fashioned physical whiteboard with post-it notes or a digital board. Shaver was not religious about insisting on the 'right' terminology, but found that introducing concepts such as backlog and prioritisation were very helpful in making the team more effective.

Another simple idea, borrowed from agile, was encouraging the teams developing products regularly to speak to the end user, rather than rely on assumptions about what the lawyers might want or need. According to Shaver, this was particularly important as so many of the team were former lawyers, who tended to rely on their own preconceptions about how lawyers would think. The discipline of iterative development paid dividends; where this approach was taken, adoption challenges were minimal.

The third simple approach borrowed from agile involved the introduction of (optional) agile meetings for the whole team; once a week, for 15 minutes only. This allowed the team to share ideas and learnings – and discover new applications for existing solutions across different practice groups. This in turn allowed for much more effective scaling of solutions across the firm.

I asked Shaver whether she felt that agile could ever be adopted at a larger scale within a law firm, and be applied to the delivery of client-facing legal work itself. Her view was that there may be elements of legal matters that could benefit from agile delivery (for example, matters requiring a large amount of project management such as post-merger integrations or complex mass claims litigation). However, she was not convinced that high-end bespoke advisory work could be delivered in this way – not least because lawyers can be highly resistant to radical changes to the way that they work.

As the case study shows, to harness agile ways of working and build the muscles needed for continuous delivery of change, a pragmatic first step is to move away from working in siloes. This requires a conscious decision to reorganise the business teams, creating digital delivery teams that cross all functions and which are truly multidisciplinary. Any change to the established order can feel like a threat, and business function leaders may need to be incentivised to work in this way. For example, it should be made clear that benefits from digital products or solutions will be shared across the functions, rather than accruing to the team leading digital transformation.

To achieve better collaboration, and avoid arguments about who pays when lending resources to a digital team, a portion of the business services budget can be ring fenced and dedicated to funding teams working on digital initiatives. The budgeting for these digital teams needs to be agile, too; traditional approval processes and funding requests can be too slow and bureaucratic. Funding should be dynamic and revisited regularly, released to the teams when defined success criteria or KPIs are achieved. Similarly, if progress is not being made, funds can quickly be withdrawn and reallocated elsewhere. This keeps things moving, and allows the roadmap to progress.

> **Key points**
> A strategy is only a paper document until there is a plan for execution and the right team to deliver. The mix of capabilities in the team will depend on the strategy, but it is important that the teams be multidisciplinary, including technology professionals and lawyers with deep domain knowledge. Although the team should have a roadmap for execution, delivery should be agile, as should the processes for funding. This will help in maintaining momentum and will keep the client at the heart of the delivery.

## 2.7 Step 7: Create your vision and strategy document and communications plan

The digital transformation vision and strategy document is an important part of the toolkit. It will be the touchstone for all communications about the transformation – with current employees and partners, with clients, with potential recruits, lateral hires, partner law firms and strategic delivery partners, with competitors and with the wider world. It needs to be multi-purpose. It will be used to inform, to persuade, to stimulate enthusiasm for the transformation and to temper it with realism. It also needs to resonate with everyone that reads it, regardless of their digital literacy. Perhaps most importantly, the vision and strategy must explain to the partners of the firm how digital transformation will make the business that they own more successful.

### (a) The devil is in the detail
It may sound like an issue of form over substance, but it is important to choose the right format for presenting the vision and strategy. Every

significant law firm change programme in which I have been involved has turned on the quality and impact of the documentation that supported it. Lawyers will either engage with the strategy or they will ignore it. You can't do too much about those that ignore it – they are either too busy or have simply disengaged. Those that do engage with the strategy, however, will definitely be interested in the detail and will expect a high-quality and thoughtful product.

When seeking partnership approval to establish the Freshfields global centre, under the leadership of a visionary litigation partner, Paul Lomas, we produced supporting papers that rivalled the scale of a court bundle, with a skeleton argument and 52 tabs of supporting annexes. Every word was sweated over by the programme team. We had content in Word, business models in Excel, presentations in PowerPoint. The documentation was a real mixture of advocacy, business modelling and market and client research – something for every partner. This approach is necessary because partners, the many owners of the business, will each have a different focus. Some will be interested in the firm's legacy, and influenced by evidence of how digital transformation will future-proof the firm. Others will be interested in the impact on people, and the ways in which digital can offer new career pathways and open up diversity. Others will be focused on clients, and how transforming the firm will make it more credible with their client base. And some, of course, will be interested in the bottom line – simply wanting to know how much the transformation will cost and what benefits it will bring.

A successful strategy document will cover all these elements and invite further discussion and explanation. This is an important point to make; the strategy is not a static artefact. It should be iterative, and revisited regularly. It should invite comment and respond to change.

*(b) What should be in the strategy document?*
The contents of the strategy document will be highly specific to the firm. There is no right way to draft it. I would suggest that it should, at a minimum, cover the following four areas:
- the case for change (Why are we doing this?);

- articulation of the strategy (What will we do?);
- envisioning the strategy (What will the new world look and feel like?); and
- the roadmap for delivery (How will we do it?).

**The case for change:** It is essential to set out, right up front, why the firm needs to make the investment in digital transformation. You should not pull any punches in this section. The document needs to be highly persuasive and to capture the reader from the beginning. Some suggestions:

- Provide an explanation of what is meant by digital transformation, tackling head-on the misconception that it is just about new technology adoption.
- Give evidence of how the world is changing (a macro view). Avoid using clichés (don't talk about Kodak or Netflix!) or slipping into the role of a futurologist. Your audience is a sophisticated one that understands the broader economics driving change; the challenge is to help them to recognise that it applies to the job that they do and the clients that they serve. Choose examples that are sufficiently engaging but still within the sphere of your partners' and business leaders' experience.[97]
- Offer examples from your clients of how their industry has been disrupted and how their business has responded (an obvious example is the rise of fintech and the response of the financial services industry). War stories from clients about their own digital transformation journeys will be particularly powerful. Use video if at all possible.
- Include examples of what your competitors are doing to change the way they deliver to clients, linked to performance improvement if the data is in the public domain. Do not only choose the obvious law firm competitors. Think about new entrants such as law companies and the Big 4. Include, also, examples of clients expanding their in-house capabilities and sending less work to external counsel.
- Describe where your firm is now in terms of digital maturity. Be honest, and use objective benchmarks to show that you are behind where you should be:

- Does the firm have a significant number of legacy systems that need to be upgraded or replaced?
- Are you vulnerable to security breaches?
- Is the firm currently unprepared for a move to the cloud?
- Is the day-to-day experience, for lawyers, other professionals and clients, sub-optimal?
- Is knowledge sharing an analogue process?
- Are there war stories you can recount of where partners have failed to win a pitch or to capitalise on an opportunity because of a lack of digital capability?

  Examples like this will exist, so be determined and resourceful in seeking them out. Many of the firm's partners simply won't know that the platform is burning – it is your job to call attention to it.

- Make the link between your firm's strategy and the digital strategy; demonstrate that the digital strategy is not a separate initiative. Emphasise that execution of the digital strategy is an essential part of the firm achieving its broader ambitions.

**Articulation of strategy:** Strategy documents can become corpulent and unwieldy, especially if they are very detailed. The detail is important, particularly in a law firm, but the strategy also needs a simple, visual hook that acts as its elevator pitch. Start by summarising the strategy in a simple and memorable way. Figure 2 is the visual that we developed at Freshfields.

This simple pyramid proved to be highly effective. It became the touchstone for every communication around the firm's digital transformation. The delivery teams were aligned to a particular layer of the pyramid; objectives were shaped around the pyramid and the delivery roadmap also tracked the three layers. When called upon to talk about digital transformation, everyone in global technology could speak to the three layers.

When setting out the detail behind the visual, bear the following in mind:
- Assume a low level of digital literacy, but do not patronise the

# Figure 2. Vision and strategy for digital transformation

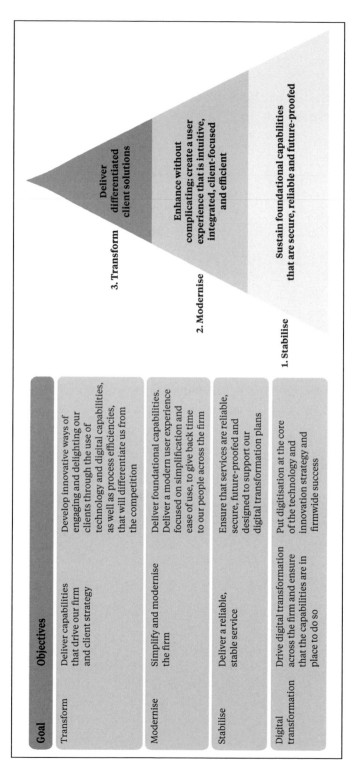

| Goal | Objectives | |
|------|-----------|---|
| Transform | Deliver capabilities that drive our firm and client strategy | Develop innovative ways of engaging and delighting our clients through the use of technology and digital capabilities, as well as process efficiencies, that will differentiate us from the competition |
| Modernise | Simplify and modernise the firm | Deliver foundational capabilities. Deliver a modern user experience focused on simplification and ease of use, to give back time to our people across the firm |
| Stabilise | Deliver a reliable, stable service | Ensure that services are reliable, secure, future-proofed and designed to support our digital transformation plans |
| Digital transformation | Drive digital transformation across the firm and ensure that the capabilities are in place to do so | Put digitisation at the core of the technology and innovation strategy and firmwide success |

*Source: Reproduced with kind permission of Freshfields Bruckhaus Deringer LLP.*

reader. Each element of the strategy should be described in non-technical language (so far as is possible).

- Ground the strategy in the reality of the working environment. It may help to show the entire end-to-end matter lifecycle or delivery value chain,[98] showing at every step how the strategy will impact the experience for lawyers, other business professionals and clients (for example, how the pitch process will change for the better, or resourcing be re-envisioned).
- Set out the benefits at every level – for the firm's people, clients, bottom line (cost reductions), top line (revenue growth), risk reduction and quality improvement. A dry business case view is not the best vehicle for this – be creative.

**Envisioning the strategy:** Paint a picture of what the new world will look like when the strategy is executed. This should be inspirational and ambitious, without being unrealistic. A helpful technique is to create envisioned user journeys for particular processes from different perspectives: lawyer, business professional, client. Choose a process from the end-to-end matter lifecycle and zoom in on the detail. How will the strategy change the experience? Make it really visual and engaging. Before and after animations can be effective here too.

**The roadmap for delivery:** This section sets out how you will deliver the digital strategy. We are not talking about a project plan or a sterile Gantt chart here, but a deeper analysis of what delivery will involve, including the role that partners and business leaders will play in making the strategy a success.

As your audience is likely to have little patience for detailed project plans and dependencies, it will be helpful to set out the principles that will govern delivery of the strategy. These principles, agreed up front, will help to guide decisions and set expectations. The guiding principles might include the following:

- **Remove waste and duplication:** Simplify the IT environment and reduce the number of applications.
- **Maximise existing technologies:** Before investing in new solutions, exploit technology the firm already has.

- **Adopt the cloud:** The cloud should be the preferred approach wherever possible.
- **Ensure reusability:** No investment in point solutions; products or solutions must have wide business application.

As well as setting out the principles for implementing the strategy, the delivery section should articulate the technologies, new ways of working and process and governance changes that will be required in order to achieve the strategy (the people, process, technology triumvirate). These changes include:

- new governance to guide and support the digital teams, and to make decisions about investments (discussed in Chapter 4);
- the introduction of a product mindset and the concept of product ownership to speed up delivery and make sure that digital solutions are truly client-centric (discussed in Chapter 4);
- new (and lighter) processes for resourcing and funding digital teams (discussed in Chapter 8);
- the creation of new career paths and incentives for digital talent (discussed in Chapter 8).

Process changes probably won't bother the partners too much, as most of the processes are (frankly) unlikely to touch their world. Other changes will. The strategy document must call out the cultural changes that the firm will need to make if it is really to commit to becoming more digitally effective. I discuss these changes at length in Part III of this book. They include conceptual and behavioural changes which lawyers, used to the established norms, may find unsettling, and which move the firm towards a culture that is:

- comfortable with failure;
- open to working in multidisciplinary teams (that means lawyers working with 'non-lawyers' (of which more later));
- diverse and non-hierarchical; and
- transparent with information at all levels of the business.

It is crucial not to exempt the partnership from the obligation to work differently. Leadership from the top will be an important success factor.

The partners will need to become familiar with the portfolio of digital technology initiatives that the team has identified. Rather than setting out the full roadmap, highlight what the team will be prioritising for delivery over the short (1–6 months), medium (6–12 months) and long (12 months plus) terms. The team will be held to this schedule, so be pragmatic and be sure to prioritise some initiatives that you know can be delivered and which will add demonstrable value. Solving an obvious lawyer pain point, such as high latency leading to frustration when working from home, can win credibility for the delivery teams and buy you the time you need to make a dent in the harder, more complex initiatives.

The goals that the leadership sets in the roadmap will also be the basis of objectives for the delivery teams. This will mean that everyone in the team is aligned around delivery and knows what they are accountable for and what is expected of them.

**Key points**
The vision and strategy document is the north star of the firm's digital transformation. It should inspire and engage the firm around a vision, while also instilling confidence that the firm can deliver on the change. The digital vision and strategy document will form the basis of the team's communications, both internal and external, so it is worth investing the time in getting it right. Words matter to lawyers, so the messaging must be crisp and clear, and the end goals tangible. The document should paint a picture of what a 'transformed', digitally effective firm will look like for the firm's people and, most importantly, its clients. The document must be open about the challenges, too, setting out the level of financial investment and the cultural change that will be required for a digital transformation to be successful and sustainable.

## 2.8 Step 8: Communicate and manage the change
Communication and change management in any organisation (particularly a large one with lots of different stakeholders) is an art. It does not begin and end with an email from the senior partner and a press release. Although most law firms will have a communications

team, very few have permanent change management capability. Firms may decide that formal change management is unnecessary, relying on traditional comms channels (email) to hammer home the message, or drawing on consultancy to support change when a large programme is being delivered.

## To change behaviour, go EAST

I have worked with a number of talented communications professionals over the years and have an appreciation for the complexity involved in changing behaviours through communication. We witnessed the UK government grapple with communicating clearly during the coronavirus lockdown. We watched the government's messages unravel as they became increasingly unclear and opaque, and as advice was disregarded by a number of key policymakers. The public's response – to take the opportunity to ignore much of the guidance themselves – shows that effective communication is really about understanding psychology. In his excellent book *Inside the Nudge Unit*, David Halpern, chief executive of the Behavioural Insights Team (BIT), which advises the government on policy, sets out BIT's approach for changing (or 'nudging') behaviour.[99] To encourage a behaviour, you should think about making it:

- Easy
- Attractive
- Social
- Timely[100]

**Easy:** If you want to encourage something, make it easy to do. Take out friction and hassle. The converse applies: to discourage behaviour, make that behaviour more difficult – put some obstacles in the way. Halpern gives the example of an individual wanting to save money for a particular item. To encourage saving, make it easy by creating an automatic money transfer to a separate account as soon as wages are paid. To discourage spending, don't have a bank card for that account.

**Attractive:** This has two elements to it. First, if you want to change behaviour then messaging needs to break through and grab the audience's attention. This means it needs to be *salient* (personalised or otherwise relevant). As an example, traffic signs that flash up a car's individual speed and number plate are much more effective at controlling speeding than a static road sign. Secondly, the suggestion or offer itself has to be attractive or persuasive. Financial incentives may work, but are only one tool. Non-financial incentives such as curiosity and fun can work, as can competition (we are attracted to things that are perceived as rare or that are associated with people we respect). Making sure the message comes from the right person (the 'messenger effect') is also key to attraction. Advice about coronavirus control coming from a politician is less attractive than when it is delivered by the chief medical officer, for example.

**Social:** As the COVID-19 crisis has taught us, the behaviour of those around us can have a powerful influence on our own actions. Research has shown that people are much more likely to drop litter in an area that is already littered. We are social beings, and conform to social norms. Halpern draws a distinction between a 'declarative' social norm and an 'injunctive' social norm. A declarative social norm is what we see others doing or what evidence indicates they are doing (dropping litter). An injunctive social norm is what we are supposed to be doing, or what others approve of (disposing of our litter in the bin). Research suggests that where the two types of norm clash, the declarative social norm (what people are actually doing) will win:

*We are influenced by what others around us are doing (declarative social norms), and particularly by the behaviour of those we know or feel are like us; by the desire to reciprocate; and even by the idea of other people observing us.*[101]

**Timely:** When trying to establish a habit or behaviour, timing is everything. There will be certain key moments when an intervention will affect an outcome or behavioural change much more effectively (the earlier a retailer knows a woman is pregnant, for example, the quicker it can capitalise on the retail opportunity that having a new baby presents). Intervening early, before a habit is established, can also be key in shaping behaviour.

EAST is a helpful framework to bear in mind when developing a communications and change plan for digital transformation. Below are some thoughts about how to apply the framework practically in a law firm.

If you want to encourage your partners to talk to their clients about digital transformation, make it *easy* for them. Provide ready-made slide decks that can be tailored to particular clients or sectors, with speaker notes and war stories. If you want lawyers to find out more about your product portfolio, make it easy by putting all the information on a mobile app on their work phone, rather than on a static document repository. Partners can look at their phone in the taxi on the way to the client meeting rather than having to search the firm's intranet.

To build interest in digital transformation, make it *attractive*: create a sense of healthy (not aggressive) competition. Give a shout-out to regions or offices that are contributing ideas for new products or that have won new work on the basis of digital credentials. If you want people to use new software, provide it on new laptops and make the provision more attractive by giving them out gradually, to influencers first. Creating a buzz around a scarce commodity can be very effective.

Use the fact that the law firm is a *social* construct to your advantage. Do not rely on an order from the senior leadership team to make people engage with the digital initiatives. An injunctive social norm will not be as effective as one that is declarative. Identify influential partners who will model the digital mindset that you are seeking to create and who will actually use the solutions and products you develop. Bear in mind that in a law firm it is not always the senior management team that exerts influence. For associates, the line partner for whom the associate works will be much more influential. Think about where the tacit power in your firm resides. Is it with the rainmakers? The culture carriers? Target as many of these individuals as you can. Do not waste time on the detractors.

Finally, *time* your interventions and messages carefully. Do not communicate when people are distracted or very busy – at quarter-end billing, for example. Intervene at key moments in a lawyer's career; for example, senior associates preparing for partnership are incredibly focused on being good corporate citizens and are very eager to learn new skills. Introduce trainees to the new tools and technologies and to new working practices. They will adopt them readily. Be aware, though, that trainees will cement their working practices in their practice teams, learning from more senior lawyers. You cannot hope to achieve real change from the bottom up only.

**Key points**

Effective communication and change management are absolutely critical to the success of the digital transformation. Use the EAST framework to 'nudge' the firm into adopting new behaviours and mindsets. Because becoming more digitally effective involves such a significant cultural change, relying on existing channels and resources is unlikely to be sufficient; you may find your digital messages slipping down the agenda. The firm should ideally invest in permanent change and communications capability to support the change, or redeploy professionals from existing teams. ∎

# Part II: Product development and technology

# Chapter 4: Products

## 1. Law firm or software development house?

During my time as chief legal innovation officer at Freshfields, our transformation team became focused on developing our own client-facing digital products. The management of the firm was supportive, but the team also encountered a degree of scepticism about our ability to build, and to sell, products to our clients. Two statements I heard a number of times were "We are not a software development company" and "We don't make widgets here." For many lawyers, developing digital products is not what law firms ought to be doing, because it is not regarded as being part of the traditional professional services offering.

It is worth defining what is meant by a 'digital product'. Hunting for a good definition, I came across some insights that might help:
- A digital product is a way to convert time, knowledge and effort into revenue at scale without hiring more people.
- Digital products are how 'new money' is made.
- "A digital product is an intangible asset ... that can be sold and

distributed repeatedly online without the need to replenish inventory."[102]
- Unlike a physical product, a digital product is only created once (but may be updated several times).

The key elements of a digital product, then, are scalability, value creation, repeatability and some level of automation of human effort. To lawyers accustomed to delivering services as blocks of advice, recorded in paper documents and charged on a time and materials basis, this concept can feel alien. Lawyers don't like to think of their work in this way. They tend to regard each transaction or case as bespoke, rather than to look for similarities. When they think about scale, they think about adding more resources. Yet even the most high-end legal work has repeatable elements, cutting across different practice groups and sectors. It is these repeatable elements that can be productised and scaled, and delivered to clients using technology.

Products should not feel like such an alien concept to law firms, particularly as other professional services organisations have been developing digital products for many years. For example, Deloitte Ventures has been working with professionals in audit to develop products to serve (or disrupt) that most traditional of Deloitte's practices. This is because Deloitte recognises that the audit practice will have to adapt if it is to survive. It is not just a defensive play; developing products can also offer great opportunity, and can help organisations reach more clients in a cost-effective way. This should be particularly appealing to law firms. Law firms are people businesses, and it is difficult to scale without hiring more people, a strategy that can be organisationally unwieldy, can lead to quality issues – and can be very expensive.

Creating products allows for cost-effective scale, and presents a genuine commercial opportunity for law firms. However, with opportunity comes challenge, as effective development and commercialisation of digital products requires some changes to the traditional law firm operating model and to established ways of working.

## 2. Embedding products into services

There is a misconception that, by developing products, law firms will move from being providers of professional services to becoming software developers or providers of technology services. This is not the case; although some changes to the operating model are required to be successful in building products, this need not amount to wholesale business model disruption. Products and services can happily co-exist.

Productising part of a legal offering, by embedding a digital product into the package of services the firm offers, is a viable and progressive approach to client service delivery and can enable scale at minimal expense. There is no disruption in this model; it does not compromise the traditional lawyer/client relationship. Because it is embedded in the service delivery, the product does not become a standalone offering, and consequently there is no disaggregation of the lawyer's role in the process. (If, however, the digital product becomes the service, this is a different proposition. At this stage, it is probably wise to take the product outside the law firm environment, as a spin-off (discussed in Chapter 7) or as part of a separate but affiliated entity with its own identity (see the discussion of aosphere, below).) Where the product is simply an enhancement, the essential function of the law firm (which is to sell professional services) is unaffected. For this reason, the embedded model can work well for both law firms and clients:

> *Services remain the center of gravity, and customers continue to buy the service offering, not the product per se. From the customer's perspective, little changes other than the pricing of the service. That drops because the value created by the new product is shared between the firm and its customers.*[103]

Pricing, an important element of product development, is discussed later in this chapter.

## 3. Law firm digital products – some examples

Digital products developed by law firms have, in fact, been around for

*The value of the product does not lie in the technology used – sometimes the more simple it is, the more successful it will be.*

quite some time (although perhaps we didn't think of them as being 'digital', as some predate the adoption of that term). Where products are being built, they vary enormously from basic automated regulatory updates through to sophisticated end-to-end platforms. The value of the product does not lie in the technology used – sometimes the more simple it is, the more successful it will be. Equally, products do not have to be client-facing to deliver value. Simple use of digital tools and technologies to make work more efficient for lawyers and law firm professionals can be highly successful – and write their own business case:

> [R]esearch has shown that companies using digital tools and technologies to help employees find what they need are much more likely to succeed in their digital transformations. Key features often include single sign-on access to databases, a simple process for submitting knowledge, and networking to allow easy-to-use access to various databases.[104]

Over the past three to five years, the market has seen more and more law firms dip their toes into product development. There are numerous different models that law firms are using to develop and deliver digital products to their clients. Four of the most common:

- subscriptions;
- partnering;
- client-facing apps; and
- digital platforms.

### 3.1 The subscription model
The subscription model, where the journey started, is long established. Under this model, law firms package up repeatable elements of legal advice and make them available to clients online in return for an annual subscription. The model is simple and sustainable and has stood the test of time, but does not quite have the glamour that we would associate with digital product development.

Allen & Overy forged the way back in 2001. The firm established Derivatives Services, which offered client-facing products focusing on the over-the-counter derivatives market. In 2015, Derivative Services was relaunched as aosphere, a wholly owned affiliate of A&O. The relaunch was a response to increased regulation in the financial services sector; the products that aosphere offered to clients were online compliance and legal risk solutions, which gave a view of regulatory obligations across different jurisdictions. According to the 2015 press release:

> *Each product turns these complex areas of the law into easy-to-use, colour-coded guides to the myriad rules that apply in different jurisdictions.*[105]

Since its launch in 2015, aosphere has grown into a successful standalone revenue-generating unit (recording nearly £5 million of profit in 2019), serving its own clients in the regulatory and compliance sectors. Its product offering has expanded. At the time of writing, there are 18 products on offer. Many continue to focus on OTC derivatives, but others go into new territory, for example by providing an analysis of global data privacy regulations or the rules relating to e-signatures in various jurisdictions.

Clifford Chance was another early pioneer of the subscription model, providing automated contract templates to its clients, using document automation platform Contract Express. This offering, CC Dr@ft, has now been wrapped into Clifford Chance Applied Solutions, the product development arm of the firm, which was formed in 2018 as a wholly owned subsidiary.

Significant revenue is being generated for Allen & Overy by aosphere and consequently it is easy to understand the firm's motivation for embracing the subscription model. In other cases, where revenue is not significant, the upside is not as clear. Why would elite law firms sully themselves with the client's low-end work, when the real money (and the interesting work) is at the premium end? One explanation is that servicing clients at the more commoditised end of the scale creates client stickiness. Dealing with, for example, a client's corporate housekeeping may not be terribly exciting or cutting edge for the law firm, but it does give the firm lots of valuable client data. That data could be a useful weapon in the hands of a smaller, cheaper firm or law company.

The subscription model may be where it all started, but the model itself is far from dead. As Bas Boris Visser, global head of innovation and business change at Clifford Chance, observed in 2017:

> *Going forward, a greater percentage of work will be sold through subscriptions and licences, rather than hourly charge-out rates. At the moment, this trend is in its initial stages, but the legal sector is capable of developing it further.*[106]

The idea of licensing is an interesting one; if law firms were able to become really sophisticated in developing software solutions that are standalone and non-advisory (solutions to support the business of law, such as a matter management platform, for example), then licensing could be an attractive option for additional revenue generation.

### 3.2 Partnering to develop and deliver products

The market has seen a progression from simple, multi-jurisdictional compliance advice to more complex digital products. In 2020, A&O announced that it was partnering with Factor (a managed services provider, formerly part of Axiom) to bring to market a product to help financial institutions manage the transition from IBOR to alternative risk-free interest rate benchmarks. The implications of the IBOR transition for financial services institutions are far reaching, as IBOR is deeply embedded in firms' operating models and financial products. This means that a huge volume of documentation (estimated at over 50 million documents) needs to be amended and future-proofed (or 'repapered') before the IBOR benchmarks cease to be used – a task which is at the same time complex and tedious.[107]

This is exactly the right space for digital product development, in which the product and the service are inextricably linked. The 'front end' of the product was conceived by A&O's markets innovation group, a team of partners who focus on creating digital solutions for financial services clients. This team has built a suite of products to deal with documentary repapering required by regulatory change (such as Brexit). The front-end solution is marketed as 'IBORMatrix' and essentially involves the review of a large corpus of documents using machine learning extraction technology (to identify whether or not the documents contain language governing the fallback position when IBOR is discontinued) and document generation technology to produce revised draft documentation on an automated basis. The technology review will allow contracts to be triaged by complexity to the most cost-effective resource to review and amend, with the less complex volume work being undertaken by Factor. IBORMatrix combines A&O's legal expertise, Factor's scale and project management expertise, and technology. What makes this particularly interesting is that it is not a standalone product, but embedded within the services the law firm provides – a complement to, rather than a replacement of, its legal expertise.

Other firms have spotted similar opportunities. In 2019, Hogan Lovells launched Engage: LIBOR, its own AI-based LIBOR solution. The product was developed in collaboration with Cognia Law (an alternative legal services provider or 'law company') and FTI Consulting (who, in conjunction with Kira Systems, provided the technology for the solution).

What is the appeal of these particular products? It is not clear precisely how much revenue they bring into the firms that develop them. Indeed, revenue may not be the main play here. There are other benefits: these propositions, particularly those that involve partnering with more cost-effective reviewers, allow large and expensive law firms to remain 'full service', combining high-end legal advice with the development of products at the commoditised end of the spectrum. Because the products are scalable and don't depend on hiring more people, full service is still competitive. This protects law firms against the threat of disaggregation by cheaper providers, and enables them to keep hold of their largest and often most valuable clients.

### 3.3 Client-facing apps
Over the past three years, there has been an increasing trend for law

firms to produce simple mobile or web-based applications to deliver high-level, generic legal advice to clients dealing with crisis situations. One example is the ubiquitous 'dawn raid' app, a client-facing application that delivers practical guidance in the event of an unexpected investigation by competition or antitrust authorities. A quick Google search shows at least 10 examples of dawn raid apps developed by large corporate law firms. There have also been a number of web-based applications developed by law firms to help clients respond to the COVID-19 pandemic – see, for example, Shearman & Sterling's Global COVID-19 Legislation tool.

Most firms do not charge for these products, which are more of a marketing play than a revenue generator. Yet there is always a dollar value to be attached to good marketing, and these solutions help make firms look innovative, modern and responsive, for relatively little investment. Other firms offer a free version of the application as a teaser, with an upgrade to a premium version coming at a cost. See, for example, Freshfields' Antitrust 101 App.

Technology is constantly evolving, and the emergence of low-code and no-code platforms means that law firms can go beyond these simple mobile apps to develop more complex products, still at a relatively low cost, without having to invest in expensive development teams.

### 3.4 Digital platforms

Using technology to deliver simple advice at scale is one thing. Developing software platforms that address the way law firms and legal teams deliver their work is another. There is intense competition in this space, with software vendors, law companies and certain law firms vying to be the first to provide the definitive legal platform solution. Some law firms have made significant investments in this area. One example is Lupl, launched in May 2020 as an open industry platform for legal matters. Lupl is a collaboration between three law firms – CMS (a large international UK-based law firm), US firm Cooley LLP and Rajah & Tann Asia (a Singaporean law firm) – supported by a legal department advisory board with GCs from corporate legal teams such as Airbnb and Deutsche Bank.

The **platform** is still in development at the time of writing (June 2021), in **private**, invite-only beta, and according to the Lupl website, a public release **is** scheduled for later in the year.[108] According to the website and press **releases**, the aim of the Lupl platform is to allow law firms and legal **teams** to work together more effectively on matters, regardless of the **platforms** or systems they use in their own organisations. Because the **platform** is open (Lupl's website explains that the platform will **integrate** with "everything except fax"),[109] and matter-centric (**organised** around a matter rather than a particular channel) all **information** relating to a particular matter will be accessible in one place, **resulting** in what the Lupl team call 'matter synchronisation':

> *What does that mean? It means bringing everything for a legal matter together in one place, rather than all over the place. By bringing together all of those moving parts – the people, the conversations, the documents, the systems – our hope is that situational awareness becomes easier. It's important of course that Lupl doesn't become "yet another channel" that you need to check to figure out what's happening. That's why Lupl is a totally open industry platform – bridging multiple solutions to enable users to plug in their systems and get everything they need in one place. This open approach is the core of what we're trying to do with Lupl ...*[110]

I have **not** seen Lupl in action, but it certainly sounds impressive, the law **firms** involved are progressive, and the concept of an open industry platform **is** a sound one. I will be watching with interest to see how the story **unfolds** once the product is launched.

I **include** details about the platform to highlight two elements that I will discuss **in** more detail in this chapter. The first is the scale of ambition that **some** law firms are demonstrating to develop products and platforms **that** change the way lawyers work. The second is the challenge **involved** in actually developing products, and how marketing **materials** can make product development sound much easier **than** it actually is.

Building **a** platform of this scale does not come cheap. According to the legal press, the three firms involved in Lupl have invested $25 million to date in the development of the platform, which, as noted above, is still in beta.

Development is also a logistical challenge. According to Duncan Weston, CMS executive partner for global development, the development of Lupl will:

> ... *set an example for how to bring together a diverse ecosystem of innovators, in-house and private practice lawyers as well as other professionals to create transformational change in our industry for the decades to come.*[111]

That sounds exciting, and collaboration can undoubtedly generate really innovative solutions. However, this kind of development, which has been resourced through a 36-strong development team, primarily based in the United States, must have presented significant logistical challenges for the teams and the investing law firms. The inputs from the business are many and diverse (good), but you cannot help but wonder how that development team coped with "thousands of hours of inputs from people at legal departments and law firms around the world", the group representing "10,000+ lawyers in 100+ jurisdictions". The website gives the following example to illustrate how the development approach works in practice:

> *Let us give you an example. The initial idea for our 'Matter Pulse' feature came from a chat we had with a startup GC and a Head of Legal Ops in San Francisco. When we met a telecoms lawyer over coffee in London, she told us it needed more depth – so we improved it. Then, we got a call from a law firm partner in Singapore, to tell us how Matter Pulse might be used in his region, and we refined it again.*
>
> *Lupl is and always will be in development because our goal is to build something that real people in legal departments and law firms actually want, not what we or anyone else thinks they want.*[112]

This description of the development approach has of course been

*At the risk of sounding like a Cassandra, any law firm feeling inspired to invest millions in new product development should look long and hard at the realities of making the product journey before jumping in.*

written for marketing purposes, but does tend to give the impression that product development is an easy and pleasant exercise in consultation and collaboration. This is somewhat removed from the gritty reality and daily grind of product development that I and others on the ground have experienced. At the risk of sounding like a Cassandra, any law firm feeling inspired to invest millions in new product development should look long and hard at the realities of making the product journey before jumping in.

## 4. Digital products – the pros and cons

In a legal technology landscape that is groaning with shiny new toys, why would a law firm consider developing its own digital products at all?

There are many arguments against moving into product development. Some lawyers perceive the development and commercialisation of products as a devaluation of their legal expertise which, they fear, can only lead to dilution of the firm brand. Others might question whether the firm has the expertise and the capabilities to move into product development. Certainly, product development is not an easy pivot, as it requires new ways of working and new capabilities that many law firms simply don't have and don't know how to acquire. Then there is the question of money: the business case for new products can be speculative, and standalone bespoke client products may not generate sufficient revenue to justify the investment. Even if products are successful and do generate revenue, the ROI will not be immediate and may even take years to be recovered. This can be a difficult sell in a partnership where revenue realisation is built around a quarterly billing cycle. In addition, some partners may baulk at the idea of charging for what they have been giving away for free to favoured clients for a very long time. Finally, there is a governance challenge: law firm management may fear that embracing product development will result in partners wanting a different bespoke product for every client who expresses an interest – leading to a non-strategic patchwork of point solutions.

Yet, despite these valid concerns, more and more law firms are starting to develop digital products. There are a number of possible reasons for this trend. The legal technology market is still relatively immature and fragmented. There is (currently) no Microsoft or Amazon of law that can provide a cost-effective end-to-end technology solution for each part of legal services delivery. Instead, point solutions proliferate, each one developed to serve a particular vertical in the legal domain (think real estate lease reviews or prospectus generation and drafting). Although the providers of these software solutions are looking to expand their reach, and 2020 saw a good deal of consolidation in the legal technology market, a definitive best-in-class solution feels as though it is some way off.

The lack of maturity in some areas of the commercial off-the-shelf market is one of the reasons why law firms might look to develop their own products – because the solutions on the market can require a lot of customisation to make them right for the firm. I have sat through numerous vendor software demonstrations where I have started out being really enthused by what the solution promised. So often, the enthusiasm wanes as it becomes clear that the product is built for a completely different type of law firm, with a very different way of working. Gaining adoption for new technology in a law firm can be incredibly difficult. Even if the product is a good one, when it does not look and feel like a tool you would use in your own firm, or reflect the way your lawyers work, you are faced with a difficult choice. Do you incur the effort and expense of customising the product to the way the lawyers work now, hoping to drive adoption? Or embark on the Sisyphean task of persuading the lawyers to work in a different way?

One consideration to weigh in the balance is that developing your own solutions (and the skills and capabilities to build them) can also be a very smart long-term investment for a law firm that is fully committed to the digital journey. Best practice for digital organisations suggests that relying on external vendors to develop essential technology is not the best approach, particularly for large companies, as it does not give them the ability to learn and adapt quickly in an increasingly digital world. Instead, companies should build their own products, by upskilling their own people or by acquiring digital capabilities:

*[The] 'build-it-here' approach is a key characteristic of successful digital companies. Some 52 percent of the most digitized companies build AI capabilities in-house, for example, compared with just 38 percent of other companies ... Top-performing companies are also more aggressive in building up their capabilities by buying, acquiring or hiring ... On average, top-performing companies use 30 percent of their M&A investments to acquire digital capabilities, companies with just 24 percent for other companies.*[113]

This is all very well for a law firm that has decided to go all out on digital transformation, but those at the start of their digital initiative should be wary. Product development should not be entered into lightly, and certainly should not be considered to be a cheaper alternative to buying commercial off-the-shelf products. Product development requires investment: financial investment, of course, but also investment in finding the right resources, in choosing the right partners, in training and upskilling lawyers, and an investment of time in putting the right structure and governance around the development process.

Jack Shepherd started out as a restructuring and insolvency associate at Freshfields Bruckhaus Deringer. He moved into the firm's innovation team and became the head of the firm's product development, with accountability for the in-house development of a number of client-facing products. Shepherd then moved to iManage, a software company specialising in work product management solutions for the legal sector, as AI legal practice lead. Jack has a very pragmatic take on the law firm 'buy' versus 'build' debate:

*I think there's a tendency, not just in law, to jump to the most exciting thing and not look at whether this is really the right way of driving business value. Often this manifests itself in bespoke product development. I have seen instances of people wanting to build something, because this is personally exciting to them. Before doing that, it's always necessary to scour the market to see if there is an off-the-shelf solution that might meet needs first.*

*I've found that in law firms, this type of analysis is often rushed. It's also often performed by the person most interested in wanting to go down the 'build route'. So it is not uncommon for people to spend time and money building something that perhaps could have been bought in for an equivalent or cheaper price.*

*More often than not, this leads to failure in the long term because law firms do not have the financial or risk appetite to invest in the long-term success of a product. Law firms are used to earning their money back within a matter of months. For a product that is being sold to the market, you would do well to get your money back in years, yet alone months. Most partners don't understand that – and even if they do, the chances are they will start demanding results long before the product reaches a sufficient level of maturity.*

*While I haven't always thought this, I think law firms should be developing software very sparingly. When they do so, it should be done within an appropriate structure and environment. Software development cannot occur alongside 'old school' teams. Such teams will expect requirements to be laid out from the start. They will not be with you on the journey of the product. Rather, they expect to be involved at specific checkpoints, and will object if facts have changed between these checkpoints (which, of course, is the nature of agile software development). This can result in blockers being raised. Often these can be overcome, but at the cost of significant time and expense.*[114]

Jack's insight injects a healthy dose of realism and illustrates very well the challenges of successful product development. To do it well, a law firm will need the right governance, the right level of financial investment, the right skills and capabilities, changes to established ways of working, and – perhaps most important of all – patience.

## 5. How to develop products successfully

Digital product development is a huge topic. Many books have been written on the subject and there are professionals and product specialists in all industries, including legal services. I am emphatically not a product specialist – but I do have some battle scars from being part of a team leading client-facing product development in a large global law firm, and have seen first-hand what does and does not work. Consider this to be a very high-level guide to how to approach thinking about product development in the context of a digital transformation strategy. If a law firm decides to embark on the product development journey, there are a number of key success factors to bear in mind.

### 5.1 Talk to customers

Product development cannot be driven by instinct. The product team must establish that there is a genuine client need for the solution that is being proposed. 'Build it and they will come' is the wrong approach. This means asking the right questions of the client and really listening to the answers. As discussed in the context of human-centred design in Chapter 2, this is a particular skill that not all lawyers have. It will need to be acquired or taught.

### 5.2 Use process

Boring as it may sound, a process for converting ideas to products is essential. Experimentation and innovation cannot flourish without discipline – absent a defined process, it will likely descend into chaos.

### 5.3 Establish product ownership

To build a successful product requires the client voice and the business voice. Both inputs need to be maintained throughout the life of the product – ideas can't just be 'thrown over the wall' to a product team. The lawyers must be involved in the development of the product by establishing product ownership (explained below) – this gives the lawyers skin in the game.

### 5.4 Build a team

There are particular skills and capabilities that will be required to build a product and take it to market. Consideration must be given up front to how and where to acquire those skills. How will the firm attract the best product and development people? Once found, how will the firm reward and incentivise them?

## 5.5 Work in an agile way

It is crucial to approach product development in an agile way. Law firms are all too familiar with the consequences of a waterfall approach (taking client requirements up front, then developing a solution and rolling it out, without continuously testing with clients). Products developed in this way often require a huge investment in professional services to implement, are slow to deliver and very expensive. An agile approach is not necessarily cheaper – funding an agile team can still be expensive – but it does ensure that the final product is what the client wants and will be adopted without costly customisation.

## 5.6 Work cross-functionally

Building a product is not simply about having a great idea, a developer and a space with a ping pong table. Many people across different functions in the firm will need to help develop, test, market, price and support the product. Some will be more willing to help than others. The product team will need to gain the support of other functions within the firm and find a way to incentivise them to help.

## 5.7 Measure success

The product team will need to think very carefully about how to define the success criteria for the product, how to measure that success – and when to call it a day and decommission the product.

## 5.8 Be cognisant of the culture

As with any new way of working, the team will have to confront the firm's culture – and in all likelihood be prepared for some difficult conversations with people who just don't get what the team is trying to achieve:

> Successfully developing products to embed in a service requires more than just a sound process. A firm's culture and people's mindsets have to change.[115]

## 6. Establishing a process

There are only a handful of law firms today that are successfully building and commercialising products. This is because product development is difficult to do well, and because it is not part of the culture of a traditional law firm partnership.

For those leading digital transformation in a law firm, there is a real tension between encouraging new ideas for products and making sure that those ideas can be converted into solutions that deliver real value to the firm. This tension needs to be carefully managed. Too much encouragement can be counterproductive if the teams can't convert ideas to action. On the other hand, too much process can turn people off altogether and stifle innovation before it begins.

A colleague working as part of an innovation team in an international law firm recounted a story that will be familiar to many working in similar roles. During the early days of the firm's innovation initiative, they invested a lot of time and money on an 'ideation' solution (a platform for crowdsourcing ideas for new products and solutions from the lawyers). The team spent months defining the governance around creating and managing the platform, which allowed them to create 'challenges' to stimulate creative ideas from the lawyers in the firm. The team agonised over selecting the right challenge and how to word it. They finally launched a challenge to find use cases for a piece of software they had licensed but didn't know what to do with (another common issue!). The team selected the best idea after a competitive process and set to work building it. It fizzled out for lack of fee-earner time (the lawyers were just too busy to commit) and the team was left with a half-built product, a bunch of ideas that they didn't know what to do with and an expensive ideation platform lying idle.

Many firms (and corporate legal teams) who have used the ideation approach have found themselves faced with similar issues. Lawyers, excited by the possibilities, may begin to submit their ideas directly to the innovation team. Unless the team can find a way to meet (or manage) demand, these same lawyers, who are used to a service mentality and a rapid turnaround, will quickly become frustrated. Some may even take matters into their own hands, buying software solutions under the radar and relying on local IT to install them. From the perspective of the CTO, this is a very dangerous place to be.

Any law firm team looking to build digital products must find a way to coordinate efforts, to prioritise ideas in a transparent way, and to be responsive to both internal customers and external clients. In short, to behave like a digital product team.

## 7. The product lifecycle

To manage a portfolio of products from idea through to delivery requires a defined process. This process should not be the preserve or sole responsibility of the technology department. It must involve lawyers (and, where a client solution is being developed, clients) throughout.

This can be challenging, for two reasons. First, lawyers in general do not react well to process. It suggests the factory floor with its production line of commoditised goods, which is unlikely to resonate with a lawyer's own view of their skills and capabilities. Secondly, the language of product development is new to lawyers. As discussed in Chapter 1, lawyers are sceptical of professional language that is outside of their own lexicon. This barrier can, of course, be overcome by translating back into language that is more familiar to the lawyers – and as a technique for winning sceptics over to your digital transformation proposals, this makes good sense. However, when it comes to the business of delivering digital products, translation can become very burdensome, and won't ultimately advance digital learning. If lawyers are to be involved in developing products and to assume the role of product owner/manager, they will need to understand the terminology that is used, at least at a working level. For this reason, it is important to retain the integrity of the language of product development, and make sure that it is understood.

The 'product lifecycle' is a model borrowed from software development. It refers to a set of commonly identified stages in the development and delivery of a commercial product. The product delivery lifecycle (PDLC) is typically divided into seven phases (although it can be more, or fewer):
- concept/idea;

- enablement/feasibility;
- validation;
- proof of concept;
- minimum valuable product (MVP)
- continuous delivery; and
- legacy.

Just as with Agile, there are many different flavours of the product lifecycle, and each has its proponents and detractors. The diagram below shows one view of the various stages, but there are many other versions, and the naming conventions and deliverables for each stage will vary.

The product lifecycle governs the different stages in the development of a product, with various 'gates' for each stage. The aim is to ensure that progress can be monitored regularly and the development stopped if things are not progressing as they should be, or if the idea proves not to be viable. There are defined inputs and outputs for each step, and funding should only be released if each stage gate is successfully passed.

As with any process, the product lifecycle needs to be owned, and tightly managed. Decisions around release of funds or progressing to the next stage in the cycle must be transparent and made on a consistent basis. Without governance and transparency, frustrations can arise, with lawyers feeling that their idea has been ignored or passed over for reasons unknown to them. It is also important that the owners of the process have overall visibility of the entire product portfolio across the firm, and sufficient seniority and backing to communicate tough decisions. The group cannot be too senior, however, as managing the product portfolio is an absorbing job that requires a lot of granular analysis. It is good practice for the group owning the process to meet regularly (once a week?) and to report on the status of ideas in the lifecycle so that anyone interested can see where things stand.

It is also critical to evaluate all ideas for products that come into the

**Figure 3. Product lifecycle model**

| | Idea | Enablement | Validation | Proof of concept | Minimum valuable product | Continuous delivery | Legacy |
|---|---|---|---|---|---|---|---|
| | | 1 | 2 | 3 | 4 | 5 | 6 | 7 |

**1 Idea**

I think I can solve a business or customer problem

I think I have a market-worthy solution to a business need

**2 Enablement**

Is there market value in this?

Is this technically achievable?

What outcomes do we want to measure?

**3 Validation**

Does this meet customer expectations?

Do customers think this is valuable?

Can we measure the outcomes?

**4 Proof of concept**

How may we achieve this technically?

Can we productionise this?

How much do we need to invest?

How long will it take?

**5 Minimum valuable product**

Did we meet the outcomes we expected?

Have all production criteria been satisfied?

Do we have mature quality metrics that will allow us to scale?

**6 Continuous delivery**

Do we continuously deliver value in an incremental way?

Are our deliverable increments aligned with our product roadmap?

Are our deliverable increments aligned with the enterprise roadmap?

Is there benefit in continuing this work?

**7 Legacy**

Have we completed all agreed decommissioning steps?

Have we addressed supersession of the product?

*Source: Reproduced with kind permission of Equal Experts and Freshfields Bruckhaus Deringer LLP.*

product lifecycle against a consistent set of criteria, aligned to the firm's strategy. There is unlikely to be an unlimited pot of money available for product development and product ideas will need to be assessed and prioritised consistently and transparently. For example, depending on the firm's strategy, more weight might be given to an idea for a product that serves clients in a growth area for the firm, or that supports a practice group or revenue line that is strategically important.

### 7.1 Stage 1: Idea

The idea stage, the first step in the process, requires the submission of an outline of the idea – an 'idea on a page' or a value statement. The value statement should set out a basic summary of the proposed product or solution, an overview of the clients or practice areas that would be served by the solution and the value it would bring to the business. This is an opportunity for the team running the process to undertake a sanity check, to make sure there is a genuine problem to solve and that there is no duplication of activity (for example, by checking that work on a solution is not already underway). It is also an opportunity to verify that the idea has some level of support or sponsorship within the relevant practice group or team.

### 7.2 Stage 2: Enablement

The next stage is enablement/feasibility. During this stage of the process, the idea generator and the team running the process will assess whether there is market value in the idea and whether it is technically feasible, and will give some thought to the outcomes that should be measured. The person coming up with the idea should provide a lightweight business case to support the proposal. The business case should, at a minimum, cost out the solution, describe the client or market research underpinning the idea, give a view of technical feasibility and include a high-level estimate of the target ROI.

It is worth noting that preparation of a business case is not part of the standard training for lawyers. Consequently it can be quite a challenge to persuade the lawyer who came up with the idea to prepare a business case, no matter how light. Although lawyers at all levels are acutely aware of the importance of billing and generating revenue, in general they are not trained to think about the firm as a business (certainly not until they are close to partnership). For this reason, the idea that a fee earner should have to justify investment in a solution she or he sees as valuable for a client is an unpalatable one.

Lawyers are also likely to be entirely unaware of the hidden costs of buying or developing a technology solution. The business services teams in law firms are generally viewed as a free resource, so lawyers will often only be aware of the headline cost of, for example, licensing software. They are unlikely to consider the cost of installation, support, integrations, training and adoption, or change management. A pro forma can help to tease out some of these hidden costs, and the team running the portfolio is likely to need to provide support to lawyers in preparing a business case (at least in the early days, until the lawyers get used to the concept and discipline).

### 7.3 Stage 3: Validation

After enablement comes the validation stage. This is the point at which the team will assess whether the proposed solution meets customer expectations. The idea generator will be asked to validate that the product or solution is viable and that outcomes can be measured. The output from this stage of the process is a prototype of the proposed solution. This sounds disconcertingly technical – a prototype suggests a build requiring an engineer or a developer. The reality is much more simple. Prototyping is simply the "intentional testing of ideas",[116] the practice of building something 'quick and dirty' to test an approach or product with customers. A prototype can be anything, from a wireframe to a clickable digital prototype through to a paper prototype or process flow. In the words of IDEO:

> That time you built a spreadsheet for collecting data from your team and adjusted it based on their feedback? That was prototyping. When you ran your big presentation with a couple colleagues and swapped out a few slides because someone said it didn't quite flow? Also prototyping.[117]

The prototype should allow the client to interact with the product so that the team can validate assumptions about its value. This should give the team enough information to ascertain whether the solution will meet the client's needs, and enough information to allow the holders of the purse strings to decide whether make an investment decision.

In order for the product to progress to the next stage, the validation stage must provide evidence of user or customer feedback that validates assumptions around the value of the product to that user or customer.

### 7.4 Stage 4: Proof of concept

If investment is released, the team can move to the next stage, which is proof of concept. This is where things get a bit more technical. The proof of concept should demonstrate that the concept is compliant to infrastructure, architecture, security and operational needs – which essentially means proving that it can be put into a (non-client-facing) production environment. The proof of concept is sometimes referred to as a 'thin slice of the end product, live'. This sounds confusing, but is actually relatively simple:

> *It basically means the least amount of features you can release that provide an end-to-end experience for users that you can release into the wild because it's valuable, usable, delightful and viable.*[118]

To bring this to life, consider the example of a development team working on a digital shopping experience. One team might be working on checkout, another team on the act of shopping itself (selection and comparison of goods), another on internal customer support features, another on payments. Delivering a thin slice would involve bringing all the disparate teams together to deliver a representative online shopping experience – but only delivering the simplest possible, usable, end-to-end slice of functionality:

> *[T]he thin slice was now to release a site where users can buy one blue t-shirt (no colors, styles, or sizes to choose from), and you checkout and pay with one payment option (16 digit MasterCard with 3 digit*

*code on back), generate the ID and confirmation email. The user calls a number on the site and the customer support picks up, views the shopping ID and info and assists the person. Then, from there, add the option to choose between two t-shirts, or multiple sizes, or multiple payment options, PayPal, multiple shipping options, or the ability to compare, share, etc. Everything is in production as you go. That's a solid first thin slice.*[119]

At the end of the proof of concept stage the team should have a detailed business case that will answer the following questions:

- How will the product be developed, technically?
- Can it be put into production?
- How much will the firm need to invest?
- How long will it take?

In answering all these questions, the business case should set out the estimated ROI and costs for developing the product to the next stage – the MVP.

### 7.5 Stage 5: Minimum valuable product (MVP)

This stage of the process is all about releasing the first marketable version of the product – something that can actually deliver business value to the customer. At the end of the MVP stage, the product is finally put into the client's hands and the team will start to measure whether the product can deliver the target ROI. This will, of course, require the team to have defined a set of metrics to capture that ROI data.

### 7.6 Stage 6: Continuous delivery

Just because the product is in the hands of the client, this does not mean that it is finished. The next stage, continuous delivery, means that the product team will continue to release new features in accordance with a product roadmap and deliver value in increments, taking feedback from the client as they go. During this stage, the product team should be measuring ROI and asking themselves whether there is benefit in continuing to develop the product.

*7.7 Stage 7: Legacy*
The final stage is legacy, when the team has taken the view that it is time to terminate the product, or supersede it with another.

## 8. Managing the product delivery lifecycle: product ownership

The PDLC is an involved process, and the route from good idea to valuable product can be a complex one. Importantly, the process is not intuitive. It needs to be learned, and managed. For the process to be successful, there must be a product owner sitting at the centre, acting as the 'glue' between the lawyers (and the external client) and the development team.

The product owner acts as the single source of truth for a product's scope, value realisation, direction and prioritisation. The product owner is a Janus – *facing in* to the product team, to make sure the team receives well thought-out requirements, and providing feedback and direction; and *facing out* to the lawyer and clients, to capture requirements and feedback, to communicate value and report on progress against KPIs. The product owner must understand the business perspective and the product team perspective and be able to mediate between the two camps. Proximity to the client is key. Creating customer-facing products is all about understanding client needs, which is itself a core component of successful digital transformation. Being able to identify and understand those client needs requires a very deep understanding of the law firm's business and the client and lawyer mindset.

Which leads to the question: Who, in a law firm, can fulfil that product owner role? In an ideal world, the product owner should be the lawyer who identified the client need that led to the idea for the product. That lawyer will be closest to the client and best positioned to understand and articulate their needs. This sounds easy, and neat, but the reality is likely to be very different. Good client-facing lawyers are usually very busy people, and are focused on billing their hours and meeting their clients' short-term demands. In my experience there are few who would willingly step out of a revenue-generating role to take on the role of a product owner.

## 9. Product owner skills

Even if they are willing to take on the role, are lawyers likely to have the requisite skills to perform it? As very few law firms have adopted the product owner model, there is no accepted framework that adequately describes the requirements of the role as it applies to law firms. However, the skills might be summarised as five core capabilities:

- **Business skills:** the ability to understand the firm's strategy, to prioritise the portfolio to reflect the strategy, and to track performance of a product against metrics relevant to the firm's business.
- **Market knowledge:** understanding of legal market trends, potential partner opportunities, and what competitors are doing.
- **Customer experience skills:** understanding of human-centred design and how to envision the client/customer journey.
- **Technical skills:** high-level understanding of technology, and issues around technology architecture, security and compliance.
- **People skills:** the ability to lead teams, to translate between lawyers and technologists, and to effect change at each level of the firm.

Without any disrespect to a profession full of brilliant over-achievers, arguably very few lawyers have all of the five core capabilities set out in this model. This does not mean that lawyers do not possess any of them, or that they cannot be trained to acquire them. Training a lawyer to perform the role of a product owner may be a better investment than recruiting for experienced product owners from outside the law firm. There are a number of reasons for this:

- The success of the product owner (and of the product) depends on a relationship of trust with the business. Lawyers are reluctant to trust anyone who does not walk and talk like one of their own, no matter how talented a professional they may be.
- The product owner has to have a deep understanding of the business and culture of the law firm and its clients. This cannot easily be taught to those who have not operated in a law firm environment – and certainly can't be taught quickly.
- The alternative, which may involve outsourcing the role to

outside contractors, or leaving it to the technology teams, with lawyers providing subject matter expertise and 'oversight', can be disastrous. There is nothing more likely to derail agile development than lawyers dipping in and out, applying pressure to get the thing built faster.

The answer is to find lawyers who are prepared to act as product owners, and upskill them for that role. This will require training, not just on the process itself, but on all the elements that support the process, such as generating a business case, managing business stakeholders, and defining and measuring success.

Lawyering skills can be useful in performing the role; the product owner will need the persuasive skill of a litigator, the tenacity and resilience of a transactional lawyer and the diplomacy of a senior partner. Lawyering skills can also be a hindrance. The product owner cannot approach product development in the same way that they would a transaction or a case – it is not deadline driven and all problems cannot be solved simply by working harder or by finding more bodies to work on the issue. To be successful in the role, the product owner will sometimes need to stop thinking like a lawyer and to put aside the ways of working that have been part of his or her law firm training.

If the team leading digital transformation is successful in finding someone with these skills from amongst the associates in the law firm, or in training them to acquire these skills, another challenge may present itself. How to incentivise and reward former lawyers, who have grown up viewing partnership as the mark of achievement? What is the career path for these stellar individuals? I discuss this in more detail in Chapter 8.

**10. What does success look like?**

One of the most significant cultural adjustments that a law firm will need to make when building products is to accept that products can't be delivered like legal services. You cannot expect to develop a product

*One of the most significant cultural adjustments that a law firm will need to make when building products is to accept that products can't be delivered like legal services. You cannot expect to develop a product to a schedule in return for guaranteed revenues.*

to a schedule in return for guaranteed revenues. The return from a product will be much more speculative and will take longer to recover – if indeed the product ever makes a return at all.

Having spoken to a number of firms who are considering developing their own products (and some that are well advanced on the journey), I know that many make the mistake, early on, of approaching the development of a digital product in the same way that they would the delivery of a legal matter. This is unsurprising, as many lawyers will never have worked outside a law firm environment. There may be a degree of arrogance at play here, too. Although few would admit to it, some lawyers believe deep down that 'IT projects' always take a long time because people just aren't working hard enough. If the lawyers could only apply their work ethic and rigour to the problem, more progress would be made, faster. However, developing a product is emphatically *not* like delivering a legal matter. You cannot simply throw more resource at the problem, or work for longer hours, and expect a better result.

Just as product owners need to unlearn some of their lawyering skills in order to be successful, so it is crucial, when embarking on product development, to think carefully about two things. First, how to commercialise the product; and secondly, how the team is going to demonstrate success to the rest of the business. Both will require a new way of thinking, and a mindset change within the law firm partnership:

> *[C]lient-facing units within services firms have a tendency to examine and evaluate their performance and budgets almost daily. Product-management organizations can't work this way, and it's important to get the organization to really value long-term goals, because the benefits of product-enabled services may take time to blossom. To measure an embedded product's performance, therefore, professional services companies have to change how they define success. Instead of focusing on classic service-based metrics (such as client satisfaction or process efficiency), use product-based metrics (such as ideas generated, prototypes created, or level of automation achieved).*[120]

## 10.1 *The right measures*

In the product world, measurement of the right things becomes very important. This is especially true where development of products is experimental, or new to the firm, and the continued existence of the product team depends on being able to demonstrate some success. Traditional law firm metrics (revenues, profit per partner point, revenue per lawyer) are blunt instruments when it comes to product development. KPIs will need to be more nuanced and tailored. It is the job of the product owner to define product metrics up front that align to the strategy and the vision of the product. The business case for the product is the starting point for this.

Look to the strategy behind developing the product. Are you building the product to bring in revenue? To build brand? To create operating efficiency? Then, create metrics that will help measure whether that strategy has been achieved. Some ideas:

- **Revenue generation:** For a standalone product that is intended to generate revenue, measuring success ought to be straightforward (the bigger challenge may be in making sure that you price at the right point (see below)). To track the success of a revenue-generating product, simply measure revenue from sales. Of course, this becomes trickier if the product is embedded in a broader service (such as the IBOR transition products referenced above).
- **Subscriptions:** If the product is sold on a subscription basis, capture the number of subscriptions and the monthly recurring revenue (all new subscriptions in a month minus customer attrition).
- **Client experience:** If the strategy behind the product is to deliver a better client experience, then look to a customer satisfaction score or net promoter score (or simply to customer feedback). Over time, as a portfolio of products is developed, these scores will become more meaningful.
- **Marketing:** If the strategy behind the product is to create client 'stickiness' or increase brand awareness, then surveys, web traffic metrics or focus groups may generate valuable data around which to build metrics.

- **Efficiency:** If the product is targeting internal efficiency, track the value of the time that is saved by removing steps from a process or by automating those steps.
- **Adoption:** If the product relies on internal adoption for its success, then track adoption (and usage) as a key metric.

Whatever the measure of success that is chosen, it is important that the metrics align with a desired business outcome and with the firm's strategy; that they are specific and quantifiable, introduced sufficiently early in the process to be meaningful (no retrofitting); and that they are kept under review – and updated if they are not giving the team meaningful data.

### 10.2 The go-to-market strategy

In order for a product to be successful, it needs to sell. This translates to internal adoption (if it is an internal product) and external use (if it is a client-facing product). No matter how good the product is, it will not sell itself. Jack Shepherd describes the challenge:

> [O]ne of the main issues I see in a lot of software projects is thinking that you can build a product, and the rest will be history. That's not the case. Particularly if you are building a strategic product, you need to invest at least as much in the marketing and positioning of that product. Many software builds are blamed for not attracting users. Yet it is not the product's problem, it is everything that goes around it. You can build the most fantastic product in the world, but if nobody knows about it, nobody will use it.[121]

Commercialisation is both a marketing and a pricing challenge. It can be very difficult in an immature market to know how much to charge for a digital product that has been developed by a law firm for its clients. There is no established frame of reference (clients will know as little about what might be appropriate in terms of pricing as law firms), and in a culture that is very focused on revenue generation as a measure of success, there is likely to be nervousness about pricing at the wrong level.

A knee-jerk response to this difficult decision is simply to give the product away for free. This is a common response amongst partners in law firms, for whom the cost of developing and maintaining a digital product has no real visibility. For those partners, once the thing is built, the costs are sunk. Because they regard the real law firm business as being the provision of technical legal advice on an hours-billed basis, why shouldn't they gift a product that the team has already developed to favoured clients?

To protect against this, it is very important to give some thought up front to pricing. How should a law firm, used to hourly rates and time and materials, approach this challenge, particularly as law firms usually don't have a strong sales culture or the infrastructure to support it?

Pricing will depend on a number of factors, including the nature of the product, the reputation of the individual firm (elite law firms are unlikely to want to join a race to the bottom), the size of the addressable market, and what competitors are charging. With so many variables, a one-size-fits-all approach is impossible to develop. Below are some basic factors to bear in mind when thinking about product pricing.[122]

- **Don't go in too low.** Once the price is out in the market, it is difficult to hike it. According to McKinsey, "80 to 90 percent of all poorly chosen prices are too low."[123]
- **Cover your costs plus a margin.** The firm needs to make some profit for the product to be viable for the business. To set a base price, you will need a view of the total cost of the product (including support, if that is part of the deal). Then add a margin that represents the smallest acceptable return on investment. This is the lowest reasonable price you can charge for your product.
- **Research the size of the market.** It sounds obvious, but it does get overlooked. Although your product may be exactly what one of your clients has been looking for, and developed in response to that client's need, the addressable market needs to be bigger than that single client for the product to be successful. There must be a pipeline of customers, and that pipeline must be large enough to make the development viable.
- **Beware discounting.** Discounting the price of a product to speed

up market penetration can have a negative impact, leading to the market questioning the product's benefits. A better alternative might be to give the product away for free to clients who might act as advocates.

If pricing still feels like an overwhelming task, another solution (if the firm has the product portfolio to justify it) is to look for outside help. This is what Kennedys chose to do in the early days after spinning off their product house, Kennedys IQ (see Chapter 7 for an overview of Kennedy's product portfolio and organisational structure). In April of 2020 the firm recruited a commercial development manager from established software vendor Luminance Technologies to manage this part of the process.

## 11. Products – or product thinking?

Not all law firms will be interested in making the financial investment and structural changes that are necessary for developing and commercialising digital products. But for law firms looking to future-proof their business model in a digital age, there is still a lot to learn about business agility and customer focus from the product world. Just as an organisation does not have to train all its people in agile to benefit from the agile mindset, so an organisation does not need to build digital products to benefit from a product mindset. The fundamental tenets of product design – product thinking – can be applied to projects and programmes within the traditional firm partnership to change the firm's focus from outputs (documents, advice papers, legal opinions) to outcomes (a successful result for the client).

This all goes back, again, to client centricity. A 'product' doesn't have to be a physical, tangible thing. A product can be viewed as the way an organisation delivers and captures value to its customers. A really effective product team, as described above, will focus with laser precision on understanding the customer needs and on continuously improving products and services to meet those needs. Non-product functions, such as HR or Finance, can benefit from a mindset shift towards product thinking:

*But what if you don't work in product? What if you work in Human Resources and are in charge of learning and development? What if you work in the legal department and your remit is cybersecurity policy for the company? Do you still make a product? Do you have customers? If you believe in bringing agility to the entire organization, the answer to both questions is yes.*[124]

Large programmes and projects within law firms (and not exclusively technology roll-outs) often suffer from a box-ticking mentality. If the firm is bringing in a new enterprise resource planning (ERP) system, replacing its document management system (DMS) or rolling out a values or diversity programme, too often success is measured by just getting the thing done, with no real analysis of whether the desired outcomes have in fact been achieved. A shift to product thinking, even in teams that are not product or technology focused, can help to address this:

*If we're going to bring our non-product teams along with us on our journey to business agility we have to reframe their work with the language of products and customers. This begins by rethinking the initiative not as a set of boxes to tick but rather as a problem to solve for a specific set of customers. The measure of success for that problem is not the deployment of a product but instead a measurable positive change in the behavior of those customers. In other words, we're working towards outcomes, not outputs.*[125]

So instead of a product, for non-product teams the outcome of product thinking is a customer-focused, agile culture.

## 12. Products – some final thoughts

The decision about whether to develop digital products is, of course, an issue for each individual firm. Although the press releases and market hype might suggest that every large law firm is developing a suite of cutting-edge products, this is unlikely to reflect reality. Very few law firms are developing products in a strategic and effective way, and fewer still are commercialising them successfully.

This does not mean that law firms should dismiss product development altogether. There are many opportunities to partner with technology vendors, strategic delivery partners or other law firms or law companies to develop products that bring value to clients. Firms adopting this approach will be able to benefit from the end product and experiment 'safely', without having to take the risk of finding (or developing) the skills and the expertise to build products in-house.

For law firms that are truly committed to digital transformation, product development has an important role to play in the overall strategy, and nurturing the capabilities to develop products is a valuable investment for teams that are prepared to be patient and take the long view.

Firms that cannot (or decide not to) move into the product space can still derive value from adopting some of the fundamentals of product thinking (a focus on the client experience) when looking to modernise delivery to clients. The client-centric discipline that the product lifecycle instils – genuinely listening to clients, understanding what value means to them and measuring whether the firm is delivering it – is not limited to digital products, and can be applied to many areas of law firm delivery. ■

# Chapter 5: Technology

## 1. Legal tech

How to address the subject of technology in a book about law firm digital transformation? Experience tells me that anyone reading about digital transformation in a law firm will have questions about technology choices – indeed, I suspect that some readers will skip the 'soft' stuff around culture and ways of working and move straight to the chapter on technology. This is entirely understandable, given the digital immaturity of the legal sector, the pervasive fear of missing out and the hunger for impartial advice in a vendor-saturated market.

I am not a technologist, so anyone looking for guidance on technology choices for particular problems will not find the answers here. However, I have worked with and led teams that aligned into global technology, and driving technology adoption amongst lawyers has been a significant part of all my law firm roles. Working with the team to develop the digital transformation strategy for a global law firm has given me a pretty good grounding in what is strategically important (and how to avoid making expensive mistakes).

We all know that technology is only one part of the digital story; other elements, including culture, are equally (or even more) fundamental to success. Simply adopting technology will not result in digital transformation being achieved. However, faced with pressure to digitise and a dizzying number of choices, how does a law firm make the right technology decisions?

One answer is to look outside the legal sector and learn lessons from other industries that have successfully transformed; this would certainly be considered best practice. However, law firms are insular in nature and, as we have discussed on a number of occasions in this book, are not always ready to learn the lessons from other industries (or, indeed, from their clients). There is a tendency, both in law firms and in corporate legal teams, to default to point solutions – that is, technologies that have been developed to solve individual problems in particular legal domains.

The proliferation of point legal technology solutions in recent years has led to a fragmented market, which law firms and corporate legal teams alike find very difficult to navigate. This has given legal tech something of a tarnished reputation, which is not deserved. There are some mature and reliable solutions in the legal tech market, that have been around a long time and that have moved the dial for legal digital transformation. There are also some very exciting start-ups. However, anyone who has spent time analysing the market will agree that, as in any industry, there are also a fair number of products that promise more than they deliver, that are duplicative, or solve a very niche problem, without much thought being given to integration with the law firm enterprise technology or the other tools that lawyers (or the business) are using.

To get a sense of the sheer volume of these offerings and the scale of the challenge that this presents for law firms and corporate legal teams, one only needs to look at the database developed by Nicola Shaver, managing director of innovation and knowledge at Paul Hastings (interviewed for Chapter 3 above) and her husband Chris Ford. In October 2020, Nikki and Chris launched Legaltech Hub,[126] a website to help legal professionals chart their way through the maze of legal tech offerings. The website allows users to search by functionality (eg, contract automation), by tools (eg, iManage) and by sector (eg, e-discovery). The user can also filter by language. The taxonomy comprises 85 separate functionalities – and in all, 1,680 tools are listed.

Legaltech Hub is a really useful resource for those looking to understand what individual legal tools deliver, and it has filled a much-needed gap in the market. Two interesting perspectives that the Hub offers are the Graveyard section, which inscribes gravestones with the names of those legal tech companies that are sadly no longer with us, and the Consolidations section, which shows which legal tech companies have been acquired, and by whom.

## 2. Simplification and convergence: making use of what you have

The sheer quantity of legal tech tools out there can be a huge distraction from the foundational technology work that needs to be done within law firms. As discussed in Chapter 3, in the context of developing digital strategy, simplification of the technology environment should be a guiding principle when making technology choices. Ideally, the number of applications a lawyer or a client interacts with should reduce over time, and law firms should resist creating overlapping solutions that add cost and complexity. Before investing in a new solution for a particular problem, the team leading the digital transformation or managing the portfolio should consider whether an existing tool to which the lawyers have access could be adapted to do the job.

For example, many law firms (and their clients) have moved or are moving to Microsoft Office 365 in the cloud. The apps in the suite can do a number of the tasks that legal tech solutions offer – and may already be within the law firm environment, supported by the global technology teams, and simply underutilised – as this extract from Lawtomated, the collaborative legal tech learning resource, explains:

*Unlike the traditional on premises enterprise version of Microsoft*

*Just as law firms should only build a product when it gives competitive advantage, so they should only buy legal tech solutions if there is no existing tool that will do the job.*

*Office, cloud-based Office 365 includes a wealth of natively integrated apps that potentially do away with countless legaltech specific point solutions, including document management, document automation, RPA, AI data extraction, search and knowledge management. Don't believe us? Well, with Office 365 you could (and can) use ...*

- *Microsoft Power Automate (formerly Microsoft Flow) to automate a decision tree of knowledge, a self-service NDA creation, approval, execution and filing workflow.*
- *Microsoft Azure AI to automate basic data extraction and contract reporting of order forms, invoices and contracts.*
- *Microsoft SharePoint's Syntex feature set to build a comprehensive knowledge management system.*[127]

Just as law firms should only build a product when it gives competitive advantage, so they should only buy legal tech solutions if there is no existing tool that will do the job. Of course, the existing tool has to be fit for purpose – it becomes inefficient and potentially more expensive if disproportionate effort is needed to adapt the existing solution.

## 3. Back to basics

Before thinking about new software tools, a law firm should go back to basics and address the fundamentals, the foundations, of technology transformation. These include:

- legacy;
- leadership;
- cloud; and
- data.

As discussed in Chapter 3, this is not to suggest that all transformative technology investment should be delayed until all the core pieces are 'fixed', as speed of change is critical to gaining competitive advantage. However, the roadmap for digital transformation must prioritise foundational elements if the value of more transformative investments is to be fully realised.

### 3.1 Legacy

One of the reasons that the legal sector is so far behind in digital transformation is a historic underinvestment in core technology systems. Chapter 3 looked at the challenge that many law firms face in paying off their 'technical debt'. Repairing aging systems that have gone out of support or been patched up with tactical repairs over a number of years, is expensive. However, before embarking on the introduction of cutting-edge technologies, legacy systems must be remediated as a matter of urgency. Failure to do this could expose the firm to significant risk, which means that remediation cannot be deferred. The effort involved in transformation of core technology systems should not be underestimated. Strong technology leadership is essential to manage the change. McKinsey outlines three different approaches:

> *There are three major archetypes for approaching core-technology transformations: "repaint" by making the minimum investment required to maintain existing operations and digital channels; "renovate" through gradual but persistent upgrades of the core and more substantial improvements when necessary; and "rebuild and replace," by building or buying a completely new IT stack (or large portions of it) and migrating the existing business to it. As companies progress on their transformation journey, they may switch from one archetype to another.*[128]

The approach that a law firm chooses to take will depend on a number of different factors. 'Repainting' might be the only choice for a law firm that is under significant financial pressure and just does not have the stomach (or the funds, or the capabilities) for a more strategic approach. However, this archetype really does just kick the can down the road, at a time when the pressure to transform has never been greater.

The full 'rebuild and replace' approach might be feasible for an ambitious law firm with money to spend. This approach will require leadership commitment, significant investment and the acquisition of the capabilities and technical skills required to see the transformation through.

The 'renovation' approach is more gradual, giving organisations time to source the skills and capabilities they need to transform the core, while also setting in motion the cultural changes that are required to make the transformation a success.

### 3.2 Leadership and digital literacy

Whichever approach is taken, core transformation cannot be regarded simply as the preserve of the IT department. To be successful, it will need really strong sponsorship from the top of the law firm and to be run as a strategic effort, closely aligned with the business. The law firm leadership will need to understand what the transformation is aiming to achieve, from a business perspective, and be a champion for this change. To do this effectively, however, the leadership must have confidence in their own digital literacy – without this, they will be unable to challenge the strategy, or lead the change.

Digital fluency is a big ask, even for a CEO in a corporation. Of course, there is (traditionally) no CEO sitting at the top of the law firm. The senior partner may be a great statesperson, or a great client lawyer, but you will be very lucky to find one who is also digitally fluent. This is a common problem, and not exclusive to law firms:

> *Too many companies fail to grapple with their technology issues, preferring to push them off to the side in the IT department, making it a "CIO problem." This tendency is exacerbated by the lack of true understanding of technology at the top table. Given the importance of technology and the size of the investment required, a technology transformation cannot succeed without a true partnership between technology and the business.*[129]

Those in leadership positions in law firms need to own the transformation. This means leading from the front by investing in their own digital literacy. There are many organisations that provide courses in digital leadership, and there are other approaches that have been shown to work, such as reverse mentoring. There is an obligation to upskill; as digital becomes an increasingly important part of every law firm strategy, firms cannot continue to regard digitisation as an issue for the IT department.

Law firm leaders who need to be persuaded of the importance for firm management of a deep understanding of technology-related issues and digital strategy should look to their clients. Boards of large corporations increasingly view a failure to understand digital strategy as a failure of directors to fulfil their fiduciary duties. If the directors are not comfortable in challenging the technology leaders of the corporation they serve, it may be that they are not fit to serve on that board:

> *Directors cannot properly oversee what they don't understand. When they don't feel prepared to deeply engage management on emerging technologies and defer to others on the board, they are not fulfilling their fiduciary duties. As one director noted, 'I have seen the speed of change create discomfort in some boardrooms. Directors hold back and are less engaged.' This discomfort complicates their ability to have a robust dialogue with the technology leaders of their own companies .... One director challenged others to rethink their approach to their board service – asserting that not understanding technology trends in one's industry is analogous to not understanding one's business.*[130]

The same principles must apply to members of the leadership committees of law firms, who are accountable to their partners for the performance of the firm.

### 3.3 Cloud

Although most of us are making use of cloud applications in our personal lives, many lawyers find the idea of cloud, as applied to their practice, confusing and opaque. What are we really talking about when we refer to the use of 'cloud computing' in law? The American Bar Association (ABA), in its 2018 Legal Technology Survey Report, keeps it simple:

> *The terms 'cloud' and 'cloud computing' have become much more familiar to lawyers in the last few years, but there can still be some confusion on the standard definitions. In the enterprise IT world, you will find public, private, and hybrid clouds, and many flavors of "as a service": software (SaaS), infrastructure (IaaS), and platform (PaaS),*

*to name the three most common ... In practical terms, you can understand cloud computing as software or services that can be accessed and used over the Internet using a browser (or, commonly now, a mobile app), where the software itself is not installed locally on the computer being used by the lawyer accessing the service. Your data are also processed and stored on remote servers rather than on local computers and hard drives. Another common way to describe cloud services is to refer to 'web services' or 'hosted services'.*[131]

The corporate legal world has historically been slow to move to the cloud, not least because many clients in regulated industries (such as financial services) have, in the past, been uncomfortable with law firms storing their data in the cloud. This has been changing in recent years, slowly; it is still too early to call, but it is likely that the move to remote working driven by the COVID-19 pandemic will have accelerated cloud adoption significantly.

Before the pandemic, law firm use of the cloud was inching upwards. The 2018 ABA survey found that law firms were "still moving much more cautiously to the cloud than the rest of the business world",[132] with cloud adoption at 54.6% in 2018, up 4% from the previous year. Other reports are more bullish; according to a 2019 survey by the ILTA, 78% of law firms currently store some client data in the cloud.[133] This sounds encouragingly high; however, the reality is that most law firms have not committed to move critical core systems into the cloud. A survey by Aderant in 2019 asked respondents about the likelihood of moving their law firm practice management system to the cloud, with the following results:[134]
- 34% said this system was already hosted in the cloud or headed that way within two years;
- 37% also said this would not happen in the foreseeable future;
- 1% said it would never happen; and
- 28% were unsure.

The findings from this survey suggests that law firms are using the cloud for less critical purposes, such as email archiving, some back-office services like payroll, and for e-discovery (ironic that law firms and their clients should accept that sensitive data in a litigation or investigation can be stored in the cloud, but not, for example, firm time recording data).

Despite current low levels of adoption, many predict that, over the next five years or so, most law firms will be predominantly cloud based. Certainly law firms should be developing their cloud strategies as a priority; adoption is one of the foundations of digital transformation. If a law firm needs to create a business case for cloud, below are some of the factors to take into account.

*(a) Cost*

The economics of cloud can be compelling. You can think of cloud computing as a pay-as-you-go model; payments are based on the processing power that is actually used, rather than firms having to expend capital up front for anticipated use. This is a much more flexible model that directly aligns with business growth. Moving to the cloud can result in a significant reduction in IT infrastructure costs. This won't be true in all cases; it depends to some degree on the firm's starting point. For example, if a law firm has just invested in a new data centre, moving to the cloud could duplicate some infrastructure costs. Similarly, if the law firm is locked into long licensing agreements that are difficult to break, transitioning to the cloud may not make economic sense. On the other hand, if the firm is facing an expensive data centre upgrade, cloud adoption is likely to represent a more cost-effective alternative.

Realising the full economic benefits of a move to the cloud will require good governance, to make sure that the firm is optimising cloud consumption once the move has been made. A simple lift and shift of all applications is unlikely to result in lower costs. To maximise the benefits, firms will need to assess their current applications (many of which will not have been designed to run in the cloud) and remediate where necessary so that running costs in the cloud can be kept low.

*(b) Accessibility*

Perhaps one of the most compelling benefits of a move to cloud is accessibility. It allows a law firm's people to access their documents, emails and other essential tools from any device with one login. The pandemic has shown that lawyers need to be able to work effectively from any location. Even when lawyers return to the office, the ability to work from home, from a client site, or while travelling is essential to deliver the best client service.

### (c) Security

Historically, law firm resistance to cloud was linked to a perception that cloud service providers are less secure than the firm's own data centres. This perception is gradually changing. The major cloud service providers have invested billions in security – no law firm can compare.

### (d) Business benefits

When building a business case for cloud, it is important to quantify the business benefits that adoption can deliver. A move to cloud can enable firms to be more agile and innovative, giving access to cloud-native functionality such as facial recognition, natural language processing and data aggregation. Firms that can take advantage of this will be able to create innovative business offerings more easily, giving them a competitive advantage:

> Cloud can improve almost every aspect of an organization's products, services, or processes. Superior computing power can lead to a greater understanding of customer needs, for example, while extra processing capacity can be used to run more complex analytics or to create differentiated business insights. Innovation is quicker and less risky because experimentation and testing of new ideas cost less and take less time. All this drives revenue growth opportunities in a variety of ways, including acceleration of new-product lead time, entry into new markets, and response to competitive threats.[135]

### 3.4 Data

I observed earlier in this chapter that we are, in general, further advanced in our personal lives with our use of cloud technologies than we are in our professional lives. As with cloud, so it is with data. In our private lives, we routinely share data with third parties, from social media providers to Uber drivers to cloud-based voice services such as

*Many lawyers would argue that years of experience of running deals has given them very good intuition on how to price accurately and fairly, and that although data can be illuminating, it is no substitute for the workings of a partner's mind.*

Alexa and Siri. This data, about our likes and dislikes, our routines and our habits, translates into auto-suggestions for products we might like to buy, or music we might like to listen to, or celebrities we might like to follow. If you have an Apple watch, you will be used to checking your personalised dashboard of analytics and understanding at a glance where you stand in relation to your targets. If you use apps like Spotify or Strava, you will receive, free of charge, an end-of-year dashboard view of what you have been listening to or how many miles you have run. This is analytics in action. Whether we regard this as an invasion of privacy or a welcome convenience, its prevalence is inescapable.

Lawyers, however, do not routinely make decisions or predictions based on data. This is particularly true in traditional law firm partnerships, where the concept of 'legal data' is relatively new. In one sense, this is hard to explain. Yes, law is based on precedent, lawyers constantly look backwards to inform the path forwards, and the profession is not full of natural disruptors who like to break the established mould. And yet, lawyers often rely on gut feel, guesswork or intuition as a basis for decision making.

The potential in legal for making use of data for insight is huge. One only has to think about time recording data – six-minute blocks of activity, with narrative, that describe how lawyers have been running a particular transaction or case. This has so many potential uses, from pricing deals on a fixed-price basis with confidence, to challenging perceptions about efficiency, to tracking the diversity of teams working on a particular matter. Yet lawyers don't routinely make use of this data, other than to provide bill narratives to clients.

Many lawyers would argue that years of experience of running deals has given them very good intuition on how to price accurately and fairly, and that although data can be illuminating, it is no substitute for the workings of a partner's mind. Lawyers rely on their judgement for so much of what they do, and on their experience, rather than making data-driven decisions. They may also have a tendency to view human judgement and data-driven decisions as alternatives, rather than as complementary.

Meanwhile, other industries are moving ahead, have invested in data capabilities, and are reaping the benefits:

> *[C]ompanies with the greatest overall growth in revenue and earnings receive a significant proportion of that boost from data and analytics. Respondents from these high-performing organizations are three times more likely than others to say their data and analytics initiatives have contributed at least 20 percent to earnings before interest and taxes (EBIT) over the past three years.*[136]

A strong business case can be built around the revenue-generating potential of data analytics, and the opportunity for new business lines, products and client opportunities that data can offer.

Even if lawyers are sceptical about the revenue statistics quoted above, I am sure that most will recognise the feelings of frustration that are commonly experienced when attempting to access data that is inconsistent between systems, or difficult to get hold of, or just of poor quality. Bad data can have profoundly negative effects – on productivity and on profitability. As an example, one global COO of a major international law firm told me that she had absolutely no way of finding out how many people were employed in the firm at any given time; the HR data was so poor and badly maintained that it could not be relied on to give an accurate picture.

Add to this the wasted time that is spent pulling together dashboards of management information that rely almost entirely on manual effort, and it becomes clear that, even if law firms never get to the stage of sophisticated AI-enhanced decision making and predictive analytics, they still have a lot to gain from getting their data house in order.

### (a) Knowledge is power

Data has more to offer than back-office operational improvements, however. There are some encouraging examples of law firms waking up to the value that exploiting data can deliver. In the bad old days, knowledge management in law firms was considered to be the career parking lot for lawyers who had prioritised raising their children over working 90-hour weeks (I say this as a former knowledge lawyer myself, a mother of three, and former head of an impressive global knowledge team which was predominantly female). This perception is changing, not least because the COVID crisis has driven lawyers from their offices and they no longer have access to the lever arch files of precedents that line the wall. When operating in a digital environment, you cannot rely on serendipitous meetings with colleagues in the lift to give you access to expertise and knowledge. More than ever, now, knowledge needs to codified, so that it can be delivered digitally. This is not just a question of scanning all paper precedents and providing better search functionality (although that would be a welcome first step for many law firms). It is about rethinking knowledge as data, and modernising the way that law firms deliver that data to their lawyers.

Knowledge management lawyers are enjoying something of a renaissance as enforced remote working drives this point home. Alex Smith, global AI product lead for iManage, makes the connection between our experience of 'search' in our personal lives and in our professional lives:

> *We're all familiar with Spotify, and its uncanny mapping of nearly all recorded music. While it is very useful that Spotify allows you to search for a specific artist and – within moments – call up their catalog of songs, what is perhaps even more useful is that Spotify can proactively suggest artists or songs that you might be interested in. In other words, it can 'nudge' you to the music that you didn't even know you were looking for. This is the direction KM is heading, and AI powered search and analytics-powered knowledge graphs are the emerging underlying technological backbone.*[137]

Smith advocates moving away from advanced enterprise search as the holy grail for knowledge management, towards the use of knowledge graphs that link disparate data sources to deliver new insights to the firm. Under this model, instead of the lawyer simply searching the document management system for the search term 'sale and purchase agreement' and pulling up a bunch of precedents, chronologically filed, that may have only tangential relevance to the lawyer's specific query, a knowledge graph enables "a dynamic connection between situations, data points and entities":[138]

> *Part of the knowledge graph's power lies in the ability to pick up signals from multiple systems – not just document management systems, for example, but also billing or practice management systems. In this way, the AI-powered knowledge graphs can establish where expertise lies within a firm based on how many hours someone has billed to a certain project, or how many times people have copied a certain document to use as a template.*[139]

Knowledge graphs don't develop organically, however; they need to be built, and this requires effort and investment. It will be the task of knowledge management lawyers to develop taxonomies that map the metadata that exists in various systems across the firm, and which show the relationships between those sources. Not only do the knowledge graphs need to be created, they also need to be curated over time. Law firms will need to invest in the skills and organisational governance to make this approach successful.

### (b) Data governance and quality

Governance is essential to successful use of data. Challenges around poor quality data can feel insurmountable. Often it can be difficult to know where to start. There are law firms who have made an investment in data (Clifford Chance, Ropes & Gray, Paul Hastings to name a few). These firms have hired data scientists and are building successful analytics proofs of concept. The next step is to scale the proof of concept, which can be challenging, and requires data governance to be in place to ensure that real value can be derived from the data. As is the case with so many issues relating to digital transformation in law firms, mindset and culture change are key to success. For data to be viewed as an asset, it needs to be treated as something of value, with an owner responsible for its hygiene and its health.

To benefit from the potential data analytics can offer, the firm must first understand any data deficiencies and take steps to remediate them, then develop a data strategy supported by governance to make implementation of that strategy a success. As a starting point, consider this test from the *Harvard Business Review*, the 'Friday afternoon measurement' (FAM) method which has an elegant simplicity to it:

> *The method is widely applicable and relatively simple: We instruct managers to assemble 10–15 critical data attributes for the last 100 units of work completed by their departments – essentially 100 data records. Managers and their teams work through each record, marking obvious errors. They then count up the total of error-free records. This number, which can range from 0 to 100, represents the percent of data created correctly – their Data Quality (DQ) Score. It can also be interpreted as the fraction of time the work is done properly, the first time.*[140]

Managers are then encouraged to reflect on the results. The article describes the reactions of those taking the test as "shocked, even horrified" – and the aggregated results explain why:

- On average, 47% of newly created data records have at least one critical (eg, work-impacting) error.
- Only 3% of the DQ scores in the study can be rated 'acceptable' using the loosest possible standard.
- The variation in DQ scores is enormous. Individual tallies range from 0% to 99%. Deeper analyses (to see if, for instance, specific industries are better or worse) have yielded no meaningful insights. Thus, no sector, government agency, or department is immune to the ravages of extremely poor data quality.[141]

The simple FAM test makes the issue of data quality very concrete. When it is the productivity of your own function or practice group that is being impacted because of poor quality data, it hits home. This creates a sense of ownership, and of accountability, which can be more effective in creating a corresponding sense of urgency than a presentation about the possibilities of neural networks and big data.

When building a business case to persuade law firm management that data is worth the investment, a good place to start might be to follow the advice of the team that developed the FAM test, and apply the rule of ten: it will cost ten times as much to complete a unit of work when the data is flawed than when it is perfect.

> *For instance, suppose you have 100 things to do and each costs a $1 when the data are perfect. If all the data are perfect, the total cost is 100 × $1 = $100. If 89 are perfect and 11 are flawed, the total cost is 89 × $1 + 11 × $10 = $199. For most, of course, the operational costs are far, far greater. And the rule of ten does not account for nonmonetary costs, such as lost customers, bad decisions, or reputational damage to your company.*[142]

This is clearly hugely simplified – but the reasoning is sound and the opportunity to save wasted operational costs is likely to be compelling.

### (c) Identifying data use cases

Being aware that the firm has some data deficiencies is only the first step – how do law firms move from this to fixing the problem? If the firm is struggling with ageing infrastructure and legacy systems, integrating and cleaning all the data to create an AI-ready data pool is going to be a gargantuan task. It is also likely to take a long time, and given the increasing competitive advantage that analytics can deliver, law firms don't have that time to waste. Is the answer to hire expensive consultants to fix the problem? Or to hire a group of data scientists and put them to work in the basement until they come up with something interesting?

If you look at the approaches to data initiatives as a spectrum, with data as an esoteric science project at one end and an expensive and time-consuming master data management programme at the other,[143] the answer probably resides somewhere in the middle. Law firm management and functional business heads should work together, with the lawyers, to identify feasible data use cases that will deliver real value to the firm and its clients. By focusing on these use cases, firms can narrow the amount of data that needs to be cleaned up. This will also help to generate some early success stories to build consensus for the data initiative, and start the firm on the long road to building a data culture.

Below are some best practices that can help in identifying and building valuable use cases.

**Find the data:** To mine data for insight, the team will need a dataset that is sufficiently large to be meaningful. For example, if looking to use data for pricing analytics, it may make sense to start with the largest practice group, or the practice group with the highest frequency of deals of a sufficient size to be useful. So, rather than choosing a practice group that only does 10 mega project financings per year, choose one with a higher incidence of like matters. The more sources of data that can be identified as helpful in bolstering the use case, the better. Depending on the use case, the team may also want to identify useful external or public data sources as well as internal ones.

**Check the data adequacy:** Even if the team has sufficient data, it will be of limited use if it doesn't meet minimum quality standards. The team will need to assess the quality and completeness of the data, bearing in mind that it may be possible to compensate for some deficiencies through interviews or conversations with the lawyers themselves (although if the team is spending a lot of time enriching data in this way, it may be an indication that the use case is not the right one, or that the data is just not good enough and the use case will be difficult to scale).

**Establish governance:** If the use case is proving valuable, the data needs to be governed. This involves identifying stewards for the data sources, so that the data can be looked after by business owners (who will ensure that it does not degrade in quality), and finding ways to improve the quality of the data over time. For example, to go back to the pricing analytics example, if one of the valuable data sources is time recording narratives, the data owners may choose to put in place processes to enhance the data set. This may include asking lawyers to record time to pre-defined phases (forcing the hand of the time recorder through mandatory drop-down menus), or developing rules around wording of narratives to drive a higher level of consistency.

*Many organisations struggle with democratising data. Data is often inaccessible due to siloed legacy systems. In general, law firms are reluctant to be too transparent with data.*

### (d) Creating a data culture

Becoming a data-driven firm is as much about people and culture as it is about technology and dashboards. While sophisticated data businesses do use some automation to help to manage data, data analytics remains a very human-centric activity. Most of the processes involved – sourcing data, cleaning and enriching it, reporting on and visualising data – are led by human effort. To become a data insight-driven organisation requires new skills (skills that have probably not been part of lawyers' traditional training), and an organisation-wide mindset shift:

*[Y]ou can't import data culture and you can't impose it. Most of all, you can't segregate it. You develop a data culture by moving beyond specialists and skunkworks, with the goal of achieving deep business engagement, creating employee pull, and cultivating a sense of purpose, so that data can support your operations instead of the other way around.*[144]

Hoarding data, or simply making it impossible to access, is a common problem for businesses in all sectors. One of the first steps towards building a data culture is making appropriate data accessible to all – 'democratising' the data:

*By far the most common complaint we hear is that people in different parts of a business struggle to obtain even the most basic data. Curiously, this situation persists despite a spate of efforts to democratize access to data within corporations. Starved of information ... it's impossible for a data-driven culture to take root, let alone flourish.*[145]

Many organisations struggle with democratising data. Data is often inaccessible due to siloed legacy systems. In general, law firms are reluctant to be too transparent with data. Few law firms share strategy with the wider firm outside the partnership, for example; in some law firms, associates do not see the business plans for the practice group they are part of. It becomes difficult to create a data culture if data is not treated as a shared resource to drive the business forwards.

To address this, law firm management needs to demonstrate that it will make decisions based on data points rather than opinion, and start to model data-driven decision making in action:

> *Companies with strong data-driven cultures tend to have top managers who set an expectation that decisions must be anchored in data – that this is normal, not novel or exceptional. They lead through example. At one retail bank, C-suite leaders together sift through the evidence from controlled market trials to decide on product launches. At a leading tech firm, senior executives spend 30 minutes at the start of meetings reading detailed summaries of proposals and their supporting facts, so that they can take evidence-based actions. These practices propagate downwards, as employees who want to be taken seriously have to communicate with senior leaders on their terms and in their language. The example set by a few at the top can catalyze substantial shifts in company-wide norms.*[146]

At the same time as this top-down approach, there needs to be an investment, from the bottom up, in the skills that are needed to understand and analyse data, and make decisions based on that data. As noted above, lasting change cannot be brought about by imposing or importing a data culture – just as you can't make a law firm innovative by creating an innovation team. If the firm is going to take data seriously, it will need to make investment in new skills, by creating and recruiting new roles (data scientists, data engineers – even, perhaps, a chief data officer), as these highly desirable professional skills are necessary to build capability. Lawyers will need to be trained to think differently about data, to see its value for the firm and for clients, to know how to read it, and to be rewarded for making decisions based upon it.

### (e) Training and learning

The United States is leading the way on training for lawyers at the juncture of law and data science in the academic field. CodeX, the Stanford Centre for Legal Informatics is focused on the research and development of what it calls 'computational law', which includes aspects of law and informatics. Georgia State University offers a certificate in legal analytics and innovation, defining 'legal analytics' as:

*... using computing power to analyze text from legal documents, treating words more like numerical data. Computer algorithms, combined with the knowledge of data scientists and lawyers, can provide insights about what happened in the past and what may happen in the future.*[147]

Academic training for lawyers is so important and, as the focus increases on critical business skills such as analytics, this will start to plant the seed for a more radical mindset change in the profession. But this is a slow burn; practical application of data to real client issues and issues of practice can only really happen in a law firm setting. The focus should be on the business outcomes that use of data can deliver; on smarter decision making rather than 'big data'. This quote from the head of corporate decision services at NBCUniversal (the US media and entertainment conglomerate) expresses the concept well:

*It's not about the data itself. It's not just about the analytics – any more than taking a vitamin is only so you can claim you successfully took a pill every morning. When it comes to analytics, we have to keep in mind the end goal is to help make better decisions more often. What we try to do first and foremost is look at places where people are already making decisions. We review the processes they use and try to identify either the gaps in the available data or the amount of time and effort it takes to procure data necessary to make an evaluation, insight, or decision. Sometimes we simply start by attempting to remove the friction from the existing process.*[148]

A mindset shift towards a decision-making culture as the outcome of better use of legal data will not happen overnight. Training at every level, from law firm leaders right through to aspiring lawyers in law school, is key. Training is only one element; it will need to go hand in hand with the active pursuit of a more open culture in law firms, with more transparency about the way the law firm is run as a business. This transparency must pervade the firm, from trainees to junior associates right the way up to line partners.

*(f) The future of legal data – data ecosystems and data sharing*

In addition to being a powerful source of insight for individual organisations and their customers, data can be shared between organisations to improve the service to the end customer across a sector or industry. Data sharing, or the creation of a common data ecosystem, is a model that is increasingly being used in industries outside legal. The idea behind a common data ecosystem or data model is that cross-disciplinary (or inter-industry) collaboration facilitates the delivery of greater value to the consumer of the service. Think of the data-sharing initiatives that have characterised the global COVID-19 pandemic – collaborations that have contributed to the common good. These have involved data sharing not only by and between corporations and governments, but by individuals, with 'citizen scientists' logging in to apps such as the ZOE COVID symptom study app.[149] In July 2021, the ZOE app was the world's largest ongoing study of COVID-19, with over 4.5 million private citizens logging their health data on a daily basis.

The incentive to join together in the face of a crisis to unite against a common enemy is obvious. The incentive for private collaborations between competitors across an industry sector, which aim to improve the experience for the end customer, is less immediately obvious. Microsoft, launching its Open Data Campaign in April 2020, described the benefits of data sharing across organisational boundaries:

> *[The] Open Data Campaign is helping to close the looming 'data divide' and help organizations of all sizes to realize the benefits of data and the new technologies it powers. We believe everyone can benefit from opening, sharing, and collaborating around data to make better decisions [and] improve efficiency.[150]*

As part of the Open Data Campaign, Microsoft is promoting the use of a common data model, a shared language which allows individual business apps to make use of the same metadata and benefit from a common understanding of the data's meaning. Microsoft is working with industry partners to extend the reach of common data models beyond individual organisations, by creating industry accelerators that will develop models that apply to an entire industry, allowing industry sectors to interoperate more easily. In the financial services sector, for example, a banking component has been developed that "includes a banking data model, sample apps, dashboards, and connected experiences for both retail banking and commercial banking".[151]

What if the legal sector were to take a similar approach to building a common data model to improve service to the end customer? Standardisation is not a foreign concept to legal services. The Loan Market Association was established back in 1996, and has focused, amongst other projects, on developing standardised best practice loan documentation in consultation with loan practitioners and law firms. Similarly, the International Swaps and Derivatives Association has driven standardisation for users of derivative products. There is no reason, conceptually, why the legal sector could not commit to developing common data models to improve the client experience across the legal industry. Some lawyers, frustrated with the lack of common data and standardisation within the sector, have started to take matters into their own hands. The oneNDA Club, an initiative conceived by the leadership of UK-based law firm The Law Boutique, has as its mission:

> [T]o create a universally standardised and agreed upon NDA that will reduce legal work, increase transparency and speed up business dealings.[152]

The movement has drafted a standardised NDA, currently under review by the team's impressive steering company. The objective is to get 1000 companies signed up to use the standard NDA by December 2001.

The desired outcome of oneNDA is to speed up business dealings, which ultimately benefits clients. If common data models for certain legal domains were to be developed, adopted by corporate legal teams and applied to services traditionally offered by law firms (such as commercial property services or M&A due diligence), the rewards for the client could be significant. Analysis of unstructured data to identify connections and issues would become a much easier task, demystified and simplified, and much more easily undertaken in-house. Other players in the ecosystem that feed in to certain legal processes (the Land Registry and commercial property owners in real estate transactions, for example) could also adopt the relevant data model, creating a common understanding and shared language across all actors in the transaction. This could be very disruptive (in a positive way) for the legal sector. As with any disruption, although it would benefit law firm clients, this kind of data sharing also has the potential to disaggregate law firms from some of their most lucrative engagements. For this reason, there is currently little incentive for law firms to collaborate in this way.

## 4. Technology leadership

Referenced throughout this book is the importance of developing or sourcing the right skills and leadership to bring about digital transformation. This is particularly important when focusing on technology. As business models change in response to customer demands, the role of technology leadership in all organisations is shifting to become less operational and more strategic. Technology leaders in law firms, who may traditionally not have been invited to contribute to firm strategy, are becoming critical resources for law firm management. The most progressive law firms, focused on the importance of becoming more digitally effective, are waking up to this and recruiting talented technology professionals who are attracted by the opportunity for transformation that the legal sector presents.

The role of the CIO/CTO in law firms has been under intense scrutiny during COVID-19. The shift to remote working and the hunger for effective collaboration tools will have consumed much of the energy of law firm technology leaders (who must have experienced intense stress through the early part of lockdown). Thankfully, most large law firms have coped well with the crisis, with the move to remote working largely being hailed as a success.

One of the cornerstones of a successful digital transformation in any business is effective technology leadership. There is a tendency in law firms to parcel up technology efforts, with responsibility for operational areas the preserve of the CTO and transformative or legal tech efforts channelled to a separate innovation team, often under different leadership. This approach can work, particularly if the IT department does not enjoy a particularly positive reputation in the firm. However, this strategy also has the potential to create unhelpful divisions which could slow down the pace of change. Ideally, everyone working on technology-related initiatives should align in to the technology leadership. Just as there should be one strategy for digital transformation, so there should be one set of objectives that cascade down from the technology leadership's objectives, supported by metrics that drive the right behaviours and measure the right things. Creating an artificial distinction between 'legal tech' and 'other tech' can be unhelpful.

This only works, however, if there is strong technology leadership, and a CTO/CIO who understands (or can quickly pick up) the way that lawyers work, has experience of transforming legacy systems, and has the stomach for a gargantuan change management effort. Finding leaders of this calibre is not easy, and law firms may have to look outside the legal services sector for the best talent. Part III of this book, in the chapter on people, discusses the importance of finding and retaining these digital stars.

## 5. In summary

Part I of this book was about getting started with digital change. We looked at:
- what 'digital' really means, and what it involves in practice, with examples from companies that do it well;
- how to evaluate the costs and benefits of investing in becoming more digitally effective; and
- how to communicate the transformation and unite the firm around a shared vision.

Part II examined the role that product development and technology play in creating a more digitally effective law firm.

Part III is about sustaining the change. A strategy is of little value unless the law firm is prepared to make the organisational and cultural changes required to make it successful over the long term. In Part III, we examine the elements of culture in a traditional law firm partnership, through the prism of partnership, people, and purpose, and explore how these elements need to be reframed to enable a law firm successfully to execute its digital strategy, and sustain the change. ∎

# Part III: Sustaining the change

# Chapter 6: Petri dish or opera house? Culture under the microscope

## 1. The link between culture and digital transformation

In Chapter 2, we looked at the five defining elements of successful digital companies. Element number five, the creation of a culture in which transformation can continue to flourish, is the subject of Part III of this book. Devoting so much space to a discussion of culture in a book on digital transformation may seem disproportionate; however, there is a large body of research that suggests that culture is the single greatest barrier to effective digital change. In this chapter, we define what is meant by 'culture' and explore the degree to which culture can be changed or influenced. We also examine the common cultural traits of a traditional law firm partnership – both the strengths and the challenges – and their implications for effecting and sustaining digital change.

This discussion of law firm culture inevitably includes some generalisations about how law firm partnerships operate. These are synthesised from a wide variety of sources – my own experiences, those of colleagues and friends, and from extensive research. Of course, all law firms are different. Some will be culturally much richer and more forward-thinking than this discussion suggests. Others will be more retrograde. What I am hoping to highlight is the common cultural traits (good and bad) that are baked into the structure and fabric of traditional law firm partnerships and which can inhibit cultural (and, by extension, digital) change.

## 2. Defining culture

'Culture' is a concept with different resonances, depending on your perspective. To some, it is the breeding ground of the petri dish; to others, a black-tie evening at the opera. Personally, I like the association of the science lab. I think of culture as an organic product of the right growth medium – the result of an environment made fertile for experimentation.

There is a connection between culture and digitisation, although that connection is not easy to describe scientifically. As discussed in Part I, many of the cultural attributes required to be a digitally effective organisation are those we might associate with a 'good' or healthy corporate culture:

- organisational diversity (which fuels innovative thinking);
- transparency (which unites teams around a shared vision);
- agility (which allows organisations to be responsive to change and serve customers better); and
- customer centricity (which gives an organisation its sense of purpose).

Even if you have all the tools you need to launch your digital transformation – strategy developed, business case honed, roadmap drawn up and team recruited – without the right cultural environment, the change cannot be sustained. Without a supporting culture and mindset, the transformation will wither on the vine.

Cultural change is hard, in any organisation. But, as anyone who has worked in a transformation role in a law firm will tell you, there is something uniquely challenging about effecting change in a traditional law firm partnership. As individuals, lawyers are smart, entrepreneurial, engaging and curious. The law firm partnership, however, with its rigid hierarchy and monolithic lack of dynamism, is somehow less than the sum of its parts, and the prevailing culture in the firm can reflect this.

## 3. The cultural strengths of law firms

It would be wrong to suggest that traditional law firm partnerships are by their nature culturally sterile. There is plenty to admire about the way these firms operate and the values on which they are founded. However, when we think about a 'healthy' workplace culture, the traditional law firm partnership is probably not what initially comes to mind. Our first thought might be of a start-up style workspace: airy, bright, open-plan offices, free beer on tap, mindfulness sessions at lunchtime and stand-up meetings. When we think about the power structure of the working environment, a good culture would be non-hierarchical, free from bullying, allowing everyone to contribute ideas and giving everyone a voice. From a financial perspective, everyone would share in the profits of the company and be incentivised to make it a success. Digging deeper still, and focusing on the interplay between personal and work personas, a good culture would allow us to bring our whole self to work, celebrating diversity in all its forms. And then there is the foundational layer, the layer of purpose and values, with a healthy culture flourishing in an organisation that has a clear purpose, that is somehow 'doing good' in its organisational journey.

On the face of it, traditional law firm partnerships do not meet this brief. However, law firms must be doing something right, or they would not have survived for so long. It is too easy to idealise the culture of digital natives and to demonise the incumbents. Digital natives have the freedom to craft a culture free of the weight of years of learned behaviours. Incumbents carry much more cultural baggage. It does not, however, automatically always follow that challengers have all the advantages, or that incumbents are intrinsically culturally sterile.

Law firm partnerships have cultural strengths as well as challenges. It is important to spend some time considering these strengths, for two reasons. First, it is law firm leaders and line partners who need to be convinced about the importance of cultural and digital change – not innovation teams or cultural commentators. Partners in law firms will (quite rightly) not be persuaded by a one-sided critique of the structure in which they have grown up. Secondly, the strengths of the partnership structure should not be discounted – they create tremendous opportunity for the law firm that is prepared to commit to digital transformation and to the cultural change required to sustain it. Here are five of the cultural strengths of the traditional law firm partnership:

- **Lockstep:** In their purest form, partnerships, particularly lockstep partnerships,[153] are a beautiful model of democracy and equality. In fact, a true partnership, giving everyone a stake in the business, is a form of employee ownership that is very close to the model adopted by digital start-ups. Everyone (at least, everyone who is a partner) is invested in the organisation's success and feels a sense of personal accountability that cannot easily be replicated in a corporate structure, where senior management and the shareholders are the primary beneficiaries of the collective effort. There are not too many pure lockstep partnerships left, however. As the partnership remuneration model has shifted, and lateral moves have increased, the old-school values of the traditional partnership have begun to be eroded.

  *Lawyers used to club together in partnership to bind themselves to a shared commercial purpose, make the most of their collective talents and share the proceeds of their efforts. This ideal has come under increasing pressure as firms have increased in size and global reach, and abandoned or modified the "lockstep" approach of deciding each partner's slice of profit by seniority, in favour of the evocatively named "eat what you kill" model. It is easy to fetishise partnership, which has its flaws. But its virtues, such as the promise of collegiality and interesting work, are increasingly drowned out by the call of cold cash.[154]*

This rather scathing piece in the *Financial Times* does not take into account the soul-searching that will likely have preceded any decision in a law firm partnership to break the lockstep model. Many law firms have broken lockstep reluctantly, as a means of sustaining their business under pressure from competitors, rather than through greed. It remains the case, though, that breaking the lockstep can contribute to an individual partner 'hero culture' that can in turn be culturally divisive.

- **Teamwork:** People who work in law firms tend to have long tenure – attrition rates are low. This cannot only be because they lack imagination. Law firms can be very collegiate places to work, full of smart and motivated people, giving those who work there a real sense of identity and belonging. When lawyers from different practice groups work together, battling in the trenches to deliver a complex mandate, you see teamwork at its best.

- **Continuity:** Many law firms have been around for a long time, have weathered economic blows and withstood crises, protecting their employees through good times and bad. These firms have provided their people with long and rewarding careers. Some of the best law firms have a palpable sense of continuity and perpetuity; this can be the bedrock of positive values.

- **Deep relationships:** Many law firm partnerships have very deep client relationships, some of which stretch back over many years. Anecdotally, during the early months of the COVID-19 lockdown, 'new law' business stalled, as clients retreated to the safety of their established law firm relationships. The first set of law firm financial year-end results, which were in the main very positive, would seem to confirm this. One can understand why; in a crisis, clients don't want to take any additional risk. In an increasingly volatile world, this is good news for the establishment – provided law firms can hold on to their client relationships in the face of increasingly sophisticated and hungry competition.

- **Consensus:** Another advantage that law firm partnerships may have over alternative corporate structures relates to the consensus-based approach to decision making. This is something of a double-edged sword. The lack of a culture of command and control in law firms can be a barrier to quick

*All law firms are different, but we cannot gloss over the very public indicators of a culture under strain that have surfaced in recent years, which are representative of wider problems in the sector.*

decision making – which is a problem in the digital age that relies on agility and speed. Once a decision has been made, however, it can be easier to diffuse. There is a growing view that although top-down mandates might get the change message out more quickly, it is influence that sustains change, and that does not necessarily come from the top:

> [A] sole focus on 'tone from the top' has gradually given way to a more complex, multi-system approach to influencing culture and behaviour. While there remains an important role for senior leaders, influence happens at all levels of an organisation. The challenge is to recognise and align all levels of the system.[155]

Once consensus has been achieved, partnerships, with their complex matrix of relationships and influences, may find it easier to diffuse that cultural change across the firm than would be the case in a command-and-control corporate structure. In this way, law firm partnerships may find lasting change easier to sustain.

## 4. Law firm culture: the challenges

Even law firms that have never heard of digital transformation will have been focused on their firm's culture in recent years. All law firms are different, but we cannot gloss over the very public indicators of a culture under strain that have surfaced in recent years, which are representative of wider problems in the sector. Examples include:

- an insistence on face time that negatively impacts wellbeing;
- a culture of perfectionism that affects mental health;
- abuses of the hierarchy leading to non-fee-earning professionals being treated like second-class citizens;
- excessive drinking leading to poor judgement and sexual harassment; and
- a lack of diversity and inclusion leading to entrenched unconscious racial and gender bias.

There is widespread recognition within the legal services industry that these behaviours are a problem, and need to change. But in order to change, law firms must go through the painful process of actively scrutinising and fixing their culture. This doesn't mean launching a firmwide values initiative, or issuing branded statements about vision and purpose. What is needed is an honest examination of the hidden, coded behaviours that govern how things are done, followed by organisational change to address identified behaviours that will hold the firm back.

Law firms will tell us that they are already doing this, and give examples of where they have acted quickly when bad behaviour surfaced or was called out. This is of course true; really bad behaviours, the scandalous ones that make the headlines, demand a response. No reputable law firm could allow these behaviours to continue unchecked. However, there are many unseen and unreported cultural indicators that don't rise to the level of bullying, discrimination or sexual assault, but which are indicative of a profession that is outdated in its approach to running a business. Some of these behaviours are isolated – the product of bad people or poor management, which can be found in any organisation. Other behaviours stem from the social norms, attitudes and ways of working particular to the law firm structure and the concept of 'lawyer exceptionalism' (of which more below). These are some of the same behaviours, I would argue, that make some law firms resistant to digital change. Positive characteristics that we might associate with being a 'professional', such as tenacity, perfectionism and dedication, if left unchecked (or even worse, encouraged), can turn to something more pernicious: ruthlessness, lack of empathy, arrogance. This in turn can lead to a false sense of being protected from any external disruption, particularly in large and profitable corporate law firms, and an unwillingness to recognise that change needs to happen:

> It's notoriously difficult for companies with a long history of success to see catastrophe looming. Often they have been lulled into a belief that the protective moat around their business is a lot wider and deeper than it actually is.[156]

Law firms need to think deeply about their culture, because getting culture right is key to the success of every organisation. A healthy culture promotes organisational growth and enhances the employment proposition. In a digital world in which information is accessible and easy to share, the reputational and business consequences of allowing culture to degrade can be catastrophic. Social media and a prevailing 'cancel culture' put corporate – and law firm – culture under the microscope.

## 5. Addressing culture under strain: lessons from the financial services sector

This imperative to scrutinise culture may be a relatively new phenomenon for law firms, but culture has been high on the corporate boardroom agenda of many Big Law clients since the global financial crisis of 2008. The cultural failings in the banking sector were devastating to the sector – and to the economy. The crisis forced the financial services sector to take a hard look at what had gone wrong and how it could be prevented from happening again.

In the United Kingdom, in the 12 years since the crisis, the Financial Conduct Authority (FCA) has implemented various regulations designed to prevent a recurrence of the sector's cultural failings. The FCA has also consistently reinforced the message that creating and embedding the right culture is an ongoing obligation for financial institutions – an obligation that requires both robust supervisory, board and management oversight and individual accountability. The FCA plays an active and thoughtful part in directing financial services organisations to embed cultural change. For example, one of the priorities in the FCA's 2019/20 Business Plan is "working with firms to promote and embed healthy culture, focusing on four drivers of behaviour – purpose, leadership, rewarding and managing people, and governance".[157]

The FCA goes on to say:

> *Purpose is a driving force in creating and sustaining healthy cultures ... [W]e will look more deeply at the concept of purpose in financial*

*services and the case for creating purposeful cultures. We will be looking to assemble and review the evidence for a causal linkage between healthy cultures and business models and healthy outcomes for consumers, markets and firms.*[158]

(The link between purpose and culture is an interesting one, which I explore in the law firm context in Chapter 9.) Progress towards cultural change in financial services has been slow and steady and was preceded by a sustained period of introspection. The sector spent time in analysing what culture means in a corporate setting, defining what a 'good' culture might look like and working out how to get there. One of the conclusions was that regulation alone cannot change culture; culture is lived, and manifests itself through behaviours rather than the existence of a rule book.

Reflecting on the relationship between regulation and behaviours, William Dudley, the one-time president and chief executive of the Federal Reserve Bank of New York, described culture as "the implicit norms that guide behaviour in the absence of regulations or compliance rules".[159] The implication is that culture grows to fill a void in the absence of explicit direction about how to behave. A simpler way of expressing this is that culture is "what people do when no one is looking".[160] The fact that culture is weaved into the fabric of the organisation makes it difficult to unpick – and to change.

Although culture may be entrenched, this does not mean that it is static. The culture of every organisation must evolve over time, as leadership changes or under the impact of unplanned external events (such as the coronavirus pandemic). You might even think of culture as a defensive shield, protecting the organisation from external shocks:

*Culture is an evolutionary construct; a response to internal and external challenges in order to safeguard the organisation's effectiveness and sustainability.*[161]

The lessons of the financial crisis should be particularly relevant to law firms. As regulated industries, law and financial services face similar challenges and responsibilities. Many law firms will have been very close to the details of the cultural failings that contributed to the financial crisis, and will have made a lot of money from advising clients who were implicated. This should have acted as an early warning system for law firms, some of whom must have seen similarities between the behaviours and culture in the financial services sector and what was happening on the ground in their own firms. Law firms, however, appear to suffer from a selective schizophrenia. For example, they will happily advise clients on digital transformation while resisting digital change in their own firm, or advise on culture while ignoring the behaviours of their fellow partners. Law firms have been engaged by some of the world's leading companies to help resolve their cultural challenges; it is a source of frustration that law firms do not always seem able to apply the lessons to their own organisations.

It is perhaps unreasonable to expect law firms to police their own behaviours. After all, as a regulated industry, should not regulation and policy be tightened to prevent cultural degradation and promote the 'right' behaviours? Indeed, just as the FCA increased its regulatory scrutiny following the credit crisis, so the regulator of solicitors and law firms in England and Wales, the Solicitors Regulation Authority (SRA), is beginning to take law firm culture into account in its regulation and enforcement activity. At the end of 2019, the SRA launched its new Standards and Regulations (StaRs), which are intended to encourage ethical decision making by lawyers 'when no one is looking'. The aim of the StaRs is not to cast the SRA in the role of police, but to provide a flexible framework for how lawyers should behave, emphasising the importance of personal judgement and individual accountability.

The emphasis on lawyers as professionals who are individually accountable for their own ethical behaviour is not new. Crispin Passmore, former executive director of the SRA and now a consultant to the legal industry, has written extensively about the relationship between regulation and culture, and the role the SRA plays in protecting the public against lawyers' bad behaviour. In an interview for this book, Passmore explained to me the distinction between the FCA's active, almost interventionist, approach to regulation after the global financial crisis, and the SRA's own approach. It comes down to lawyers' status as regulated professionals:

> *When the FCA started to look at the causes of the global financial crisis it identified a lack of personal responsibility and accountability in the financial services sector. That led to the review that put in place banking standards and the senior manager regime. One of the distinctions between legal services and financial services, from a regulatory standpoint, is that the SRA has always exercised personal level regulation, including a long period of training and workplace apprenticeship that filters out the fast buck; entity regulation was formalised in 2011 with the introduction of the SRA Code of Conduct.*

The emphasis on personal responsibility does not mean that law firms are exempt from regulatory scrutiny. According to Passmore, the pattern of SRA enforcement activity shows the regulator's growing interest in organisational culture:

> *If an individual lawyer appears to have committed a serious breach – be that financial irregularity or sexual misconduct with a trainee or client – then the SRA will be looking at culture within the firm. If their review suggests that the firm was cavalier about that type of compliance, or compliance generally, then the firm will be much more likely to be in the firing line for a firm-level sanction in addition to the individual that is most directly in breach.*

The SRA publishes an annual Risk Outlook which sets out its view of the risks and challenges faced by solicitors and law firms. The 2020/21 Risk Outlook lists 'integrity and ethics' as one of the focus areas, and emphasises that an important part of maintaining trust in the profession is "having a workplace culture that encourages integrity and being open when mistakes have been made".[162] Although it is encouraging to see that law firm culture is on the SRA's radar, it is arguable that the SRA, and the law firms it regulates, have not gone far enough in putting law firm culture under the microscope.

Perhaps this is simply because the culture in the legal sector has not yet reached crisis point. Or perhaps the explanation lies in the way that professionals, particularly licensed professionals such as lawyers, are viewed by others and view themselves. The term 'professional' suggests a certain set of qualities and values; integrity, honesty, maybe even a degree of aloofness or lack of emotion. Conceiving of oneself as a professional can lead to a self-conception of technical and moral superiority, creating a culture of 'lawyer exceptionalism'. The implications of this for law firm culture are worrying. How can a law firm create a healthy culture if individual partners believe that they are better than others and, consciously or unconsciously, exempt themselves from rules that apply to others? As Passmore observes:

*The risk of 'professionalism' on culture and innovation is probably negative. It feeds or even creates 'lawyer exceptionalism'; that means lawyers view themselves as always separate to the business, not subject to usual rules and always able to justify why they are different (be that on ethics or innovation). It is almost as if they can license their own bad behaviour because as professionals they are de facto ethical and thus their behaviour is by definition ok.*

Understanding how regulators assess the culture of an organisation can be helpful for law firms who are looking at their own firmwide culture. Deloitte's Centre for Regulatory Strategy, in its 2018 review "Culture in financial services: scrutiny by the regulator, in principle and in practice" identifies the following six areas of focus:[163]

- **Mindsets and behaviours:** Regulators will look at behaviours to assess whether they reflect the organisation's target culture and values.
- **Governance and controls:** Regulators will scrutinise the governance and controls that an organisation has in place.
- **The 'tone from the top':** Regulators look at the role of the leadership in setting, communicating and (importantly) challenging the firm's culture.
- **Remuneration and incentives:** How people in the organisation are rewarded and incentivised says a lot about the organisation's culture; rewards should promote good outcomes for the firm, customers and the market.

- **Purpose and strategy:** Regulators will look for a clear sense of purpose and alignment between strategy, culture and values.
- **Individual accountability:** Regulators will expect some individual roles (or individuals with particular responsibilities) to have enhanced accountability when it comes to behaviours and values.

In law firm partnerships, some of these areas are more mature and developed than others. I consider governance, incentives and individual accountability in more detail below.

### 5.1 Governance

Governance is a structural issue, but one that is within the control of the firm's management and which ought to be relatively easy to put in place and evidence. However, the majority of law firms continue to mark their own homework when it comes to culture and behaviours. Most do not have independent representation on their governance boards. The majority are still run by a managing partner rather than a CEO. Although business services leaders may be invited to governance meetings or even be members of the executive committee or board, in my experience their voices are not given equal weight; it is a small group of partners who make the decisions. Associates are very rarely represented, if at all. This is a missed opportunity, and another example of law firms failing to learn the lessons from their clients. The UK Corporate Governance Code requires the boards of companies to which the Code applies to have an "appropriate combination" of both executive and non-executive directors.[164] This is intended to prevent the board being dominated by particular individuals or small groups. It is also a requirement of the Code that at least half the board be independent. Independence brings challenge, fresh perspectives and diversity of thought, and can help the decision-making body create a healthier culture for everyone in the organisation. Law firms tend to close ranks, and don't like outsiders looking in.

### 5.2 Incentives

Incentives are another thorny issue for law firm partnerships. A regulator in the financial services sector would assess whether rewards promote good outcomes for the company, the clients and the market. The prevailing financial metrics in a law firm partnership are PPP (profit per partner point) and RPL (revenue per lawyer). The obsession with revenue, which is inextricably linked to the billable hour, does not incentivise efficiency and drives many negative behaviours. Increasing revenue at the expense of efficiency may promote good outcomes for partners, but arguably not for clients. Similarly, awarding associates bonuses based on hours billed (which is the standard against which associates are assessed in practice, whatever the law firm PR tells you) drives a culture of presenteeism and overwork, which takes its toll on lawyers' mental health.

### 5.3 Individual accountability

Individual accountability is also worth a mention here. A regulator will assess the degree to which those in positions of responsibility are held to a higher standard of behaviour than others who work in the organisation. Often the converse is true in law firm partnerships. I have heard anecdotes from colleagues in large City law firms that show how partners, particularly those that are making the most money for the firm, can get away with some outrageous behaviours (not the kind that get into the papers, but everyday micro-aggressions, low-level bullying or boundary pushing that is recognised and tolerated). This is a structural issue that derives from the power structure of the partnership, which elevates the status of individual partners in a way that can be unhealthy.

This leaves mindset, purpose and tone from the top – arguably the most challenging of the levers – difficult both to measure and to influence.

## 6. The enduring nature of the partnership model

Although the traditional law firm partnership structure has some deep cultural flaws, it continues to subsist as an effective organisational model for delivering legal services. Commentators have been predicting the death of the law firm partnership and the demise of Big Law since the late 1990s, but very little, so far, has really changed. As John Armour and Mari Sako of the University of Oxford observe in their paper on AI-enabled business models in legal services, the partnership model appears to be able to withstand a great deal of external pressure:

*From a macro perspective, the impact of AI technology can be understood as one of a number of forces that together are putting pressure on professional autonomy and traditional forms of law firm organization. These include intensifying competition – both within and between professions – fostered by globalization and fragmentation of professional expertise, associated pressure to redefine professional standards in terms of commercial outcomes, and deregulation of professional monopolies. Consequently, large globalizing law firms face pressures to move away from the traditional professional partnership model towards more managed professional businesses. Nevertheless, lawyers have retained much professional autonomy and discretion, and the role of partners as owners and decision-makers in law firms has proved remarkably robust.*[165]

It is telling that the legal services sector has not (yet) produced a challenger fit to displace the traditional law firm partnership. It is of course arguable that this is just around the corner; law companies, alternative legal services providers and other professional organisations (including the Big 4) are coming up fast, with compelling digital propositions that are maturing at speed. In the short term, however, being an incumbent law firm is still a good place to be. Established law firms have advantages (experience, maturity, stability, a large and loyal customer base) that challengers do not. Customer loyalty could of course be worn away over time if the law firm entirely neglects the client experience – but this is the law firm's advantage to lose.

Conversely, it is also the case that no traditional law firm partnership has (yet) made a full commitment to digital transformation and to the business model and cultural change required to sustain it. The law firm that does this, building on an already loyal customer base and a valued brand, could grow its business exponentially. There are established firms that have the potential to achieve this, if they move quickly and with purpose.

If we were to pick the three defining characteristics of culture in a law firm (or perhaps, the three factors that have the biggest influence on culture in law firm) they could be summarised as a belief in the following:

- **P**artnership (the inherent value of the partnership model)
- **P**eople (extraordinary teams, and collegiality)
- **P**urpose (a sense of perpetuity – bequeathing the firm to the next generation of partners stronger than it is today)

In the next three chapters, we explore these three Ps – how they are uniquely viewed in law firms and how they play into the existing operating model. The objective is not to demonise law firms, or to suggest that they are intrinsically unhealthy places to work. The objective is to explore the degree to which established structure and entrenched culture inhibits firms from becoming more digitally effective, and to consider what changes can be made to the law firm operating model to unlock the opportunities, and sustain successful change. ■

# Chapter 7: Sustaining change – partnership

## 1. Time for a new model?

The partnership model has come in for quite a lot of criticism in recent years. Some commentators regard it as wholly problematic and outdated, and advocate wholesale change as the only solution:

> *There is nothing inherently wrong with law firms; the problem is the traditional partnership model. It no longer serves most clients. Nor does it align well with most firm lawyers and legal professionals – except a handful of generally older partners. No amount of firm marketing or self-styled "innovation" dollars will fix this. Firms that live by PPP might just die by it.*[166]

There are many for whom this view resonates and, objectively, it sounds right. However, you would be hard pressed to find a law firm partner who will admit that the model is flawed, especially as financial results remain very strong. Many firms, particularly those at the top end of the market, continue to be very profitable (despite the pandemic), and any significant decline looks unlikely in the medium term. The buoyancy of UK law firm 2020 financial results took commentators by surprise:

> *With more than a dozen top-50 UK firms having now published their results, including all four Magic Circle firms that issue on-the-record numbers, we can see that financial performance generally is hardly down on 2019/20.*
>
> *[...]*
>
> *The results seen so far confirm the impression that London's elite is emerging in good shape from the crisis, thanks to the benefits of large, cash-rich plc clients and their role as go-to counsel when the business environment goes pear-shaped.*[167]

The same is true at the top end of the US market. A survey in December 2020 by Wells Fargo Private Bank revealed that:

> *U.S. law firms are poised to close 2020 with better-than-expected results, with a large share of big firms increasing their revenues in spite of massive challenges from the COVID-19 pandemic.*[168]

Just as it is difficult to tell a roomful of millionaires that they need to change, so there is limited value in telling law firms to ditch the partnership structure to become more digitally effective. The message will simply not resonate. Also, in practical terms, it would be very difficult to achieve. Law firms have a lot of cultural baggage and, despite the entrepreneurialism of individual partners, often lack dynamism. This is why the law firm pyramid, like its Egyptian cousins, has subsisted for so long.

If law firms accept that they must adapt, most will choose to do so within the confines of the partnership structure. It may not be the fastest way, but it is achievable, provided that firms commit to the cultural change required to make it sustainable. This will involve taking a hard look at the current operating model and defining the target ways of working for the future:

*Since a digital transformation is so complex, it's ... important to take some time to determine what you want your operating model to be – essentially, how it's all supposed to work so the change can last.*[169]

This chapter looks at the relationship between law firm structure and law firm culture, and the implications for digital change. It also identifies ways in which law firms could be more creative in exploring new models to sustain digital transformation, without doing damage to the partnership structure itself.

## 2. Structure and culture

Most law firm partnerships are structured in the same way. Even firms with many global offices, in countries with significant cultural distinctions, replicate the same organisational design and hierarchy: partners at the top, counsel below, then senior associates, associates – and in English common law jurisdictions, trainees. Beneath the fee earners sit the business teams. Under this organisational model, a partner in a firm's 50-partner New York office is regarded as no different from one in the three-partner Korean office, regardless of revenues earned or level of management responsibility. Although there may be dotted lines and matrix relationships between offices and regions for law firm management purposes, from the perspective of the 'fee earners', the chain of command is very clear. Partnerships depend on this predictable structure, which defines expectations, boundaries and career progression. Predictability is arguably one of the model's strengths. The model cannot, however, be described as dynamic. In a structure where everyone knows their place, disruption is unlikely to happen spontaneously.

A rigid structure is one of the challenges that makes digital transformation in law firms difficult to achieve. It's not that everyone in law firms is patriarchal, or old-fashioned, or particularly resistant to technology (although plenty are). It runs deeper than that – the organisational design itself is inimical to radical change.

The way an organisation is structured can shape its culture and influence behaviours:

*It is easy to make the mistake of assuming that because the law firm hierarchy is so well defined and understood, the organisational design and supporting culture must also be well aligned and fit for purpose.*

*Like culture, organisational design and structure may be a powerful driver of behaviour. Their aim is to shape, direct and coordinate behaviour towards the accomplishment of common organisational objectives. Literature suggests that there is no sharp divide between culture and structure. Both mutually influence each other and, over time, tend to blend together, simultaneously exerting influence on behaviour.*[170]

Organisational design is not just drawing lines between boxes on an organisational chart. It is an exercise that goes to the heart of how an organisation works, aligning career objectives with firm strategy, defining individual accountabilities, structuring to make sure talent is managed and developed appropriately, finding the right leaders and making sure that they actually have the capabilities to lead. It is easy to make the mistake of assuming that because the law firm hierarchy is so well defined and understood, the organisational design and supporting culture must also be well aligned and fit for purpose. This has arguably been the case in the past, but there is a serious question mark over whether the traditional law firm partnership model is fit for a digital future.

John Armour and Mari Sako of the University of Oxford have recently published some interesting research in this area.[171] They explore the potential impact of AI on the traditional law firm business model and discusses the different organisational structures that might be adopted to support AI-enabled business models in the digital age. The question that Armour and Sako's paper seeks to answer is this:

*What will happen to law firms and the legal profession when the use of AI becomes prevalent in legal services? Will the profession preserve its traditional role and forms of organizing? Or else, how will their role and forms of organizing change in the face of competition from alternative legal services providers?*[172]

This is not a 'robots will take our jobs' type analysis, but a thoughtful examination of why it is that the traditional law firm partnership model "makes the achievement of radical change and innovation particularly challenging".[173] Although the research is focused on the implications of AI adoption, the analysis is equally valid for wider digital transformation. Armour and Sako's conclusion is that although the established law firm partnership structure is well adapted to support a traditional legal advisory business model, it is not the best structure to support an AI-enabled (for which we can read, digital) business model. There are three structural characteristics of the partnership model that lead to this conclusion:

- a lack of speed and agility;
- a short-term attitude to investment; and
- an excessively rigid career framework.

## 2.1 The importance of agility

Above all else, successful digital transformation requires an ability to respond at speed to customer demand and to changes in the market. Simply watching what the competition does and hoping to leapfrog to the front is unlikely to be an effective strategy. Traditional law firm partnerships can lack agility, particularly when it comes to decision making. In a law firm, the partners own the business, and decisions are made by consensus. Law firm partnerships will of course have a senior partner supported by a leadership team, who is nominally 'in charge' – but in reality, very little power is delegated to management. Power resides with the partnership.

A partnership is made up of a number of very senior, very bright and (often) opinionated individuals, who might be spread across a number of international offices. Any important decision affecting the firm requires the agreement of all or most of those individual partners. Although fundamental disagreement is relatively rare, achieving consensus can be a long and arduous process. In a fast-paced business environment, in which market conditions are changing rapidly, law firms simply don't have the luxury of time.

Most businesses are not run this way. And for good reason. As Armour and Sako note:

*The partnership form is something of a rarity in business generally.*

*Its very strengths for the legal advisory model are weaknesses in many other contexts. Consensus-oriented decision-making is a disadvantage where, as in a typical business context ... quick reactions are required to a changing environment.*[174]

The cultural implications of this structural defect are that law firms are reluctant to take risks (even calculated ones). Because every partner has a vote, any decision must be preceded by full and irrefutable evidence that will satisfy the most conservative of the group. This means that appetite for experimentation is likely to be very limited. Successful digital transformation requires a culture in which it is safe to try new things, and to 'fail fast':

*Making it safe to fail is crucial because learning happens through experimentation, and experimentation often results in failure. Recent McKinsey research shows, in fact, that respondents at successful organizations are more than twice as likely as their peers elsewhere to strongly agree that employees are rewarded for taking risks of an appropriate level. So a willingness to fail has to be embedded in a company's culture.*[175]

### 2.2 Investing for the long term

As discussed in Part I, digital transformation is not a one-off cost, or a project or a programme with a beginning and an end. It requires significant ongoing investment as part of business as usual. The level of investment will of course depend on the size and strategy of the law firm, but to realise that strategy the ambition must be matched by investment, year on year. Partnerships are not used to thinking about investment in this way – and certainly not investment in technology. The law firm investment horizon is extremely short term. Law firms do not hold significant capital reserves; profits are distributed to partners, often quarterly, and capital can only be raised by a partner capital call (asking partners to make capital contributions) or by borrowing. Partners who are approaching retirement will not be incentivised to agree to a large capital investment to enable digital transformation if they are unlikely to reap the benefits during their time as partner in the firm.

The cultural implications of this short-term investment horizon manifest in resistance to investing money on transformation when returns are not certain or not sufficiently immediate:

> *[E]mployee ownership, an essential feature of the partnership form, puts constraints on fundraising for innovative projects. Capital must either be sourced from partners' accumulated profits or take the form of borrowing. Partners only receive profits for the period of their tenure; as a result, they will only be willing to reinvest these (as opposed to paying them out) where returns will be generated prior to their retirement. This short investment time-horizon, when coupled with the delays associated with consensus-based decision making, can make reacting to new opportunities difficult for partnerships.*[176]

In a corporate structure, decisions are of course made by a board rather than by group consensus, and shareholders, rather than employees, own the company. This makes raising funds for investment and making rapid decisions much easier to achieve than is the case in the partnership structure.

### 2.3 Rigidity of career structure

Armour and Sako's research identifies three new business models for the delivery of legal services that have emerged in response to the opportunities created by new technologies and the exigencies of client demand. The first is a legal operations model, which is essentially focused on efficiency, and combines process re-engineering, design thinking and project management with digital solutions such as automation to deliver a more cost-effective service. The second is a legal technology model, which involves the design of technology solutions for use in legal operations (essentially, creating digital products to support client-facing delivery). The third is a consulting model, which is the provision of advice to clients around technology selection and implementation, and the design of legal operations processes. There is growing demand for each of these models as law firm clients (and law firms themselves) seek to become more digitally effective.

Some law firms are experimenting with one or more of these models, and I discuss them in more detail later in this chapter. What unites each of the new models is the combination of skills and capabilities that is required to make them successful. Technical legal expertise is one important part of the mix, but there are many other skills that cannot necessarily be found in a traditional law firm hierarchy. For Armour and Sako, this suggests the need for a new kind of professional, who can combine legal expertise with digital skills:

> *[S]uccessful AI implementation requires a close collaboration by lawyers and other professionals in multidisciplinary teams. Lawyers remain necessary for the successful implementation of AI in legal services, but changes in work design resulting from AI adoption are likely to alter the nature of lawyers' jobs ... The emergence of a new expert division of labor, between what only lawyers can do and what non-lawyers are permitted to do, is likely to be a contested process. There is evidence that some firms are seeking to recruit individuals with different disciplinary backgrounds (eg lawyers and data scientists separately) and integrate them in teams; other firms are seeking individuals who themselves combine multidisciplinary backgrounds (eg lawyers who can code). Either way, the diffusion of multidisciplinary teams is likely to lead to the emergence of 'hybrid professionals'... [J]ust as doctors are expected to organize good quality patient treatment, not just treat patients, lawyers may come to design and manage the provision of good quality legal services, not just give legal advice.*[177]

Hybrid professionals do exist in law firms, but they are in the minority and often treated quite differently from the 'traditional' lawyers, separated out into innovation teams and not given the same opportunities for career progression. True multidisciplinary working, in which lawyers work not just with other lawyers but with other professionals at the firm to deliver client solutions, is culturally at odds with the traditional structure of the partnership, in which the focus is on giving legal advice and billable hours are the measure of success.

*Slow decision making, a short-term view of investment and a rigid career structure are the three main structural challenges that inhibit digital change in a traditional law firm partnership. So what should law firms do about it?*

## 3. What are the options?

Slow decision making, a short-term view of investment and a rigid career structure are the three main structural challenges that inhibit digital change in a traditional law firm partnership. So what should law firms do about it? Faced with pressure to digitise and a rigid organisational structure that makes effective digitisation difficult to achieve, law firms have a choice:

- **Choose to specialise:** Firms could decide that, beyond incremental internal efficiencies, digital transformation as a growth strategy is not a strategic objective for the firm. They could choose to narrow their model to bespoke, high-end legal advisory services, reduce the scope of what they deliver, and become highly profitable at doing the thing they do best.
- **Choose to change:** Firms could embrace digital transformation as an essential part of their strategy and a means of future-proofing the firm. They could accept that the rigidity of the partnership model might be impacting their culture in a way that makes digital transformation difficult to achieve and sustain, and explore ways to address this.
- **Choose to do nothing:** Firms could of course do nothing. They could gamble that the culture of the firm will change over time as new partners come through the ranks. Or they might adopt a 'wait and see' approach to establish whether change is really necessary, hoping that they will be able to follow fast by copying firms that have made more difficult or radical choices.

### 3.1 Option 1: Specialise

Not all law firms need to adopt digital transformation as a growth strategy. There is evidence that firms that have made considered strategic choices to dominate a clearly defined specialist space can continue to grow without investing in digital as a source of new revenues or business lines. As noted in Part 1 of this book, Kirkland & Ellis is an example of a law firm that has been highly strategic in its choice of clients and sectors. At the time of writing, Kirkland & Ellis's turnover is approaching $5 billion for the twelve months to the end of January 2021, a substantial increase from revenues of $4.154 billion in

2019. Kirkland has consciously chosen not to be a full-service law firm and to concentrate on private equity and M&A, with restructuring and litigation a strong supporting cast and cyclical counterbalance:

> *Those fields are the pillars on which Kirkland's empire is built – in sharp contrast to the biggest "full service" global firms, which cover every area of law that affects a business and have offices across the globe.*
>
> *"Full service doesn't make much money," says a UK-based corporate law veteran.*[178]

It is not only firms of Kirkland's size and profitability that have made a strategic choice to specialise and to break away from the full-service model. 2020 saw a marked increase in the number of law firm partner teams splitting off from the mother ship to form tightly scoped boutique offerings. In February 2021, eight partners from Shearman & Sterling split from the firm to start their own arbitration boutique, taking a sizeable number of associates with them. In 2020, employment partners from Osborne Clarke and Addleshaw Goddard launched boutique employment firm Chamberlain Hamnett. Two partners from Linklaters' London and Moscow offices also launched a specialist finance boutique, Bott Van Kesteren, and Stephenson Harwood's former Hong Kong senior partner launched a litigation boutique, M B Kemp. *The Lawyer* magazine sees a link between the increase in these boutique offerings and COVID-19:

> *[T]he pandemic is likely to convince more than a few lawyers, stars among them, that the time is now right to go it alone … And there's one other, generally unspoken but compelling, reason: pricing. For some clients, and for some types of work, Big Law firms simply charge too much. Boutiques may not be by definition cheaper, but chances are they are likely to be. Clients like them, some lawyers love them, the market is likely to see more of them before too long.*[179]

COVID-19 will certainly have been a factor in the rise of the boutique law firm. Remote working will have demonstrated to both partners and clients that global business can be done virtually, without a physical machine to support it. However, the 'ecosystem' approach to legal services, in which clients disaggregate services and procure them from the provider who offers the requisite quality at the best price, was already in motion long before the pandemic hit. In a digital world in which platforming, crowdsourcing and consumption of 'everything as a service' is becoming standard, there must be opportunity for law firms to radically rethink their organisational design. The boutique or specialist model makes a lot of sense, for clients, for boutique providers and for large law firms:

- From the client's perspective, the law firm machine is really just a costly overhead. Why should a client looking for a particular service, such as employment law advice, pay premium law firm rates for that service – rates which factor in the fully loaded costs of teams in landmark offices in some of the most expensive cities in the world?

- From the perspective of the small boutique provider, partners will have more autonomy than in a large law firm, and low overheads give the potential for high profitability. Platforms are the only infrastructure the boutique law firm needs – you don't need a huge machine to support the generation of documents when you have your own Office 365 account, or a business development function when you can use LinkedIn.

- From a law firm perspective, the full-service law firm, in which less profitable practice groups and partners are retained as part of the lockstep because law firms want to be able to provide one integrated, branded service to their clients, is an outmoded and expensive approach. If law firms want to be full service, why would they not retain the most profitable practice groups in the firm (corporate M&A or competition, for argument's sake) and consume tax, real estate and employment law support as a service, from boutique firms of quality allied to the firm, collaborating under one cloud platform?

There are benefits to specialisation and the market is definitely trending that way. I would argue, however, that the number of law firms that can continue to sustain growth over the long term by choosing to specialise are relatively few and pretty unique.

### 3.2 *Option 2: Choose to change*

Most large corporate law firms will be in the middle category – full service rather than highly specialised, and recognising that digitisation is something they need to do something about. These are the firms that must be prepared to look hard at the partnership model. They will need to take a creative approach to organisational design if they are to sustain the change and get value from their investment in digital transformation. This doesn't have to mean dispensing with partnership. There are various, non-violent ways to break the mutually reinforcing connection between organisational design and culture, allowing a new culture to flourish alongside the traditional partnership model.

### 3.3 *Option 3: The 'wait and see' approach*

Between options 1 and 2, there is no right or wrong choice as long as it is conscious, considered and strategic. The third option, however – to sit back and do nothing – is unlikely to lead to success.

> *First movers win. That's the hard reality of the digital age. Our research is clear on this point ... Time and again we see companies that have taken a fast-follower strategy not be able to move fast enough.*[180]

The biggest threat for the firms that choose to do nothing is not, in fact, being left behind by their competitors; it is becoming disconnected from their clients. *Fortune* 500 and FTSE 100 companies are changing fast, and clients are already moving ahead of law firms, in their use of technology, in their exploitation of data, in their expectations of customer experience and in the diversity of their teams. In short, the culture of law firm clients is changing. If law firms do not change with them, the gulf between lawyer and client will increase, and the value of the traditional law firm partner as trusted business adviser will lose its currency.

## 4. Six structures that encourage cultural change

I examine six approaches below, each of which reflects a different way of influencing culture while respecting the partnership structure:

- acquisition;
- captive entity;
- intrapreneurship;
- incubation;
- spin-off; and
- international public offering (IPO).

### 4.1 The acquisition model

One way for incumbents to speed up the cultural change required for sustaining digital transformation is through 'inorganic growth': acquiring a business or a sizeable team with digital capabilities and integrating it into the existing business. This is an approach that McKinsey (itself a partnership) adopted when undergoing its own internal digital transformation. McKinsey consciously acquired digital start-ups with ways of working that were very different from the traditional consultancy arm. Rather than immediately fully integrating the start-ups into the culture of the firm, McKinsey allowed the start-ups to retain their own unique identity. The idea behind this approach is that, by a process of osmosis, the new culture that is represented by the start-up begins to filter through the walls of the legacy organisation, diluting the prevalent culture over time. This approach is not without its challenges. One Berlin-based McKinsey digital partner confided that both sides found the cultural clash uncomfortable at times, with tie-wearing consultants and bearded hipsters struggling to relate to each other.

Acquisition can offer a faster route to cultural change, particularly as incumbent organisations might struggle to attract the digital talent and skills necessary to transform the operating model more organically:

> [I]norganic growth has always played a role in helping organizations evolve their business model and find new sources of revenue. And that's true in the digital world as well. And quite frequently, we'll find particularly for incumbents, it can be long, difficult, and time-consuming to build the capabilities in house that they need. And the pace of change is such that digital M&A needs to play a role in transforming yourself to a business that's fit for purpose in this new world, particularly in one that ... is winner takes all.[181]

This approach has some precedent in the legal world, albeit at a much smaller scale. In July 2019, Simmons & Simmons, the UK-based international law firm, acquired Wavelength.law, a legal engineering firm regulated by the SRA.

**Case study: Simmons Wavelength, part of Simmons & Simmons**[182]

Drew Winlaw, partner and chief legal engineer at Simmons Wavelength, is a serial entrepreneur. Born in Australia, Drew trained in civil engineering and manufacturing management in Sydney and went on to work in manufacturing as a 'master production scheduler' – using data to guide which products the factory should make and when. It was in this role that Winlaw learned about the power of clean data, an area that still fascinates him today and is a big part of Simmons Wavelength's focus. Winlaw came to the United Kingdom just before the dot-com boom and worked for an internet start-up in London, developing and commercialising software products in the recruitment space (selling them as a service before SaaS was a thing). As part of his 'recovery' after the dot-com bubble burst, Winlaw retrained as a lawyer, completing his training contract with Taylor Vinters, where he went on to become a commercial and technology lawyer. Winlaw switched his focus to the untapped power of legal data and, after he had solved a data transparency issue for a tricky client, gained a reputation as a fixer. He was seconded to work for the managing partner, who encouraged him to seek out and solve problems in the business. Winlaw thrived in this role and made a number of positive changes – some of the systems and processes he created are still used in the firm today, including a system for 'gamifying' the matter-closing process.

Spotting an opportunity to apply these skills beyond Taylor Vinters, Winlaw and another lawyer at the firm, Peter Lee, left to establish Wavelength.law, the world's first regulated legal engineering business. Wavelength.law was acquired by international law firm Simmons & Simmons in July 2019 and became Simmons Wavelength, and both Lee and Winlaw are now equity partners at Simmons & Simmons.

Simmons Wavelength is a small (32-strong), truly multidisciplinary team of legal engineers (including legal design and legal knowledge engineers), lawyers, data scientists and legal operations specialists. Their mission is to build multidisciplinary teams that use legal data and process to unlock new value in delivering legal services. The approach, which Winlaw describes as 'agile-esque', is certainly very different from the traditional law firm way of working. The team works in small 'scrums', leveraging a mix of different skills. Depending on the area of focus, the scrum might include a data scientist, a solution owner (typically someone with a legal background), a developer and a couple of legal engineers, who act as 'translators and value creators', straddling the worlds of legal and technology and speaking the language of both. The scrum deliberately does not reflect the traditional law firm hierarchy; solution owners are not the 'leaders' of the scrum just because they have the deepest legal domain knowledge. The multidisciplinary teams in the scrum work as equals.

Simmons & Simmons' rationale for acquiring Wavelength is clear. At the time of acquisition back in 2019, Jeremy Hoyland, the managing partner, recognised that the firm needed the capabilities that Wavelength offered, and that it would take a long time to try to replicate those capabilities internally. Hoyland took the view that it was "easier to buy than build" the type of expertise Wavelength offered, adding, "There's a real shortage of talent in this area and if you try and build it organically, the chances of getting it wrong are pretty high."[183]

What was Wavelength's motivation for joining Simmons? According to Winlaw, the leadership team knew that there was a gap in the market for solving lots of separate issues where the market scale simply wouldn't justify a start-up to develop a point solution, but where significant needs existed and significant positive impact was still available through application of legal engineering principles. They knew they would need to partner in order to grow and to have greater strategic impact. The Simmons & Simmons leadership team, he says, was proactive in pursuing Wavelength and had a clear vision for how Wavelength could help the firm in the transformation of its client service delivery. This vision, combined with the "tantalising opportunity" to sit beside the legal teams as more than just a "supercharged business services department" – a fee-earning entity in its own right – made the proposition very attractive to Wavelength.

For Simmons, the acquisition was about more than access to skills and capabilities. One of the objectives was to effect cultural change within the firm.

Winlaw is pragmatic about the impact that Wavelength has had on the law firm culture so far. Change is definitely happening: "We are beginning to influence the mindset, and we are 30 people in an organisation of 1500." As expected, though, it is a healthy challenge. He likens the effort to a tug boat towing an oil tanker: "The tug boat is using a lot of energy, but it can't slow down – if we take our foot off the gas we could get run over." Success is felt by both sides when members of the Wavelength team sit beside the partners in client conversations and help to develop solutions that directly benefit delivery. Sometimes those solutions are matter-specific, for example, assisting with complex data analysis in a tax or litigation or a competition law context where Wavelength people contribute their skills to the matter on the same commercial basis as the people with legal skill. Winlaw describes that service line as "Law +".

The other key service line for Wavelength is 'productised services'. A productised service is neither a product (available to a client within five minutes of committing), or a service (the traditional high-touch legal services model), but something in between. It is a pattern of activities, many of which can be automated or supported by technology, with the most complex elements still performed by legal fee earners within a workflow.

Winlaw says these productised services will change the game in legal services because they can incorporate sophisticated risk management techniques, and also allow the work to be done by lawyers to be designed and optimised for accuracy and acceleration. As these services come to fruition, the lawyers, the legal engineers and the clients will see the positive impact.

Most law firms, however, are uncomfortable with acquisitions of this kind. Although a number of firms have hired data scientists or small teams with a particular digital skillset (for example, in February 2021 Freshfields Bruckhaus Deringer hired a team of four machine learning experts who had been part of the German legal tech start-up Rfrnz), very few firms have acquired what would be perceived as a sizeable business support team. For most traditional law firm partnerships, the effort and cost involved in acquiring and integrating a new team is only justifiable if it will immediately lead to the generation of new revenue – for example, the lateral hiring of a team of lawyers from a particular practice area that the firm wants to grow, who will bring their client base with them. In these cases, law firm partners will only vote to bring in the team if there is a clear cultural fit. There is, understandably perhaps, no appetite for lateral teams that will disrupt the prevailing culture.

Law companies and the Big 4, by contrast, are committed to acquisition as a means of achieving growth and cultural change. In 2019, pre-COVID-19, Elevate Services made no less than five acquisitions, building strength in legal advisory (acquiring Halebury, a UK-regulated law firm providing senior lawyer resource for corporate legal teams) and data science (acquiring LexPredict, a software and data solutions business), amongst other capabilities. EY Legal acquired Pangea3, a legal outsourcing services provider, and legal services firm Riverview Law, to create a legal managed services capability. More recently, in 2020, in a very interesting move, UnitedLex acquired a team from a law firm – Paul Hastings' DSAI team. And in January 2021 Deloitte Legal acquired Kemp, Little, a technology and digital media law firm.

The legal technology market is ripe for consolidation. Given the hunger of the competition and the capital to which they have access, law firms that are considering the acquisition model will need to move quickly and strategically to identify the best targets – before they disappear.

## 4.2 The captive model

The establishment of a captive delivery centre remains one of the most radical changes to the traditional law firm operating model that the industry has seen. Setting up a captive entity is now a tried and tested way for traditional law firm partnerships to offer a more cost-effective resourcing option to clients and to increase the firm's operational profitability. It is also a safe way of experimenting with cultural change, without challenging the partnership model.

As with all significant change in the legal industry, this trend was reactive and entirely client-led, a response to pressure from clients for their external counsel to deliver more efficiently and cost effectively. During the 2000s, clients became increasingly focused on obtaining value from external legal counsel, disaggregating legal work and giving it to the most cost-effective resource capable of delivering it, rather than paying top dollar for a full-service law firm to deliver end-to-end. Establishing a captive centre allowed firms to lower the cost of delivering commodity legal work (through labour arbitrage and real estate savings) and to carry on servicing all parts of a client mandate or case in a profitable way. The thinking behind the model had already been tested in other industries that had offshored their business processes, locating resources offshore or nearshore in locations that were more cost effective than legacy landmark City offices.

Orrick Herrington in the United States led the charge on this, long before the Magic Circle in the United Kingdom. Orrick's global centre was established in Wheeling, West Virginia way back in 2002. Clifford Chance was the first in the United Kingdom, establishing its knowledge centre in India in 2007.[184] Others followed: Allen & Overy in Belfast in 2012, Freshfields Bruckhaus Deringer in Manchester in 2015. At this time, the benefits of the model, from process efficiency to labour arbitrage and quality improvement were well understood. What was perhaps less well understood, certainly within the legal industry, was the potential of the captive centre to influence the culture of the legacy organisation. I remember attending a global shared services conference hosted by Deloitte in 2014, at which Rio Tinto's then head of global business services gave a presentation on how their shared service teams were using 'SMAC' (social, mobile, analytics and cloud – what we might refer to today as 'digital') to drive efficiency and a new agile culture of experimentation and innovation. As one of the few lawyers at the conference, this felt both strange and radical to me at the time (and seven years on, many law firms still have not woken up to the potential of these approaches to modernise delivery).

If a captive centre is designed well, and executed thoughtfully, it becomes a separate but connected structure in which an 'infectious' sub-culture can flourish. Ideally, this sub-culture should reflect all the best elements of the legacy culture, but also allow for an element of positive contagion, bringing fresh thinking back into the head office. Technology and innovation are also important parts of the picture. When law firms were first setting up captives, the world of legal tech was starting to take off. E-discovery platforms were already long established, but used exclusively for contentious work. New to the market were the start-ups offering solutions for transactional work; machine learning-enabled contract analysis software to help speed up and de-risk due diligence and other contract review exercises. The natural home for these new technology investments was in the law firm captive centres, where adoption would be much easier to achieve.

### Case study: Orrick Herrington & Sutcliffe[185]

Orrick Herrington & Sutcliffe opened its Global Operations and Innovation Centre (GIOC) in Wheeling, West Virginia in 2002. CIO Wendy Butler Curtis explained to me how the GIOC had matured over time, from a cost play based on labour arbitrage and process efficiency, handling mostly commoditised work, to a revenue-generating and client-facing hub of innovation. According to Wendy, one "unintended extraordinary benefit" of the GIOC was that it attracted to it a large number of high-quality business professionals from outside the world of legal. These professionals brought with them new approaches and skills that had not traditionally been part of the law firm world: making decisions based on data, for example, and a relentless focus on the customer. Bringing these talented professionals into one place gave them a support network and cultural value that is not often seen in a traditional law firm partnership. The 'non-lawyer' title, and the associated diminution in value that comes with it (see Chapter 8) were stripped away, and the GIOC became a beacon for a new way of working at Orrick.

The GIOC is now home to Orrick Analytics, a team of lawyers, statisticians, developers and structured data experts that supports both the transactional and litigation practices in document-heavy client engagements. Orrick Analytics operates as a separate business unit, independent of the GIOC, and the team have become fungible subject matter experts, forming part of the client teams on live matters to advise on the best technologies to apply and on how to price.

Wendy sees the GIOC and Orrick Analytics as having a significant influence on the culture of the firm. The teams' ability to go where the work is and to support matter teams in a fluid and flexible way means that they are more diverse, and consequently more successful. Although not conceived as a cultural experiment, the GIOC and the analytics team have penetrated the fabric of the legacy offices and had a positive cultural impact.

Establishing a captive is certainly not a cheap shortcut to cultural change and innovation. For a captive entity to impact culture in a positive way requires a significant investment of time and effort. In Orrick's case, the GIOC was established almost two decades ago, and has had plenty of time to mature and add value to the firm. The primary driver for a law firm in establishing a captive centre is likely to be cost savings and process efficiencies, rather than cultural experimentation.

## 4.3 The intrapreneurship model

Intrapreneurship, which involves establishing a digital or innovation team within the law firm itself, is a model that has been adopted by a number of law firms. The idea is to create a team made up of home-grown talent, to support both the client-facing and internal digital efforts of the firm. The team may combine lawyers (who have moved from practice to become legal engineers/product managers) and global technology professionals with an understanding of client expectations and how the lawyers work. From a cultural standpoint, the intrapreneur model aims to drive cultural change from the bottom up, by building on momentum and enthusiasm generated within the firm.

There are advantages and disadvantages to this model. On the one hand, this is a very safe option, and one that is unlikely to upset the firm's cultural balance. Because lawyers are more likely to listen to other lawyers, having individuals leading digital change who are known to the partnership helps with credibility and with navigating the inevitable law firm politics. As a number of the intrapreneurs will also have been practising lawyers at the firm, they will have insight into the firm's clients and ways of working. The team can use this insight to help in development of digital solutions, which in turn increases the likelihood of those solutions being adopted. Intrapreneurship breeds trust; lawyers are more likely to trust other lawyers in front of clients, and for digital transformation to be successful, proximity to clients is essential.

On the other hand, if the model feels too safe, it is probably insufficiently radical to drive real cultural change. The partner/associate relationship runs deep, and it is highly unusual for the apprentice to question the master. Intrapreneurs who have grown up as associates in a law firm can find it difficult to break out of the servant mentality and to challenge inefficient working practices, or suggest disruptive new models. Some law firms recognise this and use partner sponsorship as a kind of protective shield. This can work (much depends on the character and influence of the partner). It can also be a hindrance, preventing the team from achieving autonomy and earning respect and credibility on its own terms.

Creating an effective intrapreneur team is not easy. The team must strike a delicate balance between looking recognisable and credible to lawyers and modelling new ways of working and thinking. Location plays into this. Should the team be integrated but somehow visibly different (working in open plan, using different tooling, working in a visibly agile way)? Or should it be located outside the office in an

*From a cultural change perspective, keeping the team in the office works best. The team feels accessible, people can see what they are working on, and the team has ready access to the lawyers. However, from the team's perspective, shoehorning new ways of working into a legacy office environment does not always work.*

entirely new working environment? Approaches vary, and may depend on what the firm is trying to achieve from a cultural standpoint. I have worked with intrapreneur teams using both models. From a cultural change perspective, keeping the team in the office works best. The team feels accessible, people can see what they are working on, and the team has ready access to the lawyers. However, from the team's perspective, shoehorning new ways of working into a legacy office environment does not always work. For an intrapreneur team operating inside the law firm, where the very fabric of the building reflects the established order, radical change can feel unachievable. Working outside the office environment (for example, in a co-working space) can be very liberating for an intrapreneur team. It is, however, a less visible statement of cultural change.

The intrapreneur model is particularly effective for a law firm that is just starting its digital transformation. Trusted associates with credibility and legal domain knowledge can raise the profile of digital very effectively, and use their network to spread the word across practice groups and global offices. At Freshfields, when the innovation team was first formed, it was supported by a self-selecting global group of associates interested in doing things differently. They received training on what innovation and digital change really involve, helped to assess new solutions, and reported back on the client needs particular to their jurisdictions and on what competitors and clients were doing in the digital space. This worked very well for a year or so, and from this group emerged the future leaders of innovation in the firm.

The intrapreneurship model is difficult to sustain, unless the firm is committed to creating new career structures and rewards to support it. For intrapreneurship to flourish, the law firm must align the firm's and the team's incentives and be thoughtful and creative about career progression. Intrapreneurship requires committed funding, leadership and resource – it cannot be successful as an 'edge of desk' activity. If lawyers are to become product owners (see Chapter 4) they must be given the time and space to commit to the job, and should not combine this with fee earning. It is unreasonable to expect busy associates to commit time to innovation when they have a day job to do – especially when their bonus is tied to the hours they bill. Equally, a career framework is important to lawyers, who are used to the predictability of the law firm pyramid structure. For associates in a law firm, success is partnership – if this is not on the table, then the firm will need to get creative about reward structure if it is to retain this kind of talent. Similarly, technology professionals who are part of the intrapreneurship team and contributing to revenue-generating client-facing digital products are within their rights to expect different rewards than are available to those in more traditional, back-office IT roles. I discuss rewards, career incentives and people in more detail in Chapter 8.

### 4.4 The incubation model

Another approach to changing the established culture in a law firm partnership is incubation. Incubation involves a law firm giving early-stage start-ups space in the office to work and develop digital solutions (usually legal tech solutions), and access to the firm's lawyers and data to build and test MVPs. The firm may also decide to make a financial investment in the incubatee, or to license its software for use in the firm. The incubator model is symbiotic. The law firm:

- gains access to interesting start-ups;
- gets early sight of their technology solutions;
- bolsters its external reputation for experimentation; and
- is able to expose lawyers and clients to a different way of working in a safe and controlled way.

If the firm has office space to spare, incubation can also be very cost effective.

There is no shortage of big-name firms experimenting with this model, particularly in the United Kingdom, including Allen & Overy, Slaughter & May, Mishcon de Reya and Deloitte Legal. Outside the United Kingdom, Indian law firm Cyril Amarchand Mangaldas created Prarambh, India's first ever legal tech incubator in a law firm, in 2019, and Iberian firm Cuatrecasas has also established an incubator in Spain.

From a culture change perspective, the incubation model works by exposing lawyers (and their clients) to entirely new ways of working. Much depends on physical demonstration of the products – and the people working on them – with something of a 'show and tell' culture prevailing. For the model to impact the culture, a significant number of lawyers need to be exposed to what A&O refer to as the "entrepreneurs-in-residence".[186] Perhaps for this reason, the incubation model has its critics. Cynics see incubators as innovation theatre, goldfish bowls lacking real substance. Others note that a number of legal tech start-ups have simply moved from one law firm incubator to the next, which somewhat devalues the offerings. However, the model has survived remote delivery during COVID-19, with A&O's incubator, Fuse, now into its fifth cohort, and Mishcon de Reya's offering, MDR LAB, maturing into a series of three programmes for start-ups at different stages. Something must be working.

The MDR LAB, led by Nick West, the chief strategy officer at Mishcon de Reya, was founded in 2017 and has grown into a credible and highly professionalised offering. From a purely financial perspective, there have been some stellar successes to come out of the MDR LAB. One example is Time by Ping, an AI-powered timekeeping solution that learns from how individual lawyers work and automatically builds timesheets for review. At the end of 2019, Time by Ping raised $13.2 million in a Series A funding round and Mischon benefitted, having spotted the potential and invested in the start-up back in 2017. Success is not just about money, however; the cultural impact of MDR LAB has also been significant, as Nick West explained:

> *The reason we're doing this is to change the culture of this firm. Success will look like this: lots of Mishcon lawyers working with lots of start-ups and realising tech can do things differently. That's what the LAB's about.*[187]

Incubation is not as simple as opening up the basement to a bunch of start-ups and installing a coffee machine. It requires ongoing commitment. For incubation to be successful in influencing the culture of a law firm partnership, it needs experienced leadership and significant investment and resource. Both A&O and Mishcon have a reputation as highly innovative law firms that have developed a number of digital offerings as part of a holistic firmwide strategy. Incubation is unlikely to have cultural impact as a standalone initiative. Incubators are also uniquely of their time. As the legal technology market matures and consolidates, it is possible that incubation may lose its cultural impact.

### 4.5 The spin-off model

A spin-off is a new entity that is independent of the law firm, but is wholly or partially owned by the partnership and continues to provide services to it. A spin-off will have its own distinct management structure, name and branding, but will remain connected to the parent brand in a number of ways. For example, the new entity will usually be managed by employees who were formerly part of the partnership and will often depend on the partnership for technology and other business support.

The spin-off is not a common model amongst law firms. Some have experimented with it (and there are rumours that more law firms will soon follow suit) – but it is still pretty edgy. It reflects a maturity of approach that is not (yet) common amongst law firm partnerships and is more likely to be employed by firms with a clear innovation strategy and a product mindset – generally those who are further along in their digital transformation.

From a cultural perspective, this model gives the new entity autonomy to develop a new product, service or way of working, while retaining a close association with the partnership. A new entity that still bears the law firm brand can attract new digital talent, and the separation from the partnership can provide an alternative career structure and remuneration model for those interested in digital product development.

**Case study: Kennedys**[188]
Kennedys is an international law firm with a strong UK presence, and particular expertise in insurance and reinsurance. With 2,300+

people globally, of whom 290 are partners, and global revenues that increased to £264 million in 2020/21, Kennedys is a very successful mid-market firm. It also has a reputation as one of the more innovative and progressive law firm partnerships.

Kennedys is one of a small number of firms successfully developing and commercialising client-facing digital products. The product suite comprises a number of solutions to automate and manage the insurance claims process. There are a number of component products in the Kennedys IQ platform, including Defence Lawyer, previously known as KLAiM, a web-based platform that enables clients' claim handlers to have access to Kennedys' claims expertise. The platform aggregates the lawyers' expertise into guidance notes, uses it to populate automated template documents, and overlays a simple workflow to guide the client through the litigation process. The beauty of the solution, from a client perspective, is that the tool disaggregates the lawyer – speeding up the process, lowering costs and reducing reliance on face time.

This could be a difficult sell to a partnership in which insurance claims management is a core service. Yet Richard West, head of the liability division at Kennedys and the force behind its innovation group, has always been entirely up front with the partnership about his objectives. For West, the principle that underlies Kennedys' product development is that products should enable clients to reduce their dependence on their lawyers. According to West, developing a digital product is no different from providing clients with a copy of a legal textbook. Clients can become "addicted" to their lawyers, and it is not sustainable to continue to charge for a service that does not need human legal advice.

Although not everyone in the partnership was initially supportive of this principle, as West's practice continued to grow it became clear that digital products were meeting a genuine client need. Not only was West's approach creating client stickiness, it was also leading to the firm winning new work.

I asked West about commercialisation. Pricing is a real challenge in an industry that is used to a time and materials model, particularly as so few law firms actually develop and sell digital products. Neither partners nor clients really know where to start. West told me about the early days of developing Kennedys' first product, on a shoestring budget in what he refers to as "after school club", with one part-time developer. The team provided the first product free to their client – and then, once successfully embedded and used, asked that client how much they would have been prepared to pay. This was the starting point. As product development became more sophisticated and the team more experienced, the firm adopted a standardised approach. The client will be charged a small percentage of the overall saving (the efficiency) that the product delivers.

Transparency has paid dividends. In February of 2020 Kennedys launched Kennedys IQ, a technology and services spin-off. The new entity, wholly owned by the LLP, is led by a team made up of the former heads of IT and R&D and innovation at Kennedys, with the senior partner and West on the board; it has over 30 employees, houses all Kennedys' digital products and is tasked with developing further client-facing technology solutions.

The primary driver of the spin-off was a cultural one. Developing software products within a law firm partnership is not easy, and even for the most sophisticated law firm there is likely to be a clash between the product mindset and the traditional services mindset. West explained that the kind of digital talent he wanted to attract to the product team was not incentivised by the distant promise of becoming an equity partner. In addition, West recognised that the talent he needed to help him grow the business was very different in terms of skills and experience from the talent that sits in the law firm. Kennedys formed a strategic delivery partnership with a 12-strong development team in Kerala, India, who they wanted to bring into the firm – but the partnership structure would not work for them. The team has now been successfully subsumed into Kennedys IQ, incentivised through payment of bonuses based on a percentage of the revenues generated by the products they develop.

The other cultural consideration was client related. Feedback from clients confirmed that they were not entirely happy buying their software products from the same place as their legal services. Clients wanted to avoid a situation in which the client chose to switch provider of legal services but still wanted access to the digital toolkit. It became clear that for the product team to be sustainable, it needed to become autonomous. West put it like this in an interview with *Legal Business*:

> *The LLP model is tried and tested for delivering law services, it's not tried and tested for delivering technology and software services.*[189]

### 4.6 The IPO

The most radical model of all involves dispensing with the partnership entirely and becoming a listed company through an IPO. Six UK law firms have to date taken this route, the largest of which is DWF (in fact at the time of writing DWF is the largest law firm in the world to have gone public). COVID-19 may have forced other firms to delay their IPO ambitions; certainly Mishcon de Reya was rumoured to be considering flotation before the pandemic upended the markets.[190]

DWF became the first law firm to list on the London Stock Exchange's main market in March 2019, raising £95 million at a valuation of £366 million.[191] In the years before it went public, DWF had been growing rapidly and building a firm made up of three businesses: a law firm giving high-end legal advice in the traditional way; a managed legal services business delivering more process-oriented legal work; and DWF Connected Services, providing services adjacent to legal services. Culturally, it was already far removed from the traditional law firm partnership model, with a digital agenda and a hunger for expansion into new products and services. Andrew Leaitherland, then managing partner and CEO of DWF, stated in an interview with the *Financial Times* that the firm saw itself as "a legal business rather than a law firm", adding that one of the drivers for the IPO was improved employee engagement (and, of course, the access to capital for technology investment).[192] After going public, DWF used some of the proceeds to acquire the legal outsourcing group Mindcrest for £14.2 million in January 2020.

It is easy to see why a firm such as DWF might choose to float. If a firm is growing quickly and has a strong digital agenda, as was the case with DWF, securing the investment for that digital initiative can be challenging in a traditional partnership structure. Partnerships looking to raise capital can only do so through a capital call (asking the partners to contribute money) or by borrowing. If the firm is looking to raise a substantial amount of money to fund acquisitions, an IPO is the best option.

From a cultural perspective, a law firm IPO amounts to a complete disruption of the traditional law firm partnership model. Following the DWF IPO, partners became employees as well as shareholders, drawing a fixed salary and receiving a dividend, and were subject to a salary cut of some 60%. Decision making became a formal shareholder matter, and the partners no longer had collective control over law firm operational matters. But perhaps the most striking impact of an IPO is on the traditional distinction between lawyers and 'non-lawyers'. The board of a listed company and its executive may well contain individuals who are not revenue-generating lawyers – and these individuals will receive the highest remuneration. This is a radical cultural change that strikes at the fundamentals of the hierarchy.

Is an IPO the natural route for a highly innovative firm that is looking to digitally transform? So far, the most profitable firms, at the top of the league tables, have not publicly expressed interest in the model. Firms that want to grow quickly, to move into new services and products adjacent to legal delivery and which have a digital agenda, are the best and most likely candidates for an IPO. However, as with any decision in a partnership, consensus will be required to push it through. It took 18 months of complex negotiation within the partnership and an alleged £20 million to get DWF to the point of listing. This is an expensive and drawn-out process and can put significant strain on the management team.

It is too early to assess the financial success of DWF's move, and the impact the IPO has had on the culture of the firm. There have certainly been some bumps in the road. DWF's share price fell dramatically during the UK lockdown, from a high of 143p to a low of 64p. The fall was attributed to both a decline in revenues and high borrowings. Then, at the end of May 2020, the then-CEO Andrew Leaitherland was ousted from the board to be replaced by Sir Nigel Knowles, the former chair.

Sceptics in the legal industry see DWF's current issues as reflective of the inherent incompatibility between law firms and the listed model. These sceptics see the listed model as too risky for a law firm to adopt, with the conflicting interests of partners and outside investors putting too much pressure on a fragile construct. Alex Novarese, former editor of *Legal Business*, is not optimistic about the model's future for law firms:

> [T]here is no getting around the fact that floating a law firm is a risky business, with uncertain rewards at the best of times. The notion of listed law firms redefining the UK legal market is now effectively dead for a decade, at the very least.[193]

## 5. Choosing the right model

How should a law firm decide on the right structure to drive cultural change and sustain digital transformation in its own organisation? Each of the models in this chapter are appropriate for a different level of digital maturity. You might think of it as a spectrum, with creating a captive entity at one end and spinning off a product business, or going public, at the other. Although there is not necessarily a linear path that law firms should follow, it would be unusual for a law firm to dive straight into building and spinning off a technology business, or making acquisitions without having established any in-house digital capability.

Law firms looking to start their digital journey should consider how adopting alternative structures will help to realise the overarching digital transformation strategy. There is no right approach; it will depend on a number of factors, including the firm's overarching business strategy and the clients it serves (or aspires to serve). For example, law firms with a large financial services or regulatory practice may want to consider incubation of fintech or regtech start-ups. Law firms who advise (or aspire to advise) large technology, telecommunications and media clients may want to grow their understanding of the sector through taking an equity share in legal tech start-ups. Firms who are focused on the digital literacy of their lawyers may want to establish an internal innovation capability to drive internal improvements. All these approaches are valid, provided they are made consciously as part of a wider strategy, and the firm is rigorous in assessing the return on investment.

## 6. Structuring for success

Digital transformation is a continuous process, not a project with a beginning and an end, and sustaining the change requires a cultural reset. This chapter has examined the relationship between organisational structure and culture in the context of the traditional law firm model. Although the partnership model has certain strengths, it is not culturally well adapted for digital change. Law firms have three options: to do nothing, to specialise or to become more digitally effective and commit to the cultural change that is required to make change stick. Firms that choose to embrace digital transformation do not need to break the partnership model; they will, however, need to be creative in adopting alternative structures that can create the right environment for cultural change to flourish.

The next chapter considers the second of the three Ps – people. ■

# Chapter 8: Sustaining change – people

## 1. Law firms are people businesses

*In most businesses a company's competitive advantage does not rely directly on the retention, motivation, and behavior of particular individuals. Instead, it turns on shelf space, brand strength, cost position, distribution systems, price, technology, product design, location, or any number of other variables that can exist apart from the individuals who created them. So except in the long term, most companies' profit performance does not necessarily correlate with their 'people assets'.*

*Not so for professional service firms. These firms depend not just on 'people assets', but on stars.*[194]

This quote is from a book written by Jay Lorsch and Thomas Tierney in 2002. *Aligning the Stars* is one of the seminal analyses of the relationship between culture, people and strategy in professional services organisations. A former (and brilliant) managing partner at

Freshfields insisted that everyone involved in firm strategy read the book – and it formed the basis of workshops he would deliver for senior associates and business function leaders. At the time, I considered myself too busy fee-earning to engage with 'strategy' (one of the challenges that the book itself highlights), so didn't give it the attention it deserved. The book must have made an impression on me, though, as I was drawn to re-read it as I was thinking about the people element of law firm culture.

*Aligning the Stars* harks back to a pre-digital era, when top graduates were vying to work for professional services firms. At that time, law firms paid the most, provided the best training, and created a path either to lucrative partnership or to a stellar career in-house. The authors write at length about the tension between serving clients and attending to 'stars' (high-performing partners), arguing that "the people you pay are more important than the people that pay you"[195] and that the emphasis should be "stars first, clients second, firm third"[196] – an extraordinary statement to our client-centric ears in 2021. Anachronisms aside, the main argument of *Aligning the Stars* still resonates. Its thesis is that professional services organisations are uniquely dependent on their best people (their stars), and vulnerable to the economic consequences of those stars leaving the partnership. This vulnerability informs and shapes the people culture of a law firm partnership.

It says a lot about the speed of change in law firms that cultural observations made in a book written 18 years ago still hold true today. To sustain digital transformation – indeed, to sustain any type of organisational change – you need the right people, thinking and working in the right way. In traditional law firm partnerships, the 'right' people means the best technical lawyers, with the best grades, from the best schools, who look the part. Attracting the right people to a large and successful corporate law firm has, historically, never been a problem. The opportunity to become one of the stars used to be a very compelling proposition. The predictable, rigid structure of the law firm pyramid put partners, with their deep legal expertise and their longstanding client relationships, firmly at the top. The lockstep, with its promise of huge financial rewards in return for tenure, provided scaffolding for the structure. Associates were willing to work ludicrously hard in order to be admitted into the club. All this worked very well in the analogue business world.

Times are changing, slowly. Working as a lawyer in a global elite law firm remains a very attractive and well-remunerated career proposition, but arguably does not have the cachet it did 20 years ago. There is now significantly more competition to recruit the brightest and best, particularly from technology companies and high-end consultancy firms. Today's graduates are demanding more from their careers than the graduates of the past – more balance, a sense of purpose, opportunities to progress more quickly through the ranks. Most law firms have not yet woken up to this. Many partners still believe that the carrot of partnership is sufficient to attract the best people to the firm and, as discussed elsewhere in this book, law firms are not always sufficiently creative in rethinking organisational structure to respond to changing employee expectations in a digital world. Add to this a culture of lawyer exceptionalism that prizes technical legal skills above all else, and undervalues the professional credentials of non-lawyers. This has the potential to be a real issue, both for the law firm employment proposition in the future and for law firms' ability to become more digitally effective. In this chapter, we look at the intersections between successful digital transformation, people and culture in law firms, and the work that needs to be done to address the disconnect.

## 2. The law firm people problem

From a digital transformation perspective, traditional law firm partnerships have a people problem. The reassuring rigidity of the partnership structure and the long tenure of professionals in law firms have created a false sense of security, and people issues have not been given the attention they urgently require. This has, in turn, created some significant cultural challenges that will need to be addressed if law firms are to become more digitally effective.

*Diversity should arguably be the law firm's highest people priority, even more urgent than hiring the right digital professionals.*

These challenges run deep, and the consequences go way beyond a negative impact on digital change. Throughout this book, we have observed that many of the cultural attributes required to be a digitally effective organisation are those we might associate with a 'good' or healthy corporate culture. This is particularly true when applied to people and talent. Successful digital businesses think carefully about their employee value proposition, and craft it to appeal to the very best people. This means:

- meaningful and flexible career paths;
- an organisation with a clear purpose (beyond just making money);
- a deliberately diverse and inclusive culture;
- an engaging and modern workspace (or virtual/remote workspace) which supports multidisciplinary ways of working;
- clear strategy and objectives, with rewards and incentives which align to that strategy; and
- a culture of transparency around management information.

Most traditional law firm partnerships have a lot of work to do to get close to this ideal.

In this chapter, we look at law firm people through two different lenses:
- who law firms hire; and
- what law firms reward.

## 3. Who law firms hire

### 3.1 The lawyers

As noted throughout this book, successful digital transformation in law firms requires a multidisciplinary approach, with lawyers and other professionals working together to define and deliver the very best client experience. One response to this challenge is to recruit lots of new ('non-lawyer') people with digital skills and throw them into the law firm mix. This is not sufficient to address what is perhaps the most fundamental cultural issue of all – the profile of the lawyers law firms choose to employ, and how they treat and train them.

Diversity should arguably be the law firm's highest people priority, even more urgent than hiring the right digital professionals.

One characteristic of the law firm partnership model is a "homogeneity of human capital".[197] One of the reasons that consensus-based decision making in a decentralised model is able to work is because of a high incidence of peer control. This is made possible by all the partners in the firm being from similar backgrounds, with similar education and training, similar values and similar ambitions. You can trust your fellow partners to make the right decisions because they walk, talk and think like you. This is another example of organisational design influencing culture; traditional law firms are insufficiently diverse, because for the operational model of the law firm partnership to work, it requires conformity.

The 'homogeneity of human capital' amongst the lawyers in a law firm is a problem on many levels. There is plenty of evidence that diversity makes for better business, and that multidisciplinary and agile teams are more productive – but this evidence does not seem to be resonating with law firms. To give a sense of the scale of the issue, you need only look at the most recent diversity statistics within law firm partnerships. The SRA regularly monitors and reports on diversity statistics for UK law firms. The most recent data collection was in 2019, and the most recent report was issued in March 2020.[198] The results are unsurprising, and depressing. In firms with 50-plus partners, 50% of the lawyers are women. However when it comes to the percentage of female partners in the same group, that drops to an average of 29% (no change since 2017). Of the 'non-lawyer' staff working in a law firm (those that I would argue are the most disenfranchised), 75% are female. The statistics show that the proportion of black, Asian and minority ethnic (BAME) lawyers working in law firms is 21% (no change since 2017). On its face, this number does not look too bad, given that in 2018, government figures on employment showed that 13% of the workforce in England, Scotland and Wales was BAME. However, the SRA report notes that:

*[D]ifferences become apparent when we look at the breakdown of partners in firms by size. Both black and Asian lawyers are*

*significantly underrepresented in mid to large size firms (those with six or more partners). The largest firms (50 plus partners) have the lowest proportion of BAME partners – only 8% (no change since 2017).*[199]

When you start to look at social mobility, the statistics are even more depressing. Of the general UK population, 7% attend a fee-paying school. In firms that "mainly do corporate law", the SRA statistics indicate that the number is 54%.[200]

What are we to make of this? It is clear that large corporate law firms in the United Kingdom, despite all their money and influence, are doing a woeful job of achieving better diversity, particularly when it comes to partners. The picture in the United States is not much better:

*According to most surveys, at large U.S. law firms, only about 20% of full equity partners are women, and only about 8 or 9% are underrepresented minorities. Indeed, the data suggest that the largest 200 firms in the country as a group will not reach 50% women and 33% racial and ethnic minorities in their equity partner ranks – which would mirror the composition of recent law school graduating classes – for at least another 50 years.*[201]

Many law firms have made a public commitment to diversity and inclusion and some even have departments dedicated to achieving better balance. Yet execution continues to fall short. While I was writing this book, on 25 May 2020, George Floyd was killed in a racially motivated homicide while in police custody in Minneapolis. The default response of law firms to this horrific event would usually have been to stay silent, classifying it as a political matter on which they should remain neutral. But this blatantly racist act of murder demanded a response. Not to speak out, to hide behind 'strategic colour-blindness',[202] could be interpreted as condoning the atrocity. General counsel at a number of corporations made statements of support, the president of the US Minority Corporate Counsel Association, Jean Lee, noting:

*General counsels are making more statements. Companies are trying to do better, trying to do more because they're concerned about not only their own shareholder value but the broader global impact. What does it mean to be a good corporate citizen these days?*[203]

As corporate clients spoke out, law firms tried to step up. However, perhaps because of their poor record on diversity, law firms struggled to find words that would not sound hollow or to commit to meaningful action on which they could actually deliver.

The pressure shows no sign of abating. Diversity in law firms continues to be an issue, from both an internal business and client perspective. Clients, particularly in the United States, are increasingly demanding that law firms be transparent about the levels of diversity in their organisations and are refusing to appoint to their panels firms that are not sufficiently diverse and inclusive. In 2019, Intel, stating publicly that it could not "abide the current state of progress" of diversity in law firms, announced a new rule – the 'Intel Rule':

*Beginning Jan. 1, 2021, Intel will not retain or use outside law firms in the U.S. that are average or below average on diversity. Firms are eligible to do legal work for Intel only if, as of that date and thereafter, they meet two diversity criteria: at least 21% of the firm's U.S. equity partners are women and at least 10% of the firm's U.S. equity partners are underrepresented minorities (which, for this purpose, we define as equity partners whose race is other than full white/Caucasian, and partners who have self-identified as LBGTQ+, disabled or as veterans).*[204]

This rule holds US law firms to a high standard. They must demonstrate above-average diversity in order to be retained by Intel. Other corporates outside the United States have followed suit. In April 2020, BT, after slashing its panel from 40 firms to 15, announced that as an incentive to firms to improve diversity, the firm with the best diversity and inclusion score for the duration of the panel would be automatically reappointed.[205] Novartis, the Swiss pharmaceutical company, has taken similar steps with its panel. Law firms have had to sign up to a commitment that 30% of associate time and 20% of partner time will be billed by female, racially diverse or LGTBQ lawyers. Failure to achieve this will come with a financial penalty: Novartis will withhold 15% of the fees for a matter where the team does not make the diversity grade.[206]

This is another example of law firms not listening to their clients. To those outside the legal industry it must seem extraordinary that customers are having to push their legal services suppliers so hard to reflect the real world. Intel first called for law firms to improve their diversity back in 2004; we are 17 years on, and it should be a source of shame to law firms that progress has remained so incredibly slow. For those of us that have worked in the industry for many years, however, this does not come as a surprise. Law firms are glacial in their pace of change. The client voice is one of the few levers for driving transformation, but even that takes a long time to filter through the system, particularly when the very organisational structure of the firm is geared towards conformity and preserving the status quo.

Pushing for greater diversity is of course objectively the 'right' thing to do, but GCs are not just doing this out of a sense of social justice. Diversity is important because it is good for business, as Bradley Gayton, former GC of Coca-Cola, recognised in an open letter written to the company's external counsel in early 2021:

> [W]e believe that diversity of talent on our legal matters is a critical factor to driving better business outcomes.[207]

If law firm clients can recognise this, why does it seem so difficult for law firms themselves to accept? The explanation leads us back to the partnership model, which works much more effectively if people think the same way – and people are more likely to think like you if they look like you and have shared your privilege.

Law firms need to focus on the evidence. There is plenty of research showing that organisations that are committed to diversity perform better than those that are not. McKinsey has been researching this

*The events of 2020 and into 2021 – a global pandemic, Brexit, a mob storming the Capitol, deep racial unrest, a global recession – show how crucial it is for all businesses to be able to adapt to changing circumstances and shifting customer needs.*

topic since 2015, and its most recent report, issued in May 2020, "Diversity Wins: How inclusion matters", draws some striking conclusions. The underlying research, involving more than 1,000 large companies in 15 countries, found that:

> [C]ompanies in the top quartile of gender diversity on executive teams were 25 percent more likely to experience above-average profitability than peer companies in the fourth quartile. This is up from 21 percent in 2017 and 15 percent in 2014.
>
> [...]
>
> In the case of ethnic and cultural diversity, the findings are equally compelling. We found that companies in the top quartile outperformed those in the fourth by 36 percent in terms of profitability in 2019, slightly up from 33 percent in 2017 and 35 percent in 2014.[208]

These profitability metrics should be difficult to ignore, showing as they do that successful businesses are diverse businesses. Although the McKinsey research does not explore in depth the correlation between diversity, profitability, and digitisation, it does reference the fact that organisations that are committed to diversity and inclusion are also more likely to be innovative and customer-centric:

> [D]iverse teams have been shown to be more likely to radically innovate and anticipate shifts in consumer needs and consumption patterns – helping their companies to gain a competitive edge.[209]

Never has it been more important to be an adaptive organisation. The events of 2020 and into 2021 – a global pandemic, Brexit, a mob storming the Capitol, deep racial unrest, a global recession – show how crucial it is for all businesses to be able to adapt to changing circumstances and shifting customer needs. This level of volatility appears to be a new standard. A diverse workforce is a part of the toolkit that enables businesses to adapt and change in a sustainable way.

### 3.2 The digital professionals

One of the defining elements of successful digital transformation is the ability to attract and retain people with the right digital skills. In an environment that is relentlessly fast moving, where digital transformation is shaping business strategy, access to the best digital talent is crucial. The companies that law firms serve, the majority of which are busy working on their own digital transformations, will be acutely aware of the importance of attracting and retaining world-class professionals to deliver the change:

> *It's not surprising that the talent issue causes anxiety in the C-Suite. A McKinsey study of more than 300 senior leaders in the industrial sector identified 'capability and talent management' as the area where the gap between expected impact and business readiness was largest ... Only 27% of respondents to a separate McKinsey survey, for example, said that they had access to talent with the right skill sets to support AI work.*[210]

The approach to digital talent acquisition and retention that we see in digitally native organisations, or incumbents that have committed to a digital agenda, is far more sophisticated than we see in most law firm partnerships. Law firms are very good at identifying legal talent, but do not apply the same focus to hiring people to transform and run their business. For many law firm partners, 'digital' is simply something that the IT teams do. Most partners will never have worked outside the legal sector; many will only ever have worked in one law firm. Absent a frame of reference, is it any wonder that law firms don't really know what they are looking for?

> *Getting digital talent on board is difficult enough, given the shortage of supply in a white-hot market. But it can be harder still to identify the right talent in the first place. If you don't know what 'good' looks like, where do you begin?*[211]

### 3.3 The changing role of the law firm HR function

As digital becomes a key driver of strategy, the global technology department has to upskill, developing new capabilities that move it from a 'computer says no' operational department to a core strategic function with a seat at the board table. The HR function is just as critical to successful transformation. In the past, HR (in Big Law in particular) has had a relatively easy time of it. When markets are buoyant, there is no shortage of legal talent keen to work at a firm with an established reputation. The talent pool has been deep. Career paths have historically been clear and well charted. Pay scales are pretty much defined and well understood. Historically, the role of the HR director in a law firm was to keep a hand on the tiller, keeping the ship steady as she goes.

This is also changing. There is pressure on law firm HR teams from all quarters:

- to improve and demonstrate better diversity;
- to keep a lid on the #MeToo issues that bubble under the surface of many law firms;
- to plaster over cultural cracks created by a hierarchical partnership structure;
- to rethink career pathways and incentives as changing models for client delivery demand the creation of new skills and capabilities; and
- to redefine an employee value proposition for millennials and Generation Z.

HR needs to step up and become a true business partner to the technology/digital teams, creating the right environment and culture to allow digital transformation to take hold and flourish. For digital transformation to be sustained, HR teams need to take the lead in pushing law firm leaderships to rethink hiring strategies and reward structures. Given the demand for digital skills (and the fact that law firms are not particularly attractive propositions for digital talent), HR teams need to be agile and able to move fast to find, onboard and retain the best.

Organisations that do this well take the following actions:

- They hire digital stars (from outside the industry).
- They transform HR processes.

- They provide meaningful and flexible career paths.
- They provide an engaging work environment.
- They are clear and authentic in outlining purpose and mission.

*(a) Digital stars*

A skilled recruiter can of course help to identify good candidates. However, this is only part of the challenge. Lawyers are often sceptical about the professional capabilities of anyone who is not a lawyer (see the discussion of 'non-lawyers' below), and consequently may not recognise that really talented digital stars are as valuable to the business as rainmakers – and that they will expect to be remunerated accordingly. Talented transformation professionals will also expect a degree of autonomy and professional respect commensurate with their experience and contribution to the business. This may require law firms to rethink their reward structure and career framework – and to revisit the talismanic 'partner' title, particularly if the firm wants to retain professionals for the longer term. This is from Melissa Swift, formerly senior client partner, global leader, digital transformation advisory at Korn Ferry, the organisational consulting and recruitment firm:

> *The average tenure of digital workers today is barely 36 months, and shrinking. Tenure for the best is shorter still. For the most important contributors, establish longer-term incentives that will help keep them.*[212]

Unlike other business professionals working in law firms in the past, the best digital leaders are in high demand and tend to move on much more regularly, in search of new challenges. Retention requires thought and effort. Of course, talent attracts more talent, and law firms that invest in really high-quality leadership will find it much easier to build the right teams:

> *[A] handful of recognized star performers with the right skills and experience can have an immediate and disproportionate impact on the transformation ... You will need to pay a hefty premium for these rock stars. But the very best people will be well worth the price. In transformations, a core of exceptional talent acts as a nucleus that will ignite change.*[213]

Finding digital professionals also requires a mindset change for the firm. When recruiting into 'support' roles for a traditional law firm partnership, the job description has invariably required prior experience of working in a law firm. It is easy to understand why; a highly profitable organisation that is looking to build on its success in a steady and incremental way does not want employees who are going to rock the boat, certainly not in support roles. I have seen many talented new recruits, who were unaccustomed to the law firm hierarchy, trying to make an impact and being misunderstood (or simply ignored), until they decided to leave or were asked to leave. Communicating with the partnership in the 'wrong' way, or crossing one of the invisible political lines that are a characteristic of complex matrix-structured organisations, can be fatal. For this reason, change in a law firm partnership has historically had to be achieved by stealth, led by individuals who understand the political levers and hierarchical dynamics of the firm. As discussed in Part 1 of this book, the problem with this approach is that it takes a long time – and time is now at a premium.

Law firms should actively look outside the legal industry to find digital professionals who have successfully lead transformations in other sectors. Once they have brought in these digital stars, it is equally important that law firms embrace the fresh perspective and the energy that these individuals can bring to the firm, rather than forcing them to conform to the status quo.

Even the most established institutions are taking this approach. London's Natural History Museum, founded in 1881, is a good example. When visitor numbers started to decline, the museum made an active choice to shift to a more sustainable digital model. The museum is currently embarking on an ambitious project to digitise its 80 million specimens – everything from meteorites to pinned insects.[214] This process, involving 3D scanning and imaging of specimens, has already resulted in new discoveries – a scan of an anglerfish specimen has revealed another fish in the specimen's stomach, and yet another inside that fish, leading to new insights about the deep ocean. The museum is also committed to providing a best-in-class digital experience for its visitors. Piers Jones, who sadly died from cancer in early 2020, was the first chief digital and product officer at the museum. Jones, who built the team from scratch, had no previous experience in museum curation and was not a scientist, having worked at Amazon video and *The Guardian*'s digital business before his move to the Natural History Museum. The museum is not an organisation that one would associate with digital product development, but Jones introduced a product mindset and recruited user experience teams, all in an attempt to challenge the museum's legacy thinking. The fresh approach that Jones imported into the museum was the key to the success of the digital programme. In an interview in April 2019, Jones explained his inspiration:

*As a team we are constantly inspired by those around us, whether that's by other cultural and scientific institutions like the V&A or Calacademy, other public sector providers like GDS (Government Digital Service) or companies in 'adjacent' sectors like media and publishing, for example The Guardian and BBC. We don't have a monopoly on good ideas and share what we find all the time on Slack and so on. On the whole I think we take the most inspiration from other purpose-driven organisations that are approaching their digital strategies with a goal of engaging with broad audiences in a free and open way, just like us.*[215]

Jones also explained the importance of recruiting the right digital talent:

*We've been incredibly lucky at the museum to build a very talented digital team who come from a diverse mix of backgrounds and experiences. I'm constantly inspired by the team and the passion that they have for working at the museum and how much care they put into creating a great digital future. We have put a lot of work into our hiring process and how best to involve a wide range of the team in hiring so that we can find the best people.*[216]

If an institution like the Natural History Museum can achieve this, then so can a traditional law firm partnership.

Why would a digital star be attracted to working in a law firm at all? Many would argue that the best CDTOs would only consider working in a technology company, or in a FTSE 100 or the equivalent. Law firm HR and marketing teams will need to work hard to make sure that the law firm brand is positioned to attract the best digital talent. This is not simply a question of money; talented digital people want to be able to learn and progress, and to work in a collaborative and supportive culture. The culture and the mission will be critical to attracting the best people:

> Money matters, of course. Top talent demands top dollar. But other features matter a lot as well – and sometimes even more. Top engineers, for example, cite exposure to technologies and opportunities for professional development to be among the primary reasons for choosing an organisation. Korn Ferry research shows how culture has shot to the top of the list of reasons why a candidate chooses a particular company.[217]

The HR function has an important role to play in building digital talent at the senior level, from identifying digital stars to working to integrate them into the partnership structure quickly so that they can be successful.

### (b) HR processes

Recruiting digital talent requires a rethink of traditional processes. In many organisations, including law firms, the recruitment and onboarding process is bureaucratic and painfully slow. A process that takes six months is simply too long for the digital world, where speed of movement is key.

Sophisticated digital organisations address this issue by creating new approaches to cut through the red tape. Some even establish a 'digital talent war room', supported by a recruitment team dedicated to designing a really compelling employee value proposition. For law firms that are just beginning to think about digital change, and are not recruiting at scale, a more pragmatic approach might be to upskill a member of the HR team to focus exclusively on digital, or to partner with a recruitment firm that

*In many firms, insufficient attention is given to shaping meaningful career paths for those referred to as the 'non-lawyers'.*

specialises in digital. To move at speed, teams will need to cut through the bureaucracy that surrounds the onboarding process. To achieve this requires senior leadership support and a calibrated approach to risk management. This can be challenging in a traditional law firm environment, where due diligence on potential employees is given a high degree of importance, for obvious reasons. These issues need to be addressed, with risk balanced against the downside of losing the best candidates because of a process fraught with friction.

### (c) Meaningful and flexible career paths

The predictability and rigidity of the law firm pyramid can impact career progression for all employees. In many firms, insufficient attention is given to shaping meaningful career paths for those referred to as the 'non-lawyers'. The situation for the lawyers is not much better; new approaches to career progression are rarely considered, with the historic model (trainee – associate – senior associate – counsel – partner), and the culture of 'up or out' still prevailing. As client demands shift and hybrid skills become more important to client-facing delivery, HR leadership needs to focus on these issues.

Many law firms have lawyers who want to become digital professionals, either by moving entirely out of fee earning or by moving to a hybrid role, combining traditional fee earning with work that supports new ways of delivering to clients. In firms where there is no formal home for these skills, associates (and sometimes partners) can find themselves a lone voice in the wilderness, caught between the pressures of fee earning and 'edge of desk' innovation projects. In firms that follow the intrapreneur model, these associates often find their way to the innovation team or its equivalent. These teams are rarely large or mature enough to provide meaningful career progression options. This is a wasted opportunity. Lawyers who have hybrid skills, combining deep client knowledge, legal subject matter expertise and the ability to think creatively about delivery are rare and highly valuable. To retain these lawyers should be a high priority, but the rigidity of the law firm structure does not support a balance between fee earning and innovating. For lawyers who straddle the two camps, billable hour targets make contribution to digital change career limiting. Those who move permanently into a new hybrid role can feel lost and exposed; having always had a clear career path within the firm, suddenly they cannot see how to progress. This is a sure-fire way for a firm to lose valuable talent.

Resolving this dilemma requires urgent attention from HR professionals, who need to think creatively about how to develop, incentivise and reward talented individuals who move out of lawyering into the digital space. Some law firms have set precedents by making their innovation leads into partners; Allen & Overy was the first and Addleshaw Goddard followed, as did Pinsent Masons and Gilbert & Tobin in Australia. Although this sets a good precedent, signalling that innovation is important to client delivery, it is still rather an unimaginative approach. There must be better ways to reward and incentivise forward-thinking individuals than relying on partnership as the ultimate prize (particularly as the partnership structure represents, to many, the biggest barrier to law firm change).

The talented 'non-lawyers' who are contributing to the firm's digital transformation predictably receive even less attention than the lawyers (I explore the lawyer/non-lawyer divide in more detail below). In the United Kingdom, unless the firm has adopted an alternative business structure model, which allows 'non-lawyers' to own a share in a law firm, a legal qualification is required to become a partner in the firm. Partners, as discussed at length in this book, are the leaders of the firm, hold the power and make the decisions. What message does this send to talented transformation professionals who are actively contributing to revenue generation and strategic direction in a law firm – but who do not have a law degree?

As changes to client delivery create a need for more hybrid roles in law firms and the battle for digital talent intensifies, HR teams will need to redefine career pathways in a radical way. This is not an easy task, and will require thoughtful analysis of how client needs are likely to evolve and employee expectations change over the long term. It is, however, critical to get this right, as success cannot be sustained by shoehorning digital talent into a structure and culture that does not fit.

*(d) An engaging work environment*

Those who have worked in a business committed to a digital agenda will be used to an environment that facilitates multidisciplinary working. This does not have to mean bean bags and ping pong tables, but it will involve an element of open plan, with spaces for collaboration and quiet work, and technology to support new ways of working. This requirement applies to new lawyer recruits just as much as it does to digital professionals; for young graduates coming into the profession, the workplace can be an important differentiator. A number of pre-COVID studies suggest that, when choosing an employer, new recruits (particularly millennials) place a high value on their physical environment, and in particular on opportunities for collaboration and social interaction.[218]

Law firms are still heavily invested in cellular offices, and open-plan working is an extremely hard sell. According to a report from Barclays Corporate, from 2019:

*[S]pace-heavy cellular office configurations account for 67% of office layouts in London's 100 leading law firms.*[219]

Lawyers justify this devotion to the cellular office by arguing that their work requires high levels of concentration and is often confidential, and so cannot be done in open plan. This deep-seated belief is very hard to shift, and is an emotive issue for many lawyers. It goes against a body of evidence that demonstrates that open-plan working leads to better collaboration and greater creativity, and therefore better productivity. Many lawyers find this difficult to accept, even though most of their clients (and many other professional service providers) work in a more open environment. This is yet another example of law firms distancing themselves from their clients by working in a completely different way.

The cellular office is also a cultural issue. Just as with organisational structure, the design of the law firm's physical environment can shape and reinforce the firm's culture. Some lawyers still view the cellular office as a status indicator, with the most senior partners having the corner office or the biggest space. When I was a trainee, partners were even able to choose bespoke furnishings for their offices – so when you were summoned in for a meeting you might be confronted by patriarchal power symbols like an enormous mahogany desk or a grandfather clock. Having partners sitting in one-person cellular offices is a constant visual reminder of the law firm hierarchy. One law firm that recently relocated to new offices decided, after extensive consultation, to retain the cellular office structure for all lawyers, with 'non-lawyers' (and non-revenue-generating professional support lawyers) in open plan. The clear implication of this is that 'lawyer work' is more important and difficult, and everyone else's work – and therefore their contribution – is of a lesser value.

No discussion of the working environment can ignore the impact of COVID-19 on the traditional office set-up. On the one hand, enforced remote working during lockdown has confirmed that working more flexibly is achievable, even for law firms. Many before the crisis would simply not have accepted that a flexible model could work. On the other hand, the threat of transmission of the virus in enclosed, shared spaces also argues against the co-working model that has been so successful for digital change. It is not yet clear where this debate will land. If, as is likely, the working patterns in a post-COVID world are more fluid, with time divided between home and office working, then time in the office is likely to be reserved for face-to-face collaboration, rather than for quiet study. This would suggest more, rather than less, open-plan collaboration spaces.

For law firms that cannot – or do not want to – commit to open-plan working, creation of a dedicated space for innovation and digital teams within the existing office can be a pragmatic compromise. Many law firms have established innovation spaces, in which digital teams can model new and collaborative ways of working and showcase new technologies and collaboration tools. Many law firm clients in the professional services and financial services sector have established innovation labs, Barclays, Deutsche Bank and Lloyds among them (Barclays' Eagle Labs are dedicated to legal technology). The Big 4 consultancy firms, who increasingly compete with Big Law for the best legal talent, have also made serious investments in their working environment to enhance their employment proposition. All have innovation spaces, and many have multiple spaces within one office; Deloitte, for example, in its landmark London headquarters, has four client collaboration and innovation spaces, each with a different focus.

### (e) Clear and authentic purpose and mission

As discussed, the average tenure for those with in-demand digital skills tends to be much shorter than is typical in law firms. The partnership model, of course, rewards long tenure, but when partnership is not an option, digital talent will need a different motivation to stick around. The same is also true for younger lawyers, who are looking for a different deal from the one traditionally on offer; for balance, for a sense of purpose and a reason for coming to work that transcends financial rewards. I discuss purpose in detail in the next chapter. The firm's purpose is now integral to the employment proposition, and HR teams need to give careful thought to how it is articulated to make the firm more attractive to those outside the legal profession.

## 4. What law firms reward

### 4.1 The danger of recruiting in your own image

How do you make it as a partner in a global elite law firm? Intelligence is a given, but as well as being incredibly bright you need to work really hard, look and act like the other partners, avoid making major mistakes and be prepared to sacrifice your own time and dedicate it to the firm. This may sound a bit John Grisham – but for Big Law firms at least, it holds true. In the hierarchy of the traditional law firm partnership, the stars – the partners – are the centre of the universe; and the cultural attributes of what is described in law firms as a 'high-performance culture' – tenacity, perfectionism, dedication, resilience, professionalism, collegiality and self-control – are highly prized, encouraged and rewarded.

Also rewarded is a particular way of thinking. Earlier in this chapter we explored the homogeneity of human capital amongst lawyers and how the statistics on diversity suggest that law firms are simply recruiting in their own image. Diversity, including diversity of thought, is the key to creativity and innovation, which is itself essential for sustained digital transformation. Through their recruitment practices, training and culture, law firms risk encouraging their people to think in the same way and so stifling cognitive diversity.

### 4.2 Fee earners and fee burners

One of the most enduring cultural characteristics of law firms is the distinction made between revenue-generating lawyers and the professionals who work alongside them – the 'fee earners' versus the 'fee burners'. Having myself moved from one role to the other (I was a senior associate before I moved to what was referred to, depressingly, as 'business services'), I have first-hand experience of the diminution in status that can accompany the shift. Perhaps it was just a projection of my own insecurities – but conversations with others in the same boat suggest that there is more to it than that. It is undoubtedly the case that, in all but the most progressive of law firm partnerships, there is a marked difference in the way that lawyers and 'non-lawyers' are regarded – and a perception that lawyers can do any job a 'non-lawyer' can do, better and faster and with more attention to detail.[220] One consequence of this is that, rather than the lawyers learning new ways of thinking from business professionals who do not have a law degree, the partnership looks for and rewards conformity of thinking in all its people. This is one of the reasons that law firms are so keen to hire business professionals who have worked in law firms, rather than from outside the sector.

This comes back to the mutually reinforcing relationship between law firm structure and law firm culture. Fee earner/fee burner discrimination was baked into the law firm DNA from the very beginning. Until the passing of the Legal Services Act in 2007, 'non-lawyers' in the UK were not permitted to manage or own a share in a law firm, which meant that only lawyers could be partners. Talented business professionals who were not lawyers could never progress to the very top – and consequently there were no visible role models for more junior business professionals, nor would junior lawyers perceive senior business professionals to be leaders of the firm. Coincidentally, many of those business professionals were female (often disproportionately so in areas of expertise such as HR), so the gender imbalance at the top of the ladder was perpetuated. I genuinely remember, as a mid-level associate in the early 2000s, looking around me and thinking, Where are all the senior women? There were very few female partners and I am ashamed to admit that the female 'business services' leaders were totally invisible to me. For all these reasons and more, many lawyers have grown up with an unhealthy master/servant mentality which endures to this day, exacerbated by the fact that, historically at least, many lawyers have worked in only one firm for their entire career – so simply don't know any different.

Things improved in the United Kingdom when the Legal Services Act introduced the concept of the alternative business structure (ABS), allowing 'non-lawyers' to own a share in a law firm.[221] The stated purpose of the regulation was not to improve equality and diversity; rather, it was hoped that allowing non-legally trained professionals to be owners of law firms would open up the profession to new competition and to external investment. The first ABS licence was granted in 2012. Of the relatively few licences issued since then, a large proportion have been issued to existing law firms looking to reward 'non-lawyers' by making them partners in the firm, rather than to disruptive new entrants to the market. This is a positive development, but has not been sufficiently wide-reaching. For many who work in 'non-lawyer' roles in law firms, the demotivating reality is that no matter how senior or talented, they will never get a seat at the table.

From a business perspective, why should this matter? Every organisation has a hierarchy, and some in that hierarchy are more highly regarded and better remunerated than others. If people in 'support' roles in a law firm partnership don't like their deal, surely they can just move on to a corporate, where business skills will be recognised and rewarded?

Recognition of skills beyond lawyering does matter – and not just for reasons of professional respect. There is a wide and growing recognition that working in multidisciplinary teams, using diverse

*Law firms that concentrate solely on diversity of gender or ethnicity are missing a trick. Of course, attention to diversity in these areas is crucial, but it is not the only consideration. Diversity of thought is just as important, particularly for sustaining digital transformation.*

skillsets, leads to better business results and improved outcomes for clients.

### 4.3 Cognitive diversity: the power of mixing it up

Some types of diversity, such as diversity of ethnicity and gender, can be easier to identify than others. More difficult to recognise but equally important are elements of diversity and inclusion that often remain unobserved:

> [W]e recognize the increasingly multivariate nature of diversity – including multiple forms of acquired diversity such as educational or socio-economic background, or diversity of thought ... Although this is more difficult to measure, it is a significant additional driver of the need to focus on inclusion.[222]

Law firms that concentrate solely on diversity of gender or ethnicity are missing a trick. Of course, attention to diversity in these areas is crucial, but it is not the only consideration. Diversity of thought is just as important, particularly for sustaining digital transformation. The ability to mix it up by leveraging multidisciplinary teams to solve (or anticipate) customer problems is one of the characteristics of a successful digital company.

### 4.4 The challenge of multidisciplinary teams

Of course, lawyers in a law firm are not sole practitioners, and most would consider themselves to be good team players. To deliver complex mandates in a high-pressure environment, you have to work well with lawyers in your own team and other teams in your firm, with the client and lawyers on the other side, and with local counsel that your firm is using in jurisdictions in which the firm does not have an office. Lawyers work very well in lawyer-only teams, collaborating seamlessly to divide up the work and to ensure the quality of the end product that goes to the client. The team dynamic amongst lawyers in a law firm is positive, with high levels of commitment and trust. This positive team dynamic is a strength of the partnership model – indeed, it is this sense of team that many lawyers cite as the best bit of the job. The hierarchy is tightly defined; consequently, everyone knows their place, understands the task that they have to complete and will exercise the appropriate degree of oversight and personal responsibility over their piece of the puzzle. Teams will work for as many hours as are necessary to close the deal or draft the pleadings.

The issue with this approach is that it does not always result in the outcome the client wants or needs, particularly when firms are still charging by the hour. As data sets expand, expected response times shorten and cost sensitivities increase, the skillsets required for timely and cost-effective delivery of a legal matter are changing. Solving client problems increasingly requires more than technical legal expertise. Project management skills are essential, as is expertise in identifying which technology solutions can be applied (or developed) to support the delivery of a matter. At the pitch stage, in particular, creative ideas about how to deliver streamlined technology-supported outcomes is of high value. These are not skills that form part of most lawyers' training. In many cases, lawyers would consider these skills to be of lower value than technical legal expertise.

A colleague in a large international law firm recounted the story of an experiment the firm conducted into legal project management. A young and dynamic member of the IT team with deep project management experience was parachuted into a high-profile and complex corporate matter. The idea was that this individual, who had no legal training but was smart, articulate and experienced, would act as project manager, interfacing with the client and helping the lawyers to organise timetables and complex reporting requirements. The IT professional was to be co-located with the lawyer team; to be client-facing (and chargeable); and to work closely with the matter partner to oversee progress. After a couple of weeks, my colleague checked in on the project manager, to find him sitting back in the IT department poring over spreadsheets of bill narratives. The lawyers had not allowed him to sit with them (they had simply made him feel unwelcome), and had reduced his involvement to resolving billing issues – a pain point to be sure, but not a good use of his considerable skills. The matter partner, although supportive philosophically, did not have time to help integrate him into the team. Like a transplanted organ, he had been rejected. The project manager left the firm and, somewhat ironically, is now a highly successful project manager for one of the firm's clients.

Many lawyers find it difficult to work with those who are not lawyers. Lawyers trust other lawyers because they probably went to a similar school and university, achieved similar grades and have a similar level of attention to detail. Those outside the bubble are regarded with mistrust. This has nothing to do with snobbery or prejudice. It is simply that in a demanding, high-performance culture, lawyers constantly fear exposing the client or the firm to risk. The prevailing culture is one of perfectionism and there is very little tolerance of failure. In this kind of environment, is it any wonder that lawyers find it reassuring to work with those who understand what is at stake?

The results of a 2020 survey by Bloomberg Tax on the use of multidisciplinary teams in law firms speak volumes.[223] 82% of law firm respondents reported making use of multidisciplinary teams when delivering client services. When asked to indicate which roles were represented on these multidisciplinary teams, the top five were different grades of lawyer, from partner through to different levels of associate. Only 17% mentioned 'non-lawyers' at all, suggesting that law firms simply do not understand the concept.

Although it may be reassuring for lawyers to work only with lawyers, this can be frustrating for clients. Ultimately, clients care about outcomes. They don't care about the pedigree of the person who does their document review work (beyond an obvious hygiene factor) provided that the outcome the client needs has been achieved. Part of that desired outcome may be cost effectiveness and efficiency – sometimes at the expense of perfection. If law firms really want to serve their clients in the best way possible, and encourage the creativity and innovation that sustains digital transformation, it makes sense to mix disciplines and skillsets. Research has shown that cognitive diversity creates a better client outcome than groupthink, particularly in times of crisis or rapid change.

## 4.5 What's the alternative?

Law firms who choose to dismiss concerns about cognitive diversity, and who are slow to recognise the value to clients of multidisciplinary teams, are running a risk. There are other providers coming up fast who are acutely aware of the opportunity. Law companies[224] such as Elevate Legal Services, UnitedLex and Factor have a fresh, digitally enabled approach to the legal sector, bringing law, consulting, technology and managed services together in one client-friendly package. These are not start-ups nibbling at the edges of the law firm market – they are serious businesses, some private equity backed, with global reach and digital capability. Unhampered by the structural constraints of the law firm partnership, law companies can scale quickly. They are supported by the funds they need to acquire existing businesses, enabling them to build both their technology capabilities and their legal expertise. They are also hungry for growth. All these factors, taken together, make law companies a compelling proposition.

Law companies are culturally different from law firm partnerships, too. Focused as much on the business as the practice of law, they make no distinction between lawyers and 'non-lawyers'. Their leadership teams are more diverse than in law firms, particularly in terms of professional expertise. Law companies are also unfettered by the cultural ties that hold so many law firms back from change. They can create a culture that is right for a digital age, recognising the importance to delivery of a legal matter of many different kinds of role: lawyers, consultants, developers, data scientists, project managers and client experience professionals.

## 4.6 Cognitive diversity and psychological safety

Alison Reynolds of Ashridge Business School and David Lewis of London Business School have conducted extensive research into what makes teams successful. They have identified two key attributes: cognitive diversity and psychological safety.

To measure the impact of bringing together people who think differently, Reynolds and Lewis created an exercise to test how executive teams manage new, uncertain and complex situations. The exercise requires a group to work together, under timed conditions, to develop and execute a strategy to achieve a specified outcome. Reynolds and Lewis have run the exercise more than 100 times over a period of 12 years, using teams that are diverse in terms of age, ethnicity and gender. The results are fascinating. They found there was no demonstrable correlation between success in the exercise and diversity of age, ethnicity and gender. The teams that performed the best had another differentiator: cognitive diversity. The most successful teams demonstrated marked variances in perspective and clear differences in the way that team members processed information. The conclusion of the study was that, faced with a new, complex or uncertain situation, teams that are more cognitively diverse will perform better.

It sounds beautifully simple, but writing in *Harvard Business Review*, Reynolds and Lewis explained that cognitive diversity is easy to overlook and difficult to achieve. First, cognitive diversity is not visible in the same way as are age, gender or ethnicity, so it is more difficult to measure (you can't tell how someone thinks just by looking at them). Secondly, once individuals are hired, organisations inadvertently create cultural barriers that restrict the degree of cognitive diversity, through exercising functional bias:

> *There is a familiar saying: "We recruit in our own image". This bias doesn't end with demographic distinctions like race or gender, or with the recruiting process, for that matter. Colleagues gravitate toward the people who think and express themselves in a similar way. As a result, organisations often end up with like-minded teams. When this happens [...] we have what psychologists call functional bias – and low cognitive diversity.*[225]

This resonates strongly with the law firm experience. Many young lawyers come into firms full of creative ideas, but something in the structure squeezes it out of them. Those that don't conform tend to leave. The prevailing culture of a law firm partnership compels conformity.

For this reason, I suspect that the cognitive diversity scores for most law firm partnerships would be pretty underwhelming. The fact that lawyers like to work with people who think like them may well be holding law firms back from performing more effectively, and from approaching client problems in an innovative and creative way:

> [In successful teams] we observed a blend of different problem-solving behaviors, like collaboration, identifying problems, applying information, maintaining discipline, breaking rules, and inventing new approaches. These techniques combined were more effective than in groups where there were too many rule-breakers, or too many discipline-maintainers, for example.[226]

To this culture of conformity can be added a culture of perfectionism, the characteristic that makes it very difficult for lawyers to take risks or to fail. Reynolds and Lewis added another key observation to their study. The most successful teams are both cognitively diverse and benefit from something else that allows that cognitive diversity to be sustained – an atmosphere of psychological safety.

Reynolds and Lewis define psychological safety as "the belief that one will not be punished or humiliated for speaking up with ideas, questions, concerns, or mistakes".[227] It is a fragile state that takes a long time to create and can be quickly destroyed. Absent an environment of psychological safety, people will not contribute their thoughts and ideas, and cognitive diversity cannot flourish.

Reynolds and Lewis surveyed 150 executives from different organisations globally over a 12-month period and asked them to rate their organisation in terms of its cognitive diversity and the degree of psychological safety that predominated. The best-performing organisations were labelled 'generative' (high diversity, high psychological safety), the others 'oppositional' (high diversity, low safety), 'uniform' (low diversity, high safety) or 'defensive' (low diversity, low safety). The same executives were then asked to choose five words (from a list of more than 60) that best described the dominant behaviours and emotions in their organisation.

Where would you put your own law firm? I suspect that very few would be in the 'generative' category. Some might argue that this is as it should be – perhaps it is not a lawyer's job to be 'experimental' or 'curious'. Yet in a world that feels increasingly volatile and unpredictable, where clients' own businesses are under intense pressure to adapt and transform, a little curiosity might be a welcome quality in a client's trusted adviser. It is certainly a critical component of sustained digital transformation. ■

# Chapter 9: Sustaining change – purpose

## 1. Purpose – or perpetuity?

The third element of law firm culture to explore is purpose. Historically, in traditional law firm partnerships, purpose has been conceptualised as a sense of perpetuity – the idea of bequeathing the firm to the next generation of partners stronger than it is today. The concept of perpetuity is strong in a law firm partnership; I have seen it articulated over the years in a number of senior partner election manifestos. Purpose, in a law firm, is still closely linked to looking after your own.

## 2. The corporate view of purpose

In the corporate world, things have moved on. Just as culture and digitisation have been high on the corporate boardroom agenda in recent years, so has corporate purpose. With investors ever more focused on ESG (environmental, social and governance) considerations, corporations have been compelled actively to examine and reframe their purpose for a digital age. The long-established orthodoxy was that maximising shareholder profit should be the main objective of the corporate CEO.[228] In 2019, the CEOs of 184 of the United States' largest corporations (including Amazon and Apple) made a joint statement as part of the lobbying group The Business Roundtable (BRT), on the purpose of a corporation. The BRT statement set a new standard for corporate responsibility, with a definition of corporate purpose that takes into account not just the shareholders of the corporation, but all the company's stakeholders.

Here is an extract:

### Statement on the Purpose of a Corporation

*[ ... ]*

*While each of our individual companies serves its own corporate purpose, we share a fundamental commitment to all of our stakeholders. We commit to:*
- *Delivering value to our customers. We will further the tradition of American companies leading the way in meeting or exceeding customer expectations.*
- *Investing in our employees. This starts with compensating them fairly and providing important benefits. It also includes supporting them through training and education that help develop new skills for a rapidly changing world. We foster diversity and inclusion, dignity and respect.*
- *Dealing fairly and ethically with our suppliers. We are dedicated to serving as good partners to the other companies, large and small, that help us meet our missions.*
- *Supporting the communities in which we work. We respect the people in our communities and protect the environment by embracing sustainable practices across our businesses.*
- *Generating long-term value for shareholders, who provide the capital that allows companies to invest, grow and innovate. We are committed to transparency and effective engagement with shareholders.[229]*

It is interesting that shareholders come last in the list of stakeholders, below customers, employees, suppliers and communities. The statement is a significant departure from BRT's statement of 1997, which stated that the foremost duty of a corporation's management and board was to the corporation's stockholders.

What has driven corporations towards this fundamental change to corporate purpose? The reasons are complex, tied to a global cultural shift of consciousness on macro issues like climate change and diversity and inclusion. As you might expect, it is not only about altruism; corporations have been compelled to look inwards for reasons other than their conscience:

- **The accessibility of information in a digital age.** Information has never been easier to find, and to share, globally and at lightning speed. This makes it harder for corporations to cover up bad behaviours and easier to hold them to account. Social media has given individuals a platform to band together and call out hypocrisy. Think of #MeToo; think of the rise of shareholder activism; think of the speed at which the Black Lives Matter protests were organised; think of TikTok users sabotaging Donald Trump's rally in Tulsa with fake registrations. Digitisation forces corporations to care about wider stakeholders – not because the corporate world has suddenly found its conscience, but because individual stakeholders have much more power than was historically the case.
- **The employment proposition.** There is no doubt that having a developed, authentic and clearly articulated corporate purpose improves an organisation's employment proposition. It also helps with retention; according to research undertaken by PwC, millennials who feel strongly connected to the purpose of the organisation in which they work are 5.3 times more likely to stay.[230]
- **The bottom line.** Having a purpose with which your customers can connect creates brand loyalty and can positively impact financial returns. For example, in 2019, Unilever announced that its 'sustainable living' brands, which it defines as "those that communicate a strong environmental or social purpose, with

*From my own experience and research and the experience of colleagues in the sector, very few law firms have invested serious time in considering how the purpose of the law firm might need to be reframed for a digital age.*

products that contribute to achieving the company's ambition of halving its environmental footprint and increasing its positive social impact" were growing 69% faster than the rest of the business and delivering 75% of the company's growth.[231]

## 3. The law firm response

What is the law firm response to this fundamental shift in client focus? A Google search for 'ESG legal' shows that almost all of the large corporate law firms have an ESG offering, advising clients on ESG issues ranging from sustainable finance to environmental liability, business and human rights, climate change, governance and corporate responsibility. Some law firms also make reference to their own ESG activities in the context of their offer. Many have statements of purpose on their websites. Yet, from my own experience and research and the experience of colleagues in the sector, very few law firms have invested serious time in considering how the purpose of the law firm might need to be reframed for a digital age. What is clear is that law firms view purpose primarily as a client advisory opportunity.

This is another example of law firms failing to take their own medicine. We have seen this in the context of culture, where the law firms who acted as advisers to the financial services sector following the credit crunch did not take the cultural learnings back to their own firms. We see it in the context of diversity, where lawyers are happy to offer advice on the issues but have a woeful record themselves – so much so that it is their clients who are holding them to account on their diversity and inclusion performance. We see it in the context of digitisation, where law firms will happily advise clients on the legal and regulatory impacts of digital change while showing little interest in their own firm's digital transformation.

There are two possible reasons why law firm partnerships have not prioritised the definition of their purpose, both related to the partnership structure:
- Partnerships do not invite external investment, so law firms have little motivation to articulate their purpose. The only investors they need to think about are their fellow partners.

- Profits are often distributed quarterly in a partnership, which means that law firms are notoriously short term in their investment horizon.

Consequently, despite the emotional importance law firm leadership might attach to perpetuity, in practice law firms can be very reactive organisations. Many partners in a law firm are focused on this quarter's PPP and distributions at the expense of a long-term view of value creation. The issue is neatly described in this article from the *Harvard Business Review*:

> *Economist Alfred Rappaport is one of the fathers of the idea of shareholder value. But in his book* Saving Capitalism from Short-Termism, *he makes a compelling case that our real issue is short-termism and how we think about "value". Basically, if you manage for long-term value, of course you need to account for customers, employees, communities, and more. When we define value as this quarter's profits, we don't invest (and we certainly don't prioritize long emergencies like climate change).*[232]

If law firms are serious about perpetuity, they should challenge this culture of short-term thinking and encourage thoughtful evaluation of the firm's purpose, starting with an inclusive and broad definition of the stakeholders to which the firm owes a responsibility.

## 4. The role of purpose in sustaining transformation

Law firms need to get serious about purpose. At the macro level, large corporate law firms, as highly profitable businesses, have an opportunity to leverage their wealth, influence and global scale to benefit society. It would be a mistake, and a missed opportunity, for law firms to wait until clients compel them to take action (as will surely happen, if the client stance on diversity and inclusion and innovation is any indicator). Although a grand vision is important, investing time in examining purpose is also important for the strategic direction of the firm and consequently, for its evolution. Thinking about purpose helps organisations understand how they need to change and grow, and should be an integral part of the strategy for any law firm committed to digital transformation:

> *Purpose does more than make a brand unique. It can shine a light on a business' evolutionary path. At a basic level, purpose can simply express what an organization aspires to be and do. But at a more advanced one, it becomes a conscious expression of how an organization intends to evolve and transform itself.*[233]

Like culture, purpose should not be considered static or immutable. A firm's purpose should reflect the society and community in which it operates and the stakeholders it serves. It should evolve alongside those stakeholders and respond to their changing concerns. Customers (clients) are a very important part of that stakeholder group, and transforming alongside clients, the better to serve their needs, must be an integral part of a law firm's purpose.

## 5. Becoming purpose-driven – practical steps

Law firms must recognise that purpose is about more than perpetuity. They must take the lead from clients, reframe their stakeholder group so that it is wider than the partners in the firm, and make a clear commitment to each of those stakeholders. What is preventing leaders of the largest law firms globally from coming together, through an independent organisation such as the IBA, to release a joint statement on the purpose of a law firm, just as the members of The Business Roundtable did in 2019?[234] It could be very simple. Below, I have taken the headings from the BRT statement and suggested what they might look like adapted for a law firm.

> *We commit to the following:*
> - ***Delivering value to our clients.*** *We will deliver legal services to our clients in a way that meets or exceeds their expectations, using a resourcing model and charging structure that fully reflects the value to the client of the services delivered.*
> - ***Investing in our employees.*** *We will provide career development opportunities for all our people and a*

remuneration structure that recognises the importance of multidisciplinary skills for delivering value to our clients. We will work to close the gender pay gap and the gap between partner remuneration and remuneration at all other levels in the law firm structure. We will actively work to address the diversity issues within our firms and the profession and encourage cognitive diversity to drive innovation and change.

- **Dealing fairly and ethically with our suppliers.** We are dedicated to serving as good partners to the other companies, large and small, that help us meet our missions and we will work only with other law firms and providers that share our values and purpose. We will partner with others to help our clients succeed.

- **Supporting the communities in which we work.** We recognise that our success and high levels of profitability afford us privilege that we should use to do good. We commit to using our skills and profits to serve the communities in which we operate, including by supporting better access to justice. We will respect the people in our communities and protect the environment by embracing sustainable practices across our businesses.

- **Generating long-term value for our firms as a whole,** including but not limited to the partners that own them, by investing in growth and sustained transformation.

It would be incredibly powerful if law firms were to come together in this way, as part of an ecosystem united around a greater purpose, and proactively show leadership.

Although it is the last of the three 'Ps' (partnership, people, and purpose) to be discussed in this book, purpose is arguably the most important of all. Defining purpose for a law firm cannot be a PR exercise or be ticked off by developing a vision statement. Purpose is the nucleus around which law firm culture should be built, and a focal point for redefining the law firm partnership model and people proposition. Law firms should use the exercise of defining purpose as a strategic opportunity, both as a means of understanding how they need to grow to be fit for the future, and for sustaining digital transformation:

*We think that the future of law will belong to those firms that have a clear purpose, those that understand what matters most to their clients and their people. Additionally, it will be those firms that take their purpose and use it to drive a distinctive and sustainable culture that will survive and prosper in the long term.*[235] ∎

# Chapter 10: Final thoughts

It is inarguable that the coronavirus pandemic has changed the way businesses operate, permanently. COVID-19 forced a re-evaluation of culture, of ways of working, and of digital investment across all sectors of the economy. A 2021 cross-industry study undertaken by the Economist Intelligence Unit, sponsored by Microsoft, polled 800 senior executives across eight sectors and 15 economies.[236] The purpose of the survey was twofold:

- to understand the relationship between pre-pandemic decisions/investments and organisational outcomes; and
- to gain insight into how COVID-19 has altered business and digital priorities.

The survey results show, unsurprisingly, that those businesses that were already digitally prepared before COVID-19 gained significant competitive advantage during the pandemic. Less digitally mature companies were forced to respond by accelerating the pace of their own digital transformations. 72% of respondents to the survey reported a significant increase in investment in digital in their industry as a result of the pandemic. Even more interesting is the proportion of respondents who saw the pandemic as a catalyst for linking digital transformation with social responsibility. 76% of respondents stated that they believed the pandemic has placed an obligation on companies to contribute to society, and 75% believed that "digital transformation now needs to pivot from enabling business success to supporting broader societal improvement".[237]

It seems that business is changing, radically and permanently. The change is reflected not only through an increase in financial investment in technology, but also through a recognition of a link between digital transformation, corporate purpose and the sustainability of the business model.

This has implications for traditional law firm partnerships. I have argued throughout this book that understanding what the customer wants and needs is a foundational element of successful digital transformation and should be the driving force of a law firm's digital strategy. During a turbulent 18 months of lockdown, law firms have responded to client needs by continuing to deliver to established expectations. The staggeringly positive financial results of many (corporate) law firms over the last year is testament to their ability to service clients in times of crisis – to 'keep calm and carry on'. However, as the dust settles, and law firms and their clients return to their offices and readjust to the next normal, the impact of the pandemic aftershocks will really start to be felt. Many law firm clients will be among the 72% in The Economist Intelligence Unit survey who have significantly increased their investment in digital over the past 18 months; or among the 75% who agree that digital transformation is about societal improvement as much as business success. In short, during this period of crisis, law firms' clients are likely to have moved even further along the digital maturity curve, widening the gap and sharpening the requirement for law firms to keep pace.

I have deliberately not focused in this book on the digital transformation challenges of corporate legal teams, as this is too broad a subject to be covered here. However, as we pull the threads of successful digital transformation together, from strategy to culture and beyond, it is worth spending a little time looking at where law firms' clients are now, post-pandemic. If law firms are to continue to be trusted advisers to their clients, they need to be responsive to how their clients' worlds are changing, both at an enterprise, C-suite level and at a 'local' level within the corporate legal team (which is the law firm's most immediate point of contact).

Many corporate legal teams are under pressure to transform, and are exploring ways to achieve this by investing in technology, reassessing the way they serve their internal customers and re-evaluating the skills and capabilities that will be required to future-proof the function. Gartner's 2021 predictions for corporate legal and compliance technology up to 2025 offer an interesting view of where corporate legal teams are now, and their priorities for the future. Three points in particular are important for law firms to consider:[238]

- Spend on technology within corporate legal teams is going up, and likely to increase significantly over time (Gartner assumes that by 2025, legal departments will increase their spend on technology threefold).
- Resource mix within corporate legal teams is changing, and is likely to look very different in the medium term (Gartner assumes that by 2024, legal departments will replace 20% of generalist lawyers with non-lawyer staff).
- Automation of legal work within corporate legal teams is on the rise, and this will only increase (Gartner assumes that by 2024, legal departments will have automated 50% of legal work related to major corporate transactions).

If Gartner is correct, in three years' time there will be significantly less legal work sent to external counsel. Most corporate law firms would probably recognise this, as a continuation of the current trajectory. However, the combination of less work and the predicted change in profile of the corporate legal team could have implications that law firms have not anticipated. As the resource mix within corporate legal teams shifts towards legal operations, with a focus on technology, project management and efficiency, the selection criteria for law firms may also change. It is highly likely that there will be less emphasis on technical legal expertise, and more on value-add services that support the operations of the legal team – including use of technology and data for better insight, and of collaboration tools for more seamless integration with external providers. Law firm clients will expect a frictionless, digital customer experience – not least because that is what is being demanded of their business by their own customers. Most traditional law firm partnerships do not, today, have the capabilities to respond to this.

As ever, though, it is not just about the technology. Corporate legal teams are adapting their business models to respond to changes within the businesses they serve, in some radical ways:

- A number of corporate legal teams, particularly in the TMT and financial services sectors, are reorganising their legal teams to work in an agile way, the better to support an agile enterprise. Examples include Bosch, HSBC, ING and others – many of these traditional legal teams are moving towards non-traditional delivery.
- The adoption of principles of human-centred design are also on the increase within forward-thinking legal teams, reflecting a new focus on the importance of understanding internal and external customers (Coca-Cola and HSBC are among the legal teams leading the way here).
- There is a renewed emphasis within corporate legal teams on purpose, with some legal functions using this time of transformation to redefine their role in furthering the enterprise's corporate purpose. Vodafone is one such example, with GC Rosemary Martin putting purpose right at the centre of the selection criteria for Vodafone's 2021 legal panel:

*At Vodafone, we aim to build a digital society that enhances socio-economic progress, embraces everyone and does not come at the cost of our planet. Our purpose is now very much at the core of everything that we do and I am proud that this now extends to our legal panel. We are looking forward to these new ways of working.*[239]

The pandemic has catalysed so much change in the corporate environment, and law firm customers are no exception to this. This creates real opportunity for law firms; to initiate an open dialogue with their clients, to learn from them and to adjust the law firm business model to serve them better. This opportunity could not come at a more advantageous time, given the positive financial position that many corporate law firms are currently enjoying.

It is time for law firms to shift the internal narrative about digital transformation from use of legal tech to a far-reaching discussion about the future business model of the firm. This means looking at culture, at purpose, at strategy, and putting the client right at the heart of everything the firm does. The time really is now, and for the law firms that seize the moment, the rewards will be significant.

*Timing is everything. If you undertake these changes while your company is still healthy, while your ongoing business forms a protective bubble in which you can experiment with the new ways of doing business, you can save much more of your company's strength, your employees and your strategic position.*[240] ■

# Notes

1.  The quote was attributed to Susskind by Jordan Furlong, legal market consultant, during a video conference in October 2018 with students on the international exchange programme at Bucerius Law School. See: www.law-school.de/news-artikel/future-of-law.
2.  Alex Novarese, "Comment: Apocalypse never – City leaders' 2020 results show resilience to test the most confirmed Cassandra", *Legal Business* blog, 29 July 2020. Available at: www.legalbusiness.co.uk/blogs/comment-apocalypse-never-city-leaders-2020-results-show-resilience-to-test-the-most-confirmed-cassandra/.
3.  Amy Greenshields, "Nearly half of global CEOs don't expect to see a return to 'normal' until 2022", KPMG press release. Available at: https://home.kpmg/xx/en/home/media/press-releases/2021/03/nearly-half-of-global-ceos-dont-expect-a-return-to-normal-until-2022-ceo-outlook-pulse.html.
4.  See, for example, Bjarne P Tellmann, *Building an Outstanding Legal Team*, Globe Law and Business, 2017.
5.  Hortense de la Boutetiere, Alberto Montagner and Angelika Reich (survey contribs), "Unlocking Success in digital transformations", McKinsey & Company, October 2018. Available at: www.mckinsey.com/~/media/McKinsey/Business%20Functions/Organization/Our%20Insights/Unlocking%20success%20in%20digital%20transformations/Unlocking-success-in-digital-transformations.ashx.
6.  Andrew S Grove, *Only The Paranoid Survive: How to exploit the crisis points that challenge every company and career*, Profile Books, 1998.
7.  This definition is widely used but is perhaps most closely associated with IDEO, the global design company, which popularised the concept of design thinking. See: https://designthinking.ideo.com.
8.  I discuss this establishment of captive centres and the associated cultural benefits in more detail in Chapter 7.
9.  Salesforce, "What is Digital Transformation?", Available at: www.salesforce.com/eu/products/platform/what-is-digital-transformation/.
10. World Economic Forum with Accenture, "Digital Transformation Initiative: Professional Service Industry", white paper, January 2017. Available at: http://reports.weforum.org/digital-transformation/wp-content/blogs.dir/94/mp/files/pages/files/wef-dti-professional-services-white-paper.pdf.
11. "Kirkland & Ellis Set to Hit $5 Billion Annual Revenue", *Lawyer Monthly*, February 2021. Available at: www.lawyer-monthly.com/2021/02/kirkland-ellis-set-to-hit-5-billion-annual-revenue/. The article first appeared in the *Financial Times*.
12. One notable exception is scale legal work undertaken in response to regulatory change, such as Mifid II, Brexit and the IBOR transition. I discuss this in more detail in Chapter 4.
13. Arun Arora, Peter Dahlstrom, Klemens Hjartar and Florian Wunderlich, *Fast Times: How Digital Winners Set Direction, Learn, and Adapt*, Amazon Publishing, 2020, p22.
14. Noah Waisberg and Dr Alexander Hudek, *AI for Lawyers: How artificial intelligence is adding value amplifying expertise, and transforming careers*, John Wiley & Sons, 2021, p32.
15. Mark A Cohen, "Law is Lagging Digital Transformation – Why it Matters", *Forbes*, December 2018. Available at: www.forbes.com/sites/markcohen1/2018/12/20/law-is-lagging-digital-transformation-why-it-matters/?sh=41eb39d9515c.
16. World Economic Forum "Digital Transformation Initiative", *supra* note 10.
17. *Ibid.*
18. Arun Arora *et al*, *Fast Times*, *supra* note 13, p21.
19. Andrew S Grove, *Only the Paranoid Survive*, *supra* note 6.
20. Arun Arora *et al*, *Fast Times*, *supra* note 13, p25.
21. *The Lawyer*, "The Lawyer Market Reports: US Top 50 Firms in London 2020 Sample", June 2020. Available at: www.thelawyer.com/reports/us-top-50-2020-report/.
22. Michael Bucy, Adrian Finlayson, Greg Kelly and Chris Moye, "The 'how' of transformation", McKinsey & Company, May 2016. Available at: www.mckinsey.com/industries/retail/our-insights/the-how-of-transformation.
23. David Rowan, *Non-Bullshit Innovation: Radical ideas from the world's smartest minds*, Bantam Press, 2019.
24. Jens Engelhardt, Gerard du Toit, Frédéric Debruyne and Jeff Melton, "Firing Up the Customer Experience Factory", Bain & Company, 13 June 2018. Available at: www.bain.com/insights/firing-up-the-customer-experience-factory/.
25. See: www.ideo.com/about.
26. Jens Engelhardt *et al*, "Firing Up the Customer Experience Factory", Bain & Company, *supra* note 24.
27. Kelley was interviewed by Charlie Rose for the *60 Minutes* episode, "Design Thinking", CBS, 2013. A transcript is available on the Alexander Street website at: https://search.alexanderstreet.com/preview/work/bibliographic_entity%7Cvideo_work%7C2767381.
28. The case study is adapted from Peter Hall, "IDEO Takes on the Government", *Metropolis Magazine*, June 2011. The article is available on the IDEO website at: https://new-ideo-com.s3.amazonaws.com/assets/files/pdfs/news/Metropolis_IDEO_govt_June2011.pdf.

29    The Mindful Business Charter is available at: www.mindfulbusinesscharter.com/the-charter.

30    Ann Kim, "Busting the Myth that Regulations Impede Innovation", *The IDEO Journal*, May 2020.

31    Alex Rawson, Ewan Duncan and Conor Jones, "The Truth About Customer Experience", *Harvard Business Review*, September 2013.

32    Ann Kim, "Busting the Myth", *supra* note 30.

33    Jens Engelhardt *et al*, "Firing Up the Customer Experience Factory", Bain & Company, *supra* note 24.

34    Richard Hawker, Jeff Melton, James Wright, Maureen Burns and Jens Engelhardt, "Breakthrough Design for a Better Customer Experience and Better Economics", Bain & Company, 13 June 2018. Available at: www.bain.com/insights/breakthrough-design-for-a-better-customer-experience-and-better-economics/.

35    The case study is derived from interviews conducted by the author.

36    Quoted in David Rowan, *Non-Bullshit Innovation, supra* note 23.

37    David Rowan, "Daniel Ek: Europe's greatest digital influencer tops Wired 100", *Wired*, May 2014. Available at: www.wired.co.uk/article/wired-100-daniel-ek.

38    Arun Arora *et al, Fast Times, supra* note 13, p17.

39    This could be the chief technology officer (CTO) or chief digital and technology officer (CDTO), but in law firms it can also fall to the chief operating officer (COO) or even a chief legal innovation officer (CLIO). Sometimes responsibility is given to a particular partner responsible for innovation, or a team of partners.

40    This case study is based on Roger Peverelli and Reggy de Feniks, "The vision behind Ping An's success story", *InsurTech News*, April 2019, for which the authors interviewed Ping An's CIO Jonathan Larsen. Available at: https://insurtechnews.com/insights/the-vision-behind-ping-ans-success-story.

41    *Ibid.*

42    *Ibid.*

43    Cf agile methodology, discussed in Chapter 3.

44    It can be achieved more quickly: the digital transformation team at Freshfields Bruckhaus Deringer was able to upgrade a significant number of legacy systems within one year. This involved developing a clear strategy and roadmap, and a team working at high velocity under strong, experienced leadership.

45    Arun Arora *et al, Fast Times, supra* note 13, p131.

46    Matt Smith, "Walmart's New Intelligent Retail Lab Shows a Glimpse into the Future of Retail, IRL", Walmart, 25 April 2019. Available at: https://corporate.walmart.com/newsroom/2019/04/25/walmarts-new-intelligent-retail-lab-shows-a-glimpse-into-the-future-of-retail-irl.

47    Lauren Thomas, "Walmart CEO on buying Jet.com: We would 'do that all over again'", CNBC, 20 May 2020. Available at: www.cnbc.com/2020/05/20/walmart-ceo-on-buying-jetcom-we-would-do-that-all-over-again.html.

48    See: "Walmart and Sam's Club Now Administering Walk-Up COVID-19 Vaccines at 5,100+ Pharmacies Nationwide", Walmart press release, 4 May 2021. Available at: https://corporate.walmart.com/newsroom/2021/05/04/walmart-and-sams-club-now-administering-walk-up-covid-19-vaccines-at-5-100-pharmacies-nationwide.

49    Those born between 1995 and 2010.

50    This is of course an assumption; the effects of a global recession might result in a completely different dynamic for those joining the workplace in the medium to longer term.

51    On a more positive note, digital 'stars' from other industries may be attracted to the legal industry because of the potential for effecting real change in a sector that is digitally immature.

52    P&G 2020 Annual Report, statement by president and CEO David S Taylor. Available at: https://us.pg.com/annualreport2020/introduction-and-fy-results/.

53    McKinsey Digital, Fast Times, "Building a 'faster learner wins' culture", interview with FD Wilder, 18 February 2020. Available at: www.mckinsey.com/business-functions/mckinsey-digital/our-insights/fasttimes/interviews/fd-wilder.

54    Josh Bersin and Marc Zao-Sanders, "Making Learning a Part of Everyday Work", *Harvard Business Review*, 19 February 2019. Available at: https://hbr.org/2019/02/making-learning-a-part-of-everyday-work.

55    Connie Cheng, "Eyes on the consumer, hands on the keyboard: The mantra in CPG Analytics", Trax blog, October 2020. Available at: https://traxretail.com/blog/eyes-on-the-consumer-hands-on-the-keyboard-the-mantra-in-cpg-analytics/.

56    Jay W Lorsch and Thomas J Tierney, *Aligning the Stars – How to Succeed When Professionals Drive the Results*, Harvard Business School Press, 2002.

57    Jared Spataro (Microsoft 365 CVP), "2 years of digital transformation in 2 months", Microsoft 365 blog, 30 April 2020. Available at: www.microsoft.com/en-us/microsoft-365/blog/2020/04/30/2-years-digital-transformation-2-months/.

58    Thomson Reuters Institute and the Georgetown Law Center on Ethics and the Legal Profession, 2021 Report on the State of the Legal Market, January 2021. Available at: https://legal.thomsonreuters.com/content/dam/ewp-m/documents/legal/en/pdf/reports/2021_sotlm_web_v2.pdf.

59    "What Companies Can Learn From Facebook's Latest Reputation Challenge", RepTrak, July 2020. Available at: www.reptrak.com/blog/what-companies-can-learn-from-facebooks-latest-reputation-challenge/.

60    At Linklaters, for example, it is "Cut him and he bleeds magenta" (the firm's brand colours). At Norton Rose Fulbright, "The lifers bleed NRF red."

61   The case study is adapted from David Rowan, *Non-Bullshit Innovation, supra* note 23, pp188–205.
62   *Ibid*, p197.
63   The transcript is available on The Autodesk File website at:
      www.fourmilab.ch/autofile/www/subsection2_86_0_2.html.
64   See: David Rowan, *Non-Bullshit Innovation, supra* note 23, p193.
65   *Ibid*, p200.
66   *Ibid*.
67   See the case study in Chapter 2.
68   Harvard Law School's Center on the Legal Profession, "Steering Law Firm Strategy", *The Practice*, vol 3
      no 4, May/June 2017.
69   Arun Arora *et al*, *Fast Times, supra* note 13, p25.
70   Consultancy is expensive and needs to be carefully managed. Even the best consultants, if they don't
      land well and resonate with the lawyers, are unlikely to get much useful information from them. An
      alternative option is to build an internal team to sit in with the consultancy team when undertaking
      interviews, until you are sure that the consultancy team has picked up on the tone and approach that
      works best.
71   Such tools can be a helpful starting point, but are unlikely to be sufficient and should ideally be
      supplemented with structured and detailed interviews.
72   Jacques Bughin and Tanguy Catlin, "What Successful Digital Transformations Have in Common",
      *Harvard Business Review*, 19 December 2017. Available at: https://hbr.org/2017/12/what-successful-
      digital-transformations-have-in-common.
73   *Ibid*.
74   Arun Arora *et al*, *Fast Times, supra* note 13, p8.
75   *Ibid*, p43.
76   The Freshfields Lab is a collaborative client experience and co-working space established by
      Freshfields Bruckhaus Deringer in Berlin in 2019. The Lab was established as a space to explore digital
      technologies and develop new ways of working to address clients' digital challenges.
77   Arun Arora *et al*, *Fast Times, supra* note 13, p10.
78   Jacques Bughin, James Manyika and Tangay Catlin, "Twenty-five years of digitization: Ten insights
      into how to play it right", McKinsey Global Institute online briefing note, May 2019. Available at:
      www.mckinsey.com/business-functions/mckinsey-digital/our-insights/twenty-five-years-of-
      digitization-ten-insights-into-how-to-play-it-right.
79   Yvonne Nath, "50 Shades of White Labeling Alternative Legal Service Providers" (quoting Richard
      Levine from Deloitte), *Legaltech News*, 28 January 2001. Available at:
      www.law.com/legaltechnews/2021/01/28/50-shades-of-white-labeling-alternative-legal-service-
      providers/?slreturn=20210426093003.
80   Tanguy Catlin, Johannes-Tobias Lorenz, Bob Sternfels and Paul Willmott, "A roadmap for a digital
      transformation", McKinsey & Company, March 2017. Available at:
      www.mckinsey.com/industries/financial-services/our-insights/a-roadmap-for-a-digital-
      transformation.
81   Arun Arora *et al*, *Fast Times, supra* note 13, p20.
82   "Total Cost of Ownership of IT – post COVID-19, why this is even more important to understand",
      Costratify, 11 June 2020. Available at: www.costratify.com/total-cost-of-ownership-of-it-post-covid-19-
      why-this-is-even-more-important-to-understand/.
83   See: Justin Watson and David Wright, "The robots are ready. Are you?", Deloitte survey, 2017. Available
      at: www2.deloitte.com/content/dam/Deloitte/tr/Documents/technology/deloitte-robots-are-ready.pdf.
      The survey suggests that organisations that have implemented RPA at scale believe that 52% of FTE
      capacity could be provided by 'robots'. (Lest this terrify the workforce, the authors are also at pains to
      point out that RPA "can enable the human workforce to be redeployed to more value adding activities".)
84   Resale benefits can be subject to challenge as the model presupposes an infinite supply of work to keep
      the freed-up capacity busy. One approach is to assume only a portion of the freed-up capacity will be
      resold, with the best case being, for example, 60%, the median case 40% and the worst case 20%.
85   FCA, "Transforming Culture in Financial Services", discussion paper, March 2018. Available at:
      www.fca.org.uk/publication/discussion/dp18-02.pdf.
86   McKinsey & Company, "Driving Impact at Scale from Automation and AI", collection of online articles,
      February 2019. Available at: www.mckinsey.com/~/media/McKinsey/Business%20Functions/
      McKinsey%20Digital/Our%20Insights/Driving%20impact%20at%20scale%20from%20automation%20
      and%20AI/Driving-impact-at-scale-from-automation-and-AI.ashx.
87   See: Dave Murphy, "John Doerr: Best Entrepreneurs Attempt the Impossible", article for Graduate
      School of Stanford Business on an interview with the American investor and venture capitalist,
      1 November 2009. Available at: www.gsb.stanford.edu/insights/john-doerr-best-entrepreneurs-
      attempt-impossible.
88   See Chapter 3, section 2.2 (d).
89   Arun Arora *et al*, *Fast Times, supra* note 13, p57.
90   For more on the somewhat contentious issue of use of the term 'non-lawyer', see the discussion in
      Chapter 8, and note 220.
91   'Velocity', in the context of Agile, is defined by Agile Alliance (www.agilealliance.org) as follows: "At
      the end of each iteration, the team adds up effort estimates associated with user stories that were
      completed during that iteration. This total is called velocity. Knowing velocity, the team can compute

(or revise) an estimate of how long the project will take to complete, based on the estimates associated with remaining user stories and assuming that velocity over the remaining iterations will remain approximately the same. This is generally an accurate prediction, even though rarely a precise one."

92   Yes, people actually do use that term.

93   Arun Arora *et al*, *Fast Times*, *supra* note 13, p61.

94   The four values are as follows (see: www.agilealliance.org/agile101/the-agile-manifesto/):
*Individuals and interactions* over processes and tools.
*Working software* over comprehensive documentation.
*Customer collaboration* over contract negotiation.
*Responding to change* over following a plan.

95   Available on the Agile Alliance website at: www.agilealliance.org/agile101/12-principles-behind-the-agile-manifesto/.

96   The case study is based on the author's interview with Paul Hastings' managing director of innovation and knowledge, Nicola Shaver.

97   The impact of COVID-19 and the response of clients (and your own firm) to the disruption could provide some relevant examples that will resonate.

98   By this I mean a simple diagram setting out the various steps in the life of a legal matter, from brand and relationship building through to onboarding a client and conflict checks through to resourcing the matter, pricing it, delivering it – all the way through to billing and knowledge collection.

99   David Halpern, *Inside the Nudge Unit*, Penguin Random House, 2019.

100  The Behavioural Insights Team, or 'Nudge Unit', as it is colloquially known, is an independent body which generates and applies behavioural insights to inform UK government policy. The EAST approach described by David Halpern was first laid out in BIT's 2014 publication, *EAST – Four simple ways to apply behavioural insights*. Available at: www.bi.team/wp-content/uploads/2015/07/BIT-Publication-EAST_FA_WEB.pdf.

101  David Halpern, *Inside the Nudge Unit*, *supra* note 99, p125.

102  Braveen Kumar, "The Most Profitable Digital Product Ideas in 2021 (and How to Sell Them)", Shopify blog, 17 February 2021. Available at: www.shopify.co.uk/blog/digital-products.

103  Mohanbir Sawhney, "Putting Products Into Services", *Harvard Business Review*, September 2016.

104  Arun Arora *et al*, *Fast Times*, *supra* note 13, p114.

105  "Allen & Overy expands online services with launch of aosphere", press release, 13 January 2015. Available at: www.allenovery.com/en-gb/global/news-and-insights/news/allen—overy-expands-online-services-with-launch-of-aosphere.

106  World Economic Forum with Accenture, "Digital Transformation Initiative", *supra* note 10.

107  At the time of writing, consultation is taking place to determine whether to push the date out to 2023.

108  See: www.lupl.com/our-january-2021-update.

109  See: www.lupl.com/how-it-works.

110  *Ibid*.

111  Nick Hilborne, "Law firms invest $10m in collaboration platform", *Legal Futures*, 14 May 2020. Available at: www.legalfutures.co.uk/latest-news/law-firms-invest-10m-in-collaboration-platform.

112  See: www.lupl.com/about.

113  Arun Arora *et al*, *Fast Times*, *supra* note 13, p91.

114  In interview with the author.

115  Mohanbir Sawhney, "Putting Products Into Services", *supra* note 103.

116  Jayme Brown, "Practice Your Protyping Skills With These 4 Resources", IDEO blog, 21 February 2019. Available at: www.ideo.com/blog/practice-your-prototyping-skills-with-these-4-resources.

117  *Ibid*.

118  Lauren Barrett, "All the product management jargon, delivered", *Start it up*, 8 August 2019. Available at: https://medium.com/swlh/all-the-product-management-jargon-delivered-3bde50d79e2f.

119  *Ibid*.

120  Mohanbir Sawhney, "Putting Products Into Services", *supra* note 103.

121  In interview with the author.

122  List adapted from Michael V Marn, Eric V Roegner and Craig C Zawada, "Pricing New Products", *McKinsey Quarterly*, 1 August 2003. Available at: www.mckinsey.com/business-functions/marketing-and-sales/our-insights/pricing-new-products.

123  *Ibid*.

124  Jeff Gothelf, "Bring Product Thinking to Non-Product Teams", *Harvard Business Review*, 7 April 2020. Available at: https://hbr.org/2020/04/bring-product-thinking-to-non-product-teams.

125  *Ibid*.

126  See: https://legaltechnologyhub.com.

127  "Why you should look beyond legaltech: 4 surprising reasons to leverage non-legaltech." Lawtomated blog, 22 January 2021. Available at: https://lawtomated.com/why-you-should-look-beyond-legaltech-4-surprising-reasons-to-leverage-non-legaltech/.

128  Brant Carson, Alexey Goldov, Laurent Kinet, Warren Oakes, Giulio Romanelli and Anand Swaminathan, "Overcoming the core-technology transformation stalemate", McKinsey Digital, 28 September 2020. Available at: www.mckinsey.com/business-functions/mckinsey-digital/our-insights/overcoming-the-core-technology-transformation-stalemate.

129  *Ibid*.

130  Leslie Chacko, Rachel Lam and Friso Van der Oord, "Governing Digital Transformation and Emerging Technologies", Marsh McLennan, August 2019. Available at: www.mmc.com/insights/publications/2019/aug/governing-digital-transformation-and-emerging-technologies.html.

131  Dennis Kennedy, "2018 Cloud Computing", American Bar Association, 14 January 2019. Available at: www.americanbar.org/groups/law_practice/publications/techreport/ABATECHREPORT2018/2018Cloud/.

132  *Ibid.*

133  "2019 Technology Survey", ILTA. Available from: www.iltanet.org/resources/publications/surveys/2019ts.

134  "The 2019 Aderant Business of Law and Legal Technology Survey", Aderant. Available at: www.aderant.com/wp-content/uploads/2019/08/2019-Business-of-Law-Survey-Results.pdf.

135  Mark Gu, Rich Isenberg, Leandro Santos and Isabelle Tamburro, "Debunking seven common myths about cloud", McKinsey Digital, 5 October 2020. Available at: www.mckinsey.com/business-functions/mckinsey-digital/our-insights/debunking-seven-common-myths-about-cloud.

136  Josh Gottlieb and Allen Weinberg, "Catch them if you can: How leaders in data and analytics have pulled ahead", McKinsey & Company, 19 September 2019. Available at: www.mckinsey.com/business-functions/mckinsey-analytics/our-insights/catch-them-if-you-can-how-leaders-in-data-and-analytics-have-pulled-ahead.

137  Alex G Smith, "The Continuing Evolution of KM – Modern Management, Advanced Measurement, and More", ILTA's *Peer to Peer*, Winter 2020. Available at: http://epubs.iltanet.org/i/1323358-winter2020/21.

138  *Ibid.*

139  *Ibid.*

140  Tadhg Nagle, Thomas C Redman and David Sammon, "Only 3% of Companies' Data Meets Basic Quality Standards", *Harvard Business Review*, 11 September 2017. Available at: https://hbr.org/2017/09/only-3-of-companies-data-meets-basic-quality-standards.

141  This is an abbreviated version of the list in Tadhg Nagle *et al*'s list in their *HBR* article, *ibid.*

142  *Ibid.*

143  According to the Information Technology Gartner Glossary, master data management is "a technology-enabled discipline in which business and IT work together to ensure the uniformity, accuracy, stewardship, semantic consistency and accountability of the enterprise's official shared master data assets. Master data is the consistent and uniform set of identifiers and extended attributes that describes the core entities of the enterprise including customers, prospects, citizens, suppliers, sites, hierarchies and chart of accounts". See: www.gartner.com/en/information-technology/glossary/master-data-management-mdm.

144  Alejandro Diaz, Kayvaun Rowshankish and Tamim Saleh, "Why data culture matters", *McKinsey Quarterly*, 6 September 2018. Available at: www.mckinsey.com/business-functions/mckinsey-analytics/our-insights/why-data-culture-matters?

145  David Waller, "Ten Steps to Creating a Data-Driven Culture", *Harvard Business Review*, 6 February 2020. Available at: https://hbr.org/2020/02/10-steps-to-creating-a-data-driven-culture.

146  *Ibid.*

147  See, on the GSU website: https://law.gsu.edu/faculty-centers/legal-analytics-innovation/#:~:text=Computer%20algorithms%2C%20combined%20with%20the,approach%20to%20working%20a%20case.

148  Alejandro Diaz *et al*, "Why data culture matters", *supra* note 144, quoting Cameron Davies of NBCUniversal.

149  The ZOE COVID symptom study app was created by health science company ZOE, with scientific analysis provided by King's College London. See: https://covid.joinzoe.com/.

150  "Closing the Data Divide", Microsoft news item. See: https://news.microsoft.com/opendata/#data-sharing-today.

151  From Microsoft's Dynamics 365 financial services accelerator documentation. See: https://docs.microsoft.com/en-us/common-data-model/banking-accelerator.

152  See: https://onenda.club.

153  Lockstep is a model in which profits are shared equally between partners according to their seniority. Contrast this with an 'eat what you kill' model that compensates partners based on the amount of revenue that that partner generates.

154  "Why law firms must change how they work", *Financial Times* editorial, 14 June 2019. Available at: www.ft.com/content/81205f00-8d27-11c9-a1c1-51bf8f989972.

155  FCA, "Transforming Culture in Financial Services", *supra* note 85.

156  Arun Arora *et al*, *Fast Times*, *supra* note 13, p2.

157  Business Plan 2019/20, FCA. Available at: www.fca.org.uk/publication/business-plans/business-plan-2019-20.pdf.

158  *Ibid.*

159  William C Dudley, "Enhancing Financial Stability by Improving Culture in the Financial Services Industry", speech at the Workshop on Reforming Culture and Behavior in the Financial Services Industry, Federal Reserve Bank of New York, 20 October 2014. Available at: www.fsb.org/wp-content/uploads/Dudley-Enhancing-Financial-Stability-by-Improving-Culture-in-the-Financial-Services-Industry.pdf.

160  Attributed to Gerard Seijts, executive director, Ian O Ihnatowycz Institute for Leadership, in interview

with Rajarshi Bhattacharjee for *Business Standard*, 20 January 2013. Available at: www.business-standard.com/article/management/culture-is-what-people-do-when-no-one-is-looking-gerard-seijts-112092400046_1.html.

161 Wijnand Nuijts, Department of Governance, Culture and Organization Behaviour, Dutch National Bank, "Managing culture: the role of regulation and supervision", Essay 2.6 in "Transforming Culture in Financial Services", FCA discussion paper, March 2018. Available at: www.fca.org.uk/publication/discussion/dp18-02.pdf.

162 "Integrity and ethics", in the SRA Risk Outlook 2020/21, November 2020. Available at: www.sra.org.uk/risk/outlook/risk-outlook-2020-21/integrity-and-ethics/.

163 This list is adapted from the areas of focus listed in "Culture in financial services: scrutiny by the regulator, in principle and in practice", Deloitte's Centre for Regulatory Strategy, 2018. Available at: www2.deloitte.com/content/dam/Deloitte/uk/Documents/financial-services/deloitte-uk-ecrs-understanding-culture-in-financial-services-updated.pdf.

164 The Combined Code on Corporate Governance, FRC, 2018. Available at: www.frc.org.uk/getattachment/88bd8c45-50ea-4841-95b0-d2f4f48069a2/2018-UK-Corporate-Governance-Code-FINAL.pdf.

165 John Armour and Mari Sako, "AI-Enabled Business Models in Legal Services: From Traditional Law Firms to Next-Generation Law Companies?", paper for University of Oxford Faculty of Law as part of the programme, "Unlocking the Potential of AI in English Law", December 2019. Available from: https://papers.ssrn.com/sol3/papers.cfm?abstract_id=3418810.

166 Mark A Cohen, "Are Law Firms Sustainable? It's The Model That Matters", *Forbes*, 19 August 2019. Available at: www.forbes.com/sites/markcohen1/2019/08/19/are-law-firms-sustainable-its-the-model-that-matters/?sh=41bea145628f.

167 Alex Novarese, "Apocalypse never – City leaders' 2020 results show resilience to test the most confirmed Cassandra", *Legal Business*, 29 July 2020. Available at: www.legalbusiness.co.uk/blogs/comment-apocalypse-never-city-leaders-2020-results-show-resilience-to-test-the-most-confirmed-cassandra/.

168 Dan Packel, "Most Big Firms Are Increasing Revenue, but Performance Gap Steadily Grows", *The American Lawyer*, 2 December 2020. Available at: www.law.com/americanlawyer/2020/12/02/most-big-firms-are-increasing-revenue-but-performance-gap-steadily-grows/.

169 Arun Arora *et al*, *Fast Times*, *supra* note 13, p11.

170 Wijnand Nuijts, "Managing culture: the role of regulation and supervision", *supra* note 161.

171 John Armour and Mari Sako, "AI-Enabled Business Models in Legal Services", *supra* note 165.

172 *Ibid.*

173 *Ibid.*

174 *Ibid.*

175 Arun Arora *et al*, *Fast Times*, *supra* note 13, p51.

176 John Armour and Mari Sako, "AI-Enabled Business Models in Legal Services", *supra* note 165.

177 *Ibid.*

178 James Fontanella-Khan, Sujeet Indap and Barney Thompson, "How a private equity boom fuelled the world's biggest law firm", *The Financial Times*, 6 June 2019. Available at: www.ft.com/content/13696928-86d5-11e9-a028-86cea8523dc2.

179 Matt Byrne, "There are many escapees from BigLaw", *The Lawyer*, 19 January 2021. Available at: www.thelawyer.com/there-are-many-escapees-from-biglaw/.

180 Arun Arora *et al*, *Fast Times*, *supra* note 13, p8.

181 "Digital disruption and the role of M&A", interview of Simon Blackburn for McKinsey's "Inside the Strategy Room" podcast, 16 March 2020. Available at: www.mckinsey.com/business-functions/strategy-and-corporate-finance/our-insights/digital-disruption-and-the-role-of-m-and-a.

182 The case study is based on the author's interview with Drew Winlaw.

183 Neil Rose, "City firm acquires legal engineering ABS Wavelength", *Legal Futures*, 24 July 2019. Available at: www.legalfutures.co.uk/latest-news/city-firm-acquires-legal-engineering-abs-wavelength.

184 In early 2018 Clifford Chance acquired Carillion Advice Services (CAS), a provider of commodity legal services located in Newcastle. CAS was originally developed to support the Carillion legal team and was sold to Clifford Chance after Carillion became insolvent in January 2018.

185 The case study is based on the author's interview with Wendy Butler Curtis.

186 "Nivaura fintech specialists appointed A&O's entrepreneurs-in-residence", news announcement on the A&O website, 10 July 2017. Available at: www.allenovery.com/en-gb/global/news-and-insights/news/nivaura-fintech-specialists-appointed-aos-entrepreneurs-in-residence.

187 Hamish McNicol, "The wheat from the chaff", *The In-House Lawyer*, Summer 2018. Available at: www.inhouselawyer.co.uk/feature/the-wheat-from-the-chaff/.

188 The case study is based on the author's interview with Richard West.

189 Hamish McNicol, "'Doesn't fit a law firm': Kennedys looks to prove smarts with IQ technology arm spin-off", *Legal Business* blog, 26 February 2020. Available at: www.legalbusiness.co.uk/blogs/doesnt-fit-a-law-firm-kennedys-looks-to-prove-smarts-with-iq-technology-arm-spin-off/.

190 In April 2021, Mishcon's partners voted in favour of listing on the London Stock Exchange later in 2021.

191 This was significantly lower than the estimated valuation of more than £1 billion mooted in June of the previous year (see: www.globallegalpost.com/news/fast45growing-dwf-mulling-pound1-billion-ipo-98813556).

192 Reena SenGupta, "Law firms confront a question of identity: The line between legal and business

advice is blurring ever faster, say senior lawyers", *Financial Times*, 4 October 2018. Available at: www.ft.com/content/de0da42a-b41a-11e8-bbc3-ccd7de085ffe.

193 Alex Novarese, "Falling stock – DWF's predictable woes will hang over the listed sector for years", *Legal Business* blog, 1 June 2020. Available at: www.legalbusiness.co.uk/blogs/comment-falling-stock-dwfs-predictable-woes-will-hang-over-the-listed-legal-sector-for-years/.

194 Jay W Lorsch and Thomas J Tierney, *Aligning the Stars: How to succeed when professionals drive results*, Harvard Business Review Press, 2002, p24.

195 *Ibid*, p150.

196 *Ibid*, p151.

197 John Armour and Mari Sako, "AI-Enabled Business Models in Legal Services", *supra* note 165.

198 "How diverse is the legal profession?", SRA report, 20 March 2020. Available at: www.sra.org.uk/sra/equality-diversity/key-findings/diverse-legal-profession/.

199 *Ibid*.

200 *Ibid*.

201 Steven Rodgers, "The Intel Rule: Action to Improve Diversity in the Legal Profession", Intel Newsroom, 21 November 2019. Available at: https://newsroom.intel.com/editorials/intel-rule-action-improve-diversity-legal-profession/#gs.352zdy.

202 Laura Morgan Roberts and Ella F Washington, "U.S. Businesses Must Take Meaningful Action Against Racism", *Harvard Business Review*, 1 June 2020.

203 Phillip Bantz, "'Things Are Different Now': General Counsel, Corporations React Publicly to George Floyd's Death", *The American Lawyer*, 1 June 2020. Available at: www.law.com/corpcounsel/2020/06/01/things-are-different-now-general-counsel-corporations-react-publicly-to-george-floyds-death/.

204 Steven Rodgers, "The Intel Rule: Action to Improve Diversity in the Legal Profession", *supra* note 201.

205 Cristiano Dalla Bona, "BT throws down gauntlet to panel: 'Our most diverse firm gets rehired automatically'", *The Lawyer*, 27 April 2020. Available at: www.thelawyer.com/bt-throws-down-gauntlet-to-panel-our-most-diverse-firm-gets-rehired-automatically/.

206 Novartis has also signed up for the Legal Metrics special project, developed by a consortium of law firms, corporate legal teams, law companies and industry experts to agree and share certain metrics that define efficiency, value and citizenship for law firms and their clients. See: www.legalmetrics.com.

207 Bradley M Gayton, "Open Letter: Commitment to Diversity, belonging + Outside Counsel Diversity", LinkedIn, 28 January 2021. Available at: www.linkedin.com/pulse/open-letter-commitment-diversity-belonging-outside-counsel-gayton/?trackingId=hF5DSRHfQ6yqNW4u84LD4Q%3D%3D.

208 McKinsey & Company, "Diversity wins: How inclusion matters", 19 May 2020. Available at: www.mckinsey.com/~/media/mckinsey/featured%20insights/diversity%20and%20inclusion/diversity%20wins%20how%20inclusion%20matters/diversity-wins-how-inclusion-matters-vf.pdf.

209 *Ibid*.

210 Arun Arora *et al*, *Fast Times*, *supra* note 13, p65.

211 *Ibid*, p65.

212 *Ibid*, p67.

213 *Ibid*, p66.

214 For a video explaining more about this impressive work, see the NHM's website at: www.nhm.ac.uk/our-science/our-work/digital-collections.html.

215 Lovelace Digital, "Future-proofing the Natural History Museum, the best job in digital?", interview with Piers Jones, 4 April 2019. Available at: www.lovelacedigital.co.uk/post/future-proofing-the-natural-history-museum-the-best-job-in-digital.

216 *Ibid*.

217 Arun Arora *et al*, *Fast Times*, *supra* note 13, p79.

218 "Future Workplace" issue, *Raconteur*, January 2019.

219 Barclays Corporate, "The more flexible the better? Why professional services firms are rethinking office spaces", 5 December 2019. Available at: www.barclayscorporate.com/content/dam/barclayscorporate-com/documents/insights/industry-expertise/Future-proofing_the_workplace.pdf.

220 There is an ongoing and vigorous debate on social media about use of the term 'non-lawyer' to describe business professionals working in legal services who do not have a law degree. See, for example, posts on the subject from Julie Savarino ("Let's all stop using 'NON-LAWYER'!": www.linkedin.com/posts/juliesavarino_law-lawyer-inclusion-activity-6628283900420505600-u3zm) and John Croft ("Life as a Non-Lawyer": https://expertise.elevateservices.com/post/102g1y9/life-as-a-non-lawyer) of Elevate. See also James Goodnow, "Non-Attorney – Distinction Or Diss?", *Above the Law*, 7 February 2020. Available at: https://abovethelaw.com/2020/02/non-attorney-distinction-or-diss/.

221 Comparatively speaking, the regulatory regime in the United Kingdom is considered progressive in this regard (in the United States, the rules are much stricter with respect to non-lawyer ownership of law firms; only in Washington D.C. are non-legally trained professionals permitted to be law firm partners). There is mounting pressure in other US states for this to change, with states such as California, Utah and Arizona calling for regulatory reform.

222 McKinsey, "Diversity Wins: How inclusion matters", *supra* note 208.

223 "It's Just Us Lawyers Here, On a Multidisciplinary Team", Bloomberg Tax Daily Tax Report analysis, 22 July 2020. Available at: https://news.bloombergtax.com/daily-tax-report/analysis-its-just-us-lawyers-here-on-a-multidisciplinary-team?context=article-related.

224 'Law companies' is the term preferred by the providers themselves; incumbents tend to refer to them, rather archly, as 'legal process outsourcing providers' or 'alternative legal service providers'.

225 Alison Reynolds and David Lewis, "Teams Solve Problems Faster When They're More Cognitively Diverse", *Harvard Business Review*, 30 March 2017. Available at: https://hbr.org/2017/03/teams-solve-problems-faster-when-theyre-more-cognitively-diverse.

226 Alison Reynolds and David Lewis, "The Two Traits of the Best Problem-Solving Teams", *Harvard Business Review*, 2 April 2018. Available at: https://hbr.org/2018/04/the-two-traits-of-the-best-problem-solving-teams.

227 *Ibid.*

228 As set out by the US economist Milton Friedman in his 1970 *New York Times* essay, "The Social Responsibility of Business is to Increase its Profits". Available at: www.nytimes.com/1970/09/13/archives/a-friedman-doctrine-the-social-responsibility-of-business-is-to.html.

229 Business Round Table announcement, 19 August 2020. Available at: www.businessroundtable.org/business-roundtable-redefines-the-purpose-of-a-corporation-to-promote-an-economy-that-serves-all-americans.

230 PwC, "Putting Purpose to Work: A study of purpose in the workplace". Available at: www.pwc.com/us/en/about-us/corporate-responsibility/assets/pwc-putting-purpose-to-work-purpose-survey-report.pdf.

231 "Unilever's purpose-led brands outperform", Unilever press release, 11 June 2019. Available at: www.unilever.com/news/press-releases/2019/unilevers-purpose-led-brands-outperform.html.

232 Andrew Winston, "Is the Business Roundtable Statement Just Empty Rhetoric?", *Harvard Business Review*, 30 August 2019. Available at: https://hbr.org/2019/08/is-the-business-roundtable-statement-just-empty-rhetoric.

233 Caterina Bulgarella, "Purpose-Driven Companies Evolve Faster Than Others", *Forbes*, 21 September 2018. Available at: www.forbes.com/sites/caterinabulgarella/2018/09/21/purpose-driven-companies-evolve-faster-than-others/?sh=71f87b955bcf.

234 Business Round Table Announcement, *supra* note 229.

235 Simon Bailey, "Is purpose before profit the new law for firms?", *Global Legal Post*, 4 November 2016. Available at: www.globallegalpost.com/blogs/commentary/is-purpose-before-profit-the-new-law-for-firms-91802876/.

236 The Economist Intelligence Unit, "The transformation imperative: Digital drivers in the covid-19 pandemic", 2021. Available at: https://transformationimperative.economist.com/pdfs/EIU_MIcrosoft_The_Transformation_Imperative_Executive_Summary.pdf.

237 *Ibid*, p9.

238 Jim Murphy, Chris Audet, Nikos Drakos, Zack Hutto, Katrin Leksa, James Crocker and Will Glynn, "Predicts 2021: Corporate Legal and Compliance Technology", Gartner survey, 25 November 2020. Available at: www.gartner.com/en/documents/3993547/predicts-2021-corporate-legal-and-compliance-technology.

239 Tom Baker, "Vodafone puts emphasis on ESG in new eight-firm advisory panel", *Legal Business*, 6 April 2021. Available at: www.legalbusiness.co.uk/blogs/vodafone-puts-emphasis-on-esg-in-new-eight-firm-adviser-panel/.

240 Andrew S Grove, *Only the Paranoid Survive*, *supra* note 6.

# About the author

**Isabel Parker**
Executive director, Digital Legal Exchange
isabel.parker@cantab.net

Isabel Parker is the executive director of the Digital Legal Exchange, and works with general counsel to help corporate legal functions become more integrated with the business through digital transformation. Prior to this, Isabel was chief legal innovation officer at Freshfields Bruckhaus Deringer, with accountability for the development and commercialisation of client-facing digital products, and founder and co-leader of the Freshfields Lab in Berlin. She trained at Freshfields as a finance lawyer and is qualified to practise law in England and Wales and the State of New York.

Isabel has always been committed to driving change in the legal sector. During her time as chief legal innovation officer at Freshfields, the firm was awarded the honour of being the most innovative law firm in Europe at the FT Innovative Lawyer Awards for 2019. Isabel was herself recognised as one of the top 10 innovative lawyers in Europe in the Financial Times Innovative Lawyers Report for 2018, and in 2020 was the winner of a European Women in Legal Tech Award in the professional services category. Isabel has wide experience in advising law firms, new law companies and corporate legal teams on digital transformation, alternative resourcing and legal technology. ∎

# Index

# About Globe Law and Business

Globe Law and Business was established in 2005. From the very beginning, we set out to create law books which are sufficiently high level to be of real use to the experienced professional, yet still accessible and easy to navigate. Most of our authors are drawn from Magic Circle and other top commercial firms, both in the UK and internationally.

Our titles are carefully produced, with the utmost attention paid to editorial, design and production processes. We hope this results in high-quality publications that are easy to read, and a pleasure to own. Our titles are also available as ebooks, which are compatible with most desktop, laptop and tablet devices. In 2018 we expanded our portfolio to include journals and Special Reports, available both digitally and in hard copy format, and produced to the same high standards as our books.

In the spring of 2021, we were very pleased to announce the start of a new chapter for Globe Law and Business following the acquisition of law books under the imprint Ark Publishing. We are very much looking forward to working with our new Ark authors, many of whom are well known to us, and to further developing the law firm management list, among other areas.

We'd very much like to hear from you with your thoughts and ideas for improving what we offer. Please do feel free to email me at sian@globelawandbusiness.com with your views. ■

Sian O'Neill
Managing director
Globe Law and Business
www.globelawandbusiness.com

# Related new titles

Accelerating Trends in Law Firms

Consulting Editor **Peter Zeughauser**

The Post-Pandemic Law Firm

NEW NORMAL

EDITED BY ALEX DAVIES

The Agile Law Firm

Chris Bull

Law firm management **Insights**

Next Stage Legal Project Management

Future-proof Your Matter Management
Consulting Editor **Ignaz Fuesgen**

Go to **www.globelawandbusiness.com**
for full details including free sample chapters